SUPERMARKET SUPER GARDENS

www.jerrybaker.com

Other Jerry Baker Books:

Jerry Baker's The New Impatient Gardener
Jerry Baker's Dear God...Please Help It Grow!
Jerry Baker's All-American Lawns
Jerry Baker's Bug Off!
Jerry Baker's Terrific Garden Tonics!
Jerry Baker's Backyard Problem Solver
Jerry Baker's Green Grass Magic
Jerry Baker's Great Green Book of Garden Secrets
Jerry Baker's Old-Time Gardening Wisdom

Jerry Baker's Backyard Birdscaping Bonanza
Jerry Baker's Backyard Bird Feeding Bonanza
Jerry Baker's Year-Round Bloomers
Jerry Baker's Flower Garden Problem Solver
Jerry Baker's Perfect Perennials!

Jerry Baker's Top 25 Homemade Healers
Healing Fixers Mixers & Elixirs
Grandma Putt's Home Health Remedies
Jerry Baker's Herbal Pharmacy
Jerry Baker's Supermarket Super Remedies
Jerry Baker's The New Healing Foods
Jerry Baker's Cut Your Health Care Bills in Half!
Jerry Baker's Amazing Antidotes
Jerry Baker's Oddball Ointments, Powerful Potions, and Fabulous Folk Remedies
Jerry Baker's Giant Book of Kitchen Counter Cures

Jerry Baker's Solve It with Vinegar!
Jerry Baker's Speed Cleaning Secrets!
America's Best Practical Problem Solvers
Jerry Baker's Can the Clutter!
Jerry Baker's Homespun Magic
Grandma Putt's Old-Time Vinegar, Garlic, Baking Soda, and 101 More Problem Solvers
Jerry Baker's Supermarket Super Products!
Jerry Baker's It Pays to Be Cheap!

To order any of the above, or for more information on Jerry Baker's
amazing home, health, and garden tips, tricks, and tonics, please write to:

Jerry Baker, P.O. Box 1001
Wixom, MI 48393

Or, visit Jerry Baker online at:

www.jerrybaker.com

SUPERMARKET SUPER GARDENS

An Aisle-by-Aisle Guide to Growing
a Lush Lawn and Gorgeous Garden
Using Baby Powder, Dental Floss,
Milk, Panty Hose, and More!

By Jerry Baker
America's Master Gardener®

Published by American Master Products, Inc.

Copyright © 2008 by Jerry Baker

Published by American Master Products, Inc. / Jerry Baker

Executive Editor: Kim Adam Gasior
Managing Editor: Cheryl Winters Tetreau
Writer: Vicki Webster
Copy Editor: Barbara McIntosh Webb
Interior Design and Layout: Sandy Freeman
Cover Design: Kitty Pierce Mace
Indexer: Nan Badgett

Publisher's Cataloging-in-Publication Data
(Provided by Quality Books, Inc.)

Baker, Jerry.
    Jerry Baker's supermarket super gardens : an aisle-by-aisle
  guide to growing a lush lawn and gorgeous garden using baby
  powder, dental floss, milk, panty hose, and more!
    p. cm. -- (Jerry Baker good gardening series)
    Includes index.
    ISBN-13: 978-0-922433-87-2
    ISBN-10: 0-922433-87-9

      1. Gardening. 2. Gardening--Equipment and supplies.
3. Garden tools--Miscellanea.   I. Title. II. Series.

SB450.97.B14 2008   635
               QBI07-1628

Printed in the United States of America
18 20 19 17 hardcover

Contents

Contents

Introduction

Here's a question for you: What do these five garden-variety problems have in common?

1. Spring has sprung, and your rosebushes are covered with new buds—and Japanese beetles are eating big holes in every single one of them.

2. Droves of deer are devouring your entire vegetable garden—and just about every other plant in your beautiful backyard.

3. You've filled your deck with big pots of beautiful flowers—but the neighborhood cats think the containers are their litter boxes!

4. Your phlox start out as healthy as can be, and then bingo—mildew spores erupt and the plants are wearing white powdery coats from top to bottom.

5. As you were filling your lawn mower, you missed the mark—and now you've got a puddle of petroleum on your gorgeous green grass.

Are you ready for the super-simple answer? Here it is: You can solve every single one of these problems—and a whole lot more—using products that you'll find on the shelves of your local supermarket. In fact, many of those products are probably sitting in your kitchen cabinets right now. For example, you can use molasses to feed your plants, fend off fungal diseases, get moles out of your yard, and remove grass stains from your clothes. And that's just for starters!

This book is jam-packed with tips, tricks, and tonics that'll help you use dozens of common, everyday products to grow healthier, more beautiful—and in some cases, tastier—plants than you ever thought possible. You'll get the lowdown on:

- Getting your grass off to a great start with corn syrup and Epsom salts

- Growing show-stopping roses with banana peels and tea bags

- Using sugar and aluminum foil to make your tomatoes the sweetest-tasting in town

- Preventing damping-off disease with cinnamon and rubbing alcohol

- Keeping your herbs happy and healthy using ammonia, beer, and corn syrup

- Banishing bad bugs with a garlic, onion, and baby shampoo spray

- Sending rabbits scurrying from your trees and shrubs with buttermilk

But wait—that's not all! You'll also find fantastic features like *Do Tell!,* which contains the fascinating and little-known stories behind some of our biggest supermarket superstars. (With these tidbits at your beck and call, you'll win any trivia contest, hands down!) Here's a couple of fabulous factoids to whet your appetite: Peanut butter got its start as a source of protein for people who couldn't chew meat, and the Manhattan cocktail was invented by none other than Winston Churchill's mother!

In *Round & Round,* I'll show you hundreds of ways to turn potential trash into treasures ranging from bug traps to bird feeders, fire starters to fishing lures, and pet toys to plant foods. Sneak preview:  When you finish the last pickle in a jar, serve the remaining juice to your gardenias. They go gaga for the stuff!

 And *Here's to You* includes my fast, fun, and foolproof directions for using everyday products to make your life easier and more fun, both indoors and out. For example, you'll discover how to ease muscle aches with a potato, shine your floor with wax paper, and make a potent, baby-safe insect repellent using vinegar and fresh herbs from the Produce aisle.

Finally, in *Marvelous Mixes,* I'll share tons of my terrific tonics made with ingredients straight from the aisles of your favorite supermarket. I love mixin' and fixin' things, and you will, too.

So what are we waiting for? Get ready, get set, and above all else—get growing!

Bags & Wraps

ALUMINUM FOIL

FOOD-STORAGE BAGS

FOOD-STORAGE CONTAINERS

GROCERY BAGS

PLASTIC WRAP

TRASH BAGS

WAX PAPER

# Aluminum Foil

Speed up bloom time. You say you've planned a garden wedding at your place, but you're concerned that your roses won't reach their peak of bloom in time for the big event? Well, here's a simple trick that just *might* save the day: Spread aluminum foil on the ground between your rosebushes. The extra light reflecting off of the foil should hasten their blooming by a full two weeks. (Of course, you'll want to replace it with a more attractive mulch before the wedding bells chime!)

Prevent sunscald. This nasty condition plagues young, thin-barked trees, especially ashes, lindens, maples, oaks, willows, and nearly all fruit trees. It occurs when the sun's warmth hits the southwest side of the trunk, propelling the tree's growth cells into action. Then, when the sun sets and the temperature plummets, the cells rupture and the bark splits wide open. In most parts of the country, the prime danger period is January and February. To guard your newly planted treasures, wrap a couple layers of aluminum foil around the trunk. Be sure to remove the wrapper in early spring, when the wild temperature swings even out; otherwise, it will give insect pests a cozy place to hide. *Note:* Sunscald will pose less of a risk as your tree matures and develops thicker bark and larger branches that (even without leaves) can help shade the trunk.

Hold cuttings in place. Getting ready to start new perennials by rooting some stem cuttings in water? Stretch a piece of aluminum foil across the top of a glass and poke holes in it. Then insert the cuttings through the holes. The foil will hold the stems securely in place and keep the water from evaporating as quickly as it would in an uncovered container. *Note:* Some of the best candidates for this method are tender perennials that are commonly treated as annuals, including petunias, geraniums *(Pelargonium* spp.), and impatiens.

Cure Bald Spots (in Your Lawn, That Is)

Brown patches can appear overnight, even on the best-tended lawns. In most cases, the only cure is to dig up the dead grass and replace it. No need to worry—it's a simple matter when you keep a stock of homegrown replacement plugs on hand. Here's how to make your own supply:

1. Collect a bunch of plastic flats, like the ones that many annual flowers and veggies come in. (Make sure there are holes in the bottom for drainage.)

2. Line each flat with aluminum foil, leaving about 2 inches of foil hanging out over one side. That will allow excess water to drain off and make the soil block easier to slide out later on. Also, be sure to punch holes through the foil in the bottom.

3. Fill each flat with potting soil or a half-and-half mixture of compost and garden soil.

4. Sprinkle grass seed on top—the same type as you've got growing in your lawn, of course—and put the flats in a bright, but sheltered, place. (I keep mine by the back door so I never forget to water them.)

5. Keep the soil moist until the seeds sprout; after that, just give the grass a good drink of water twice a day.

Within a couple of weeks, you'll have nice, thick blocks of turf that you can use whenever a bare spot appears in your lawn. Just slide the soil out of the flat and pop it into place, either whole, or broken into pieces first.

Get an earlier tomato harvest. And a bigger one, too! Just stretch aluminum foil on the ground between your plants, and anchor it along the edges with stones or bricks. The reflected light can increase your yield, especially in cloudy weather, and speed up the ripening of your fruit by a full two weeks.

Grow stronger seedlings. Young flowers and vegetables that don't get enough light when you're starting them indoors tend to grow weak, leggy, and spindly. To prevent that

Round & Round
Round & Round

Question: What on earth can you do with those small pieces of aluminum foil that always seem to be left over at the end of a roll? Answer: Plenty! Just set them all aside (maybe in a plastic food-storage container). Then, when the need arises, dip into your stash and turn that potential trash into any one of these treasures:

Battery tightener. When a flashlight or portable radio starts giving you on-again-off-again performance, check the battery compartment. Chances are that the springs have lost their tension. If that's the case, fold a scrap of foil into a pad that's thick enough to fill the gap, and insert it between the battery and the spring.

Cat toy. Wad the foil into a 1$\frac{1}{2}$-inch ball, and watch Fluffy go to town with her new toy!

Dyed-eyeglass preventers. When it's time to color your hair (or have it tinted at the beauty parlor), wrap strips of foil around the temples of your specs. You'll be able to catch up on your reading and get beautiful at the same time.

Fishing lure. Wrap foil around a fishhook, and fringe it so that the foil wiggles when you move it through the water. Fish find it irresistible!

problem, just spread a long strip of aluminum foil on the shelf or table under your grow lights, and set your seed flats on top of it. Then lift up each end of the foil and tape it to the outside shade of the light fixture, using either electrical, packing, or duct tape. (Don't let the tape touch the bulb!) The foil "walls" will focus light on your baby plants and help retain heat, forcing them to grow bigger, stronger, and faster.

Keep houseplants growing evenly. When plants are growing in or near a window, they tend to lean toward the light—and if you're not Johnny-on-the-spot to turn them frequently, you wind up with a lot of bent-over greenery. The simple solution: Cut the top and one side off of a cardboard box, and cover the bottom and the three remaining sides with aluminum foil, shiny side out. Place your plants inside the box and set it in front of a sunny window. The green residents will soak up the sun's rays from all sides, so they'll grow strong and evenly shaped. *Note:* This trick also works for tender perennials that you've brought indoors for the winter.

Shine light from below. If you don't have room for a whole reflecting box (see above), simply line your windowsills with aluminum foil (again, shiny side out). It'll reflect light onto the plants from below and keep them going strong, even through the gray days of winter.

Force spring-blooming bulbs. Want to force spring-blooming bulbs like crocus and hyacinths, but lack the refrigerator space to give them the chilly darkness they need? Here's your answer: Plant the bulbs in a pot, put it on a cold windowsill, and cover the top with a cone of aluminum foil. Remove the foil when the crocus shoots are 2 inches tall and the hyacinth shoots are 4 inches tall.

Deter bark munchers. There's nothing mice and rabbits love more than newly planted trees and shrubs. Protect your treasures with heavy-duty aluminum foil. Wrap it around each trunk from the ground to a height of about 18 inches, and keep it there until the plant has established itself. The glittering, rattling surface will send the varmints elsewhere for dinner!

De-cat container plants. For some reason, most cats find large planters irresistible. But you can declare your potted plants off-limits with this simple trick: Cover the soil surface  with aluminum foil, and spread a thin layer of mulch on top of it. When Fluffy leaps into the pot to do her duty or nibble on some greenery, the rustling sound and strange feel will make her hop right out again.

Protect outdoor furniture. Having trouble keeping Fido or Fluffy (or both) off of your chair and chaise longue cushions? Just lay sheets of aluminum foil on the cushions. The crackly sound and strange feel will send them scurrying elsewhere in search of comfort. (Of course, this trick works just as well indoors!)

Make your garden cat-free. And your bird feeders, too! Fill empty 2-liter soda pop bottles half-full of water, and add a few drops of bleach, just to keep smelly algae from growing. Then put two or three long, thin strips of aluminum foil into each bottle, and set the containers every few feet around the area you want to protect. The constantly changing reflections from the foil will make any cat think twice before he or she ventures closer. After a few forays onto your flashy turf, Fluffy will seek her fun elsewhere.

Erect a flashing fence. Got four legged critters helping themselves to your harvest? Or maybe early birds snatching your seeds before they even have a chance to germinate? Here's the answer to both of those problems: Just pound stakes into the soil at 3- to 4-foot intervals all around the plot, and run twine between the stakes. Then cut aluminum foil into strips about 1 inch wide and 5 inches long, and tape them to the twine. The shiny streamers will send rabbits, raccoons, and most other varmints packin' fast!

Guard your fruit harvest. Here's a shining way to keep birds out of your fruit trees and berry bushes: Cut leftover cardboard into stars, circles, triangles, and other shapes. Wrap each one in aluminum foil, poke a hole near one edge, and

Dried Is Dandy, but Frozen Is Finer

If you grow and preserve your own herbs for cooking—or even buy them fresh at the supermarket—here's a little secret you ought to know: Most culinary herbs retain a lot more of their fresh-from-the-garden flavor when they're frozen, rather than dried (although, of course, they won't keep their good looks). There are several easy-as-pie freezing methods. Use whichever one you want, then later just pull out whatever quantity you need to cook with, and put the rest back in the freezer. Here are your culinary choices:

* Wrap up bunches of herb sprigs (one kind per bunch) in aluminum foil.

* Chop fresh herbs, and freeze them in food-storage containers.

* Puree chopped herbs with water, butter, or olive oil. (The exact amount is your call, but roughly 2 parts herbs to 1 part mixer is a good starting point.) Then pour the mixture into ice cube trays. When the cubes are frozen, pop them out of the trays and store them in food-storage containers or freezer bags.

Aluminum Foil

hang the baubles from the branches, using twine or nylon fishing line. The light flashing off the foil will make the fliers steer clear.

Foil cutworms. All flower and vegetable seedlings need protection from these greedy gluttons. One simple way to provide that security is to wrap aluminum foil loosely around the stem of each tender baby plant. The foil should extend about 2 inches below the ground and 3 inches above. You can remove the wrapping when the stalk is about $1/2$ inch in diameter—at that stage, it's too thick for the cutworms to damage.

Foil squash vine borers, too. These villains target a whole lot of vegetables, including (of course) all types of squash, as well as tomatoes, peppers, and eggplant. Protect your harvest by wrapping a 2- to 3-inch strip of aluminum foil around the base of each plant—and keep it there right through the growing season. Check it frequently, though, and loosen the foil or apply a longer strip as necessary.

Fend off slugs. It's no secret that these slimy villains will sink their jaws into just about any kind of plant under the sun. But they can't get through a coat of metallic armor. To protect single-stemmed plants, wrap a 1-inch-high band of crinkled aluminum foil around the bottom of the stem. For multi-stemmed plants, simply make a foil ring that's long enough to encircle the whole base of the slugs' target.

Deter flying insects. When placed on the soil around plants, aluminum foil will deter aphids, thrips, moths, and other destructive (and disease-spreading) insects. How? The light reflecting off the foil confuses the bugs so much that they can't land, so they head elsewhere for dinner. Just be sure to poke holes a few inches apart in the foil so that water can get down to the plants' roots. Also, check on it periodically to make sure the shiny covering isn't reflecting too much hot sun onto the foliage. If the plants' lower leaves appear dry or crinkled, remove the foil immediately.

Lighten up your yard. Make the night a little brighter by giving each one of your lamps or lanterns a reflective backdrop. Just wrap pieces of wood or cardboard in aluminum foil, shiny side up, and set one behind each light fixture.

Do Tell!

If you use a lot of aluminum foil around the old homestead, you're not alone. According to the folks who keep track of such things, every year, Americans use 500 million pounds of aluminum foil and foil containers. That adds up to 8 million miles of foil—enough to stretch from the earth to the moon and back again about 18 times!

Clean your birdbath. It goes without saying that you want your bathing and drinking water to be pure and crystal clear. Well, so do birds! If the winged wonders aren't flocking to your yard as much as they used to, it could be that your birdbath could use a little cleaning. So just sprinkle baking soda onto the surface, then crumple a piece of aluminum foil into a ball, dip it in water, and scrub-a-dub-dub! (In Chapter 2, you'll find a jillion-and-one more great, garden-variety uses for baking soda.)

Remove rust from chrome. Whether the offending spots are on your lawn mower, your car, or your (or your youngster's) bicycle, there's a super-simple way to get them off. Just crumple up a piece of aluminum foil, dip it into some cola, and rub the spots away.

Most youngsters love to play card games, but sometimes a hand of cards is too big for little hands to hold. Here's a simple solution: Give each tyke a closed, empty box that once held aluminum foil, plastic wrap, or wax paper. (Be sure to peel off the serrated cutting edge first!) Then have the youngsters stick the cards, upright, into the opening in the top of the box. The result looks a little like a wooden rack full of Scrabble® tiles. *Note:* This same trick works just as well for grownups with arthritis or hand injuries as it does for kids.

Shine your tools. When you come in from working in your yard, do you always find yourself searching for a rag to scrape mud or other gunk off of your metal tools? Well, search no more! Instead, keep a box of aluminum foil in your tool shed or workshop. Then anytime the need arises, simply tear off a piece of foil, crumple it up, and rub the dirt away. In the process, you'll also sharpen the tools' edges a little.

Clean your grill. Looking for an easy way to clean your barbecue grill? Here it is: After you serve up the last steak or burger, lay a sheet of aluminum foil on the hot grill. Then, when the metal has cooled down, peel off the foil, crinkle it into a ball, and rub the grill clean. All that burned-on meat will be gone faster than you can say, "Make mine medium rare."

Keep steel wool rust-free. After you've finished an outdoor (or even an indoor) chore with a steel-wool pad, if the pad still has some "life" left in it, don't even think of tossing it in the trash. (As the old saying goes, "Waste not, want not.") Instead, wrap the pad in aluminum foil and tuck it into the freezer. It'll stay rust-free and be rarin' to go!

Create a funnel. Need a one-time funnel for a really grimy job, like pouring oil into your lawn mower? Double over a piece of aluminum foil, roll it into the shape of a cone, and insert the small end into the oil tank's opening. Then pour away!

Make a barbecue drip pan. A grease fire in a barbecue grill is a nuisance—if you're lucky. If you're not so lucky, it could be a disaster. Well, to paraphrase Smokey, only you can prevent trouble. Fortunately, it's a snap. Just mold a double layer of heavy-duty aluminum foil around a baking pan that's about an inch bigger all around than the meat you're cooking. Set your pan under the grill, and bingo—instant peace of mind!

No more bugs in your drink. When you're kicking back in the shade of a tree, sipping a nice, cool drink, you don't want to share it with a bunch of bugs. And you don't have to. Just cover the top of your glass with aluminum foil, poke a hole in it, and push a straw through the hole. Then sip to your heart's content—and the bugs' frustration.

Here's to YOU!

There's almost nothing more frustrating than trying to cut with dull scissors—indoors *or* out. You can sharpen those blades in a hurry with this simple trick: Just fold a piece of aluminum foil into three or four layers, and cut it into strips with your dull scissors. Eight or ten slices should put those clippers back on the cutting edge again. But don't throw the pieces away! Instead, use them to keep roving cats out of your garden. (See "Make your garden cat-free," on page 6.)

Keep your buns warm. Nobody likes to put a fresh-from-the-grill burger or hot dog into a cold bun. And your family and guests won't have to if you try this simple trick: Line your serving basket with a piece of aluminum foil, add your warmed rolls, and top it off with a napkin. The rolls will stay nice and toasty until the main course comes off of the grill.

Food-Storage Bags

Germinate seeds. To get a jump on the growing season, wrap your flower or vegetable seeds in a moist paper towel, insert it into a resealable plastic bag, close the package, and set it in a warm, dark place. Every few days, open your home-made incubator and take a look: When you see little sprouts, remove the seeds and plant them, either directly in the garden or in starter pots indoors (depending on the time of year and the type of seed).

Save your seeds. When you don't use all of the seeds in a packet, don't throw them away! Instead, mix 1 part seed with 1 part powdered milk in a resealable plastic bag (one kind of seed per bag). Squeeze the air out, close the top tightly, and stash the pouch in the refrigerator (not the freezer). The milk will keep the seeds dry and fresh all winter long. Then, come spring, they'll be rarin' to grow! If you don't plant them then, don't worry: Most vegetable and annual flower seeds remain viable for two to three years.

Make a hanging garden. Are you a little short on garden space? Or maybe the only "land" you have is a balcony. Either way, here's how to gain some ground: Poke a few small drainage holes in the bottoms of heavy-duty plastic bags, then tack them to a board. Fill each bag with potting soil, add a few seeds or a small transplant, and water well. Before long, you'll have a lush and lovely vertical garden.

Grow perfect apples. If you opt for quality over quantity, even when it comes to your homegrown apples, then this tip has your name all over it: When the fruits are about the size of a marble, select those that are flawless, and slip a plastic sandwich bag over each one. Fasten the bag to the stem with a twist tie, but keep it loose enough to allow good air circulation. At harvest time, remove the "armor" along with the apples of your eye.

Here's to
YOU!

When yard work (or play) leaves you with tired, achy, or strained muscles, it's a good idea to have instant relief at hand. And you can, with the help of a heavy-duty plastic freezer bag. How you use this dandy device depends upon whether your problem calls for a cold or hot treatment. Here are your choices:

Cold treatment. Before trouble strikes, make a reusable ice pack. Just mix 1 part rubbing alcohol with 2 parts water, then pour the solution into the bag (but don't fill it; leave room for expansion). Squeeze out all of the air, seal the bag, and put it in the freezer. Because alcohol doesn't freeze, the contents will be slushy rather than rock hard—and all the more comfortable to conform to your achin' body.

Heat treatment. Put a wet washcloth in the bag, and microwave it on high for 30 seconds. Reheat it as often as you need to. It's more portable than a heating pad and a whole lot easier than fussing with a hot-water bottle.

Make a seed-collection kit. Take a tip from the Boy Scouts, and
be prepared to snag spent flower heads (with permission,
of course!) wherever you spot them—say in a friend's
yard, on a garden tour, or even in a park. Just get a resealable plastic bag that's sandwich-sized or a little larger, and
tuck a few smaller bags inside of it. Include a permanent
marker or a pen and some labels so that you can write all

MARVELOUS Mix

Homemade Seed Tape

Seed tape is one of the best planting aids that any gardener
could ask for. But it's especially handy if you've got young
helpers who tend to get the seeds everywhere except in the
holes where they belong. Most garden centers and catalogs
sell seed tape, but you'll have a much bigger choice of
plants—and have a whole lot of fun besides—if you make your
own. Here's all there is to it.

> **Paper towel**
> **Plastic wrap**
> **Resealable plastic bag**
> **Seeds**

Cut a 3-inch-wide strip from a paper towel, dampen it, and
lay it on top of a slightly wider strip of plastic wrap. Lay your
seeds on the paper towel, spacing them according to the directions on the seed packet. Cover this with another 3-inch-wide
strip of damp paper towel. Roll up your paper-and-plastic
sandwich, put it inside a plastic bag, and store it in a warm
place (the top of your refrigerator is perfect). Check it periodically, and when the seeds have sprouted, remove the plastic
wrap and carefully carry your towel strip to the garden. Set it
in the bed, cover it with soil to the depth that's right for your
seeds, and water gently.

of the pertinent details on the bags. Stash the kit in your purse or the glove compartment of your car, and you'll be all set when opportunity knocks.

Store pears safely. Pears are one of the trickiest fruits to deal with because you have to pick them when they're still hard, rather than letting them ripen on the tree. And once they've been harvested, they ripen up in a flash. Here's the best method I've found for storing homegrown or store-bought pears: Poke half a dozen or so holes in a resealable plastic bag, insert your fruit, and stash it in your refrigerator's produce compartment. Check on it frequently, because pears can over-ripen quickly. And whatever you do, don't store pears in a sealed plastic bag in or out of the refrigerator—the lack of oxygen will cause the fruit to turn brown at the core.

Help seedlings stay warm and snug. Starting seeds indoors? Slip each pot or flat inside a large, clear plastic bag to seal in warmth and moisture. Remove the bag for an hour or so each day to prevent too much humidity from building up and causing disease problems.

Keep just-cut flowers fresh. A friend has just invited you to cut yourself a big bouquet of flowers from her garden. The trouble is, you've got a long drive home, and those blooms are likely to turn as limp as wet dishrags on the way. Well, don't worry—here's the simple solution: Wrap the stems in a wet paper towel, slide the bundle into a resealable plastic bag, and close the top as tightly as possible.

Make fruit trees blossom faster. How? By bending the tree's branches downward to a roughly 60-degree angle, thereby shifting the plant's energy away from foliage growth and into producing fruit buds. To accomplish that feat, simply fill heavy-duty plastic freezer bags with sand and hang them on the branches as weights—making sure that the branches don't break! This nifty trick works with any kind of tree fruit, including apples, pears, peaches, and plums.

Take "dinner" to carnivorous plants. If you grow Venus flytraps or other green "pets" that eat bugs instead of fertilizer, sink your teeth into this tip: When you round up the necessary insects, tuck them into a zip-top plastic bag. Make sure it's the kind with a slider that you can open and close quickly. (Otherwise, the meal could escape before you get it home!)

Make sticky traps. Many flying insects find certain colors irresistible. You can turn that craving into the cause of their downfall: Just tuck a piece of appropriately colored poster board or construction paper inside a resealable plastic bag. Cover the bag with petroleum jelly or a commercial stick-um, and hang it on or next to your plagued plant. Every few days, remove the bug-covered bag and replace it with a fresh one. As for what color to use, see "Color Them Gone," on the opposite page. One word of caution: If you find that your traps are catching beneficial insects like bees, butterflies, or ladybugs along with the bad guys, change your tactics. Throughout this book, you'll find plenty of ways to get rid of destructive pests without harming garden-variety heroes.

Corral your work papers. If your garden shed is anything like mine, it's filled with owner's manuals, instruction booklets, and equipment warranties—not to mention tonic recipes, plant lists, garden plans, and seed catalogs. To keep it all clean, dry, and at your fingertips, do what I do: Use resealable plastic bags as file folders. Organize the papers in whatever way makes sense to you, placing each in its own plastic bag, and keep them in your choice of containers. (Anything goes, from a plastic milk crate or old wooden box to a fancy, rectangular planter.)

Make a fire extinguisher Unlike weather related disasters, a fire doesn't give you fair warning before it strikes. So don't take any chances. Fill some resealable plastic bags with baking soda, and keep them in your workshop, garden shed, and anyplace else you keep flammable substances. Should the need arise, just open the top and douse the flames. (For good measure, keep a couple of these fire-stoppers in your car and at least one by the kitchen stove.)

Marinate meat. And carry it, too. Has this ever happened to you? You've gotten your steaks, chops, or chicken marinated just so in the kitchen. Then, as you're toting them outside to put on the grill, you trip and spill half the marinade— or worse yet, drop the bowl and lose everything. Well, for your next barbecue, put your main course and your favorite marinade into a resealable plastic bag. That way, there's no muss, no fuss—and no disappointed diners, either!

Color Them Gone

Remember the old saying, "You can catch a lot more flies with honey than you can with vinegar"? Well, you can catch a lot more of *any* kind of bugs if you choose the right color for your traps. Here's a quick rundown of color preferences, insect-style.

COLOR	BUGS THAT FLOCK TO IT
Blue	Thrips
Green	Walnut husk flies
Red	Fruit flies (including apple-maggot flies)
White	Flea beetles, four-lined plant bugs, plum curculios, rose chafers, and tarnished plant bugs
Yellow	Most flying insects, including aphids, cabbage moths, leaf miners, psyllids, squash beetles, webworm moths, and whiteflies
Yellow-orange	Carrot rust flies

Food-Storage Containers

Start seeds. Getting a jump on the spring planting season? Plastic food-storage containers make perfect starter pots—or flats, depending on the size you prefer. Just poke drainage holes in the bottoms of the containers, fill them with seed-starting mix, and plant your flower or vegetable seeds. Then put these pots into larger food-storage containers without holes, to contain the runoff. After you've moved your seedlings to the garden, wash off your "maternity wards" and stash 'em away until next year.

Make seed-sprouting greenhouses. Most flower and vegetable seeds germinate faster and grow stronger in warm, humid conditions. But you don't need a fancy greenhouse to provide those surroundings—just invert the bottom of a food-storage container over your seed-starting flat to hold in heat and humidity. Remember to take it off for an hour or so each day, so the moisture doesn't build up too much.

Keep deer repellents working. Plenty of aromatic substances, like deodorant soap, smelly socks, or dog hair, will send deer scurrying. But rain or snow will quickly wash the scent away. So before you set out your deterrent of choice, tuck it into an old panty hose toe, or a mesh onion bag, and tie the pouch closed with a string. Then poke a hole in the bottom of a plastic food-storage container and tuck the pouch inside. (A round, 12- to 16-ounce container is perfect for this purpose.) Pull the string through the hole, and tie it into a loop. Then fasten the loop to a tree branch, and you're good to go. Your smell-emitters should keep their deer-chasing power for about a year through rain, sleet, snow, or dark of night!

Even so-called disposable food-storage containers can be reused several times, as long as you wash them thoroughly. (They come out spotless—and odorless—when you run them through the dishwasher on the top rack.) Even when they do finally get too grungy to use or the lids go astray, there's still plenty of life left in those plastic marvels. Here's just a sampling:

Wipe out mosquitoes. Fill large containers (loaf-sized or bigger) with water, add a few squirts of dishwashing liquid, and set them outside. When female skeeters set down to lay their eggs, they won't get up again.

Make plant-stake toppers. Whether you use wood or metal stakes to prop up tall plants, you always run the risk of hitting your face or, worse, your eye on the dang things when you're working in the garden. The simple solution: Put a piece of double-sided tape on the top of each stake and push a small food-storage container, upside down, over the top of it. Because the containers are transparent, they'll be all but invisible, but they'll give you a big margin of safety.

Lighten up big pots. Before you add potting mix, set closed food-storage containers on the bottom. (Be sure they're upside down if the lids have gone AWOL.) They'll take up the space, and the weight, of a lot of soil. Use this trick only for annuals and shallow-rooted perennials. Trees, shrubs, and some large perennials need all the root space they can get.

Trap slugs. Bury a food-storage container up to its rim in the soil, and fill it with the bait of your choice (you'll find some dandy ones in Chapters 3 and 13). The slugs will belly up to the bar, and they won't get out!

Make plant labels. Cut roughly 2-by-6-inch strips from the sides and bottom of an old food-storage container, and use a permanent marker to write the pertinent details on the top portion of each strip. Then insert the bottom part into the soil in your garden beds, or into the starting mix in your seed flats.

Dry flowers. This simple technique works just as well for leaves and decorative seedpods. First, get a plastic food-storage container that's big enough to hold your plant parts. Next, mix 1 part borax and 2 parts cornmeal, and pour a 1-inch layer of the mixture into the box. Lay your plant material on top, then very gently cover it with more of the mix, taking care to leave no air space around the flowers. (If you're working with many-petaled posies, such as roses or carnations, sprinkle some of the mixture directly into each bloom before you place it in the container). Put on the lid, press it tightly closed, and store the box in a dry place at room temperature for 7 to 10 days. At the end of the waiting time, pour or gently brush away the covering, and carefully lift out your newly dried beauties.

Make potpourri. Do you love to scent your rooms with homemade blends of dried herbs and flowers? Then here's a perfect mix-and-store idea for you: Just combine the ingredients of your choice, pour the mixture into plastic food-storage containers, secure the lids tightly, and stack them neatly in a cool, dark place until you're ready to use the aromatic treasure. For one fabulous, fresh-from-the-garden (rather, *dried*-from-the-garden) recipe, see my "Dazzling Basil Potpourri," on the opposite page.

Assemble a first-aid kit. For such an easy-going pastime, gardening certainly has its share of risks. For instance, you never know when you'll reach out to prune a rose and wind up with a thorn-pricked finger. And then there's all of those bugs just waiting to stick their choppers—or their stingers—into your unsuspecting skin. So do what I do: Fill a plastic food-storage container with emergency supplies like bandages, antibiotic cream, and a small bottle of

MARVELOUS Mix

Dazzling Basil Potpourri

This old-time potpourri looks as good as it smells. What's more, it's as easy as pie to make with dried herbs and flowers picked fresh from your garden.

- **4 cups of sweet basil leaves and flower spikes**
- **2 cups of dark opal basil leaves and flower spikes**
- **2 cups of rosebuds**
- **2 cups of rose petals**
- **2 cups of rose geranium leaves**
- **1 cup of lavender blossoms**
- **1 oz. of orrisroot***
- **1 oz. of sweet flag powder***

Put the dried leaves and flowers in a big bowl, and toss them gently. Add the orrisroot and sweet flag powder, and toss the mixture again. Scoop the potpourri into plastic food-storage containers, canning jars, or other airtight containers, and store them in a cool, dark place. To use your colorful, sweet-smelling creation, pour it into a basket or bowl, and set it out to be admired.

*Available in craft-supply stores, herb shops, and the floral section of some supermarkets.

antiseptic mouthwash (for use on insect bites). Then stash it with your hand tools in your gardening carryall.

Store your stuff. You can buy plastic food-storage containers that are small enough for just a single serving of applesauce, big enough for a potluck casserole, and every size in between—and in just about every shape you can imagine. Plus, they're inexpensive, waterproof, stackable, and surprisingly sturdy. In short, they're perfect organizing aids for your garden shed or workshop!

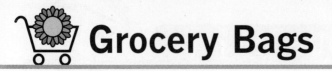

Grocery Bags

Make compost. Brown paper bags are a first-class source of carbon. To tap into their riches, just tear up the bags, or run them through a paper shredder, and toss the pieces into your compost bin. If you don't have a compost bin (or pile), just bury the scraps in the ground. They'll break down in no time, improving your soil in the process.

Get rid of weeds. It never fails: You're all geared up to plant a new garden, or maybe pour a new patio, but there's a thriving crop of weeds standing in the way. Well, don't fret. You can clear out those invaders lickety-split—without toxic herbicides. Here's my almost no-work method: First, trample any tall weeds or, if you prefer, mow them down. Then spread brown paper bags on top, overlapping them as you go, until the layer is three or four bags deep. If you're making a path, walkway, or outdoor seating area, add gravel, bark mulch, or another foot-friendly substance. To make an instant planting bed, pile on 6 to 8 inches of topsoil and compost.

Protect young plants from the cold. The calendar, and even the soil temperature, may *say* that it's time to plant your garden. But when Mother Nature is calling the shots, it pays to have a little weather insurance up your sleeve—like this simple solution: At planting time, as you dig each hole, set a brown paper bag (opened and upright) inside so that the top 10 inches or so sticks up above the soil surface. Fill it with soil, roll the top down to form a collar on the outside of the bag, and plant your seedling. At the first sign of frost, roll up the collar and fasten it with a spring-loaded clothespin or two. When all danger of frost has passed, simply cut off as much of the bag as you can, leaving the rest in place.

Harvest your seeds. If you've ever tried to save seeds from your flowers (or vegetables), you know that sometimes the little things simply blow away in the wind before you have a chance to collect them. But that won't happen if you use this simple trick: When the flowers fade and the seedpods start turning brown, cover each plant with a brown paper bag, and tie it closed at the bottom with twine. Then, when the stems turn brown, clip off the plant at ground level, flip the bag over, and take it indoors. Give the bag a good shake every few days. When you hear loose seeds rattling around, remove the twine, cut off the stems, and store the bag in a cool, dry place until planting time.

On This Date in History...

Have you ever wondered when various bags and wraps found their way into our lives? You haven't? Well, I'm going to tell you anyway. Here's a brief history lesson, so now you'll know!

IN THE YEAR	THIS HAPPENED
1883	Charles Stilwell patented a machine to make flat-bottomed, brown paper bags.
1927	Nicholas Marcalus first put wax paper on a roll in a box with a built-in cutting blade. (Before that, it was sold in bags of pre-cut sheets.)
1942	Earl Tupper discovered a method for molding polyethylene into containers with tight-fitting lids.
1947	Richard S. Reynolds introduced aluminum foil as we know it today.
1950	Harry Wasylyk and Larry Hansen invented the plastic trash bag, intended for commercial use.
1956	Saran Wrap® was first sold in supermarkets.
Late 1960s	GLAD® trash bags became available in supermarkets.
1977	Plastic grocery bags first appeared in supermarkets.

Shelter young plants with plastic. If you haven't "planted" bottoms-up weather protection for your flower and vegetable seedlings, top-down coverage will do just as well. Just push four sticks into the soil around each plant, so that the ends stick up a couple of inches above the foliage. Then pull a plastic grocery bag down over the sticks and anchor the bottom with stones. If the temperature warms up, remove the cover during the day.

Winterize your trees. To protect the trunks from sunscald and from bark-munching deer and rabbits, cut brown paper bags into strips about 6 inches wide. Then wrap the

How can a simple brown paper bag make your automotive life easier? Just look!

Here's to **YOU!**

Keep your windshield ice-free. If you have to leave your car outdoors overnight in the winter when precipitation is forecast, cut brown paper bags down the sides to open them up, spread them across the windshield, and secure them in place with the wiper blades. Come morning, strip off the bags, and toss them on the compost pile or into the recycling bin.

Keep your car's interior cool. When the summer sun is baking everything in sight and you can't find your windshield protector, use brown paper bags instead. Cut them open, lay them against the inside of the windshield, and lower the visors to hold the paper to the glass.

Keep the steering wheel cool, too. Just cut or tear a roughly 10-inch slit in one side of a brown paper bag, and slip the bag over the wheel to keep it as cool as a cucumber.

strips in spiral fashion up the trunk, overlapping as you go, and fastening the ends with masking tape. If you're worried about rabbits, you can stop the coverup about 2 feet above the ground. To guard against deer and sunscald, continue wrapping up to the height of the tree's lowest branches.

Jump-start your radishes. Radishes are naturally fast-growing vegetables. And with just a little pre-planting TLC, they'll turn into genuine speed demons. Soak the seeds in water for 24 hours, then put them in a brown paper bag and set it in the sun. Within 24 hours, the seeds will germinate, and you can plant 'em right in the ground.

Ripen tomatoes faster. If you have to pick 'em while they're still a tad green (or even *all* green), put them in a brown paper bag, and store at room temperature. The bag helps retain the natural gases that cause the fruit to ripen. If you have a ripe apple on hand, toss it into the sack, too—it'll give off gases that speed up the ripening process even more.

Ripen tree fruits, too. This same brown paper bag trick also works to bring other fruits to the eating stage faster, whether you've grown them yourself, or bought them at the supermarket. Prime candidates include peaches, pears, avocados, bananas, and (yes) apples.

Keep onions fresh longer. Whether you grow your own onions or buy them at the supermarket, you want to keep them at their peak of freshness and flavor for as long as possible. So do what I do with my crop: Put them in a brown paper bag, and store them on the bottom shelf of your refrigerator. You'll delay the bulbs' sprouting for two to three months.

Dry herbs. In order to retain their volatile oils (the secret to their fragrance and flavor), herbs need to dry in near total darkness. If no room in your house meets that requirement, you can create it this way: Gather the sprays into bunches of five or six stems each, and tie the stems together with twine. Then put each bunch upside down in a brown paper bag (making sure the herbs clear the bottom), fasten the top with a rubber band, and hang the bundles from anything that'll hold them.

Mulch your veggies. To keep your vegetable garden all but weed-free, spread brown paper bags over the soil and top them with grass clippings or shredded leaves. Besides making it hard for weeds to grow, the barrier will also conserve moisture in the soil and prevent soilborne pests and diseases from splashing onto your plants.

Make a mulching kit for tight places. The process couldn't be simpler. Tear or cut brown paper bags into strips from 2 to 6 inches wide, fold them into tidy bundles, and keep them with your garden tools. Take a supply with you whenever you go out to weed, harvest, or do other chores. Then, whenever you spot a piece of bare ground in a tightly planted bed, just lay the strips where you need them, and toss on grass clippings, leaves—or even weeds if they haven't gone to seed.

Get amaryllis to bloom every year. For a lot of folks—including yours truly—nothing cheers up a gray, winter day like these big, bold, beautiful blooms. If you always toss your bulbs into the compost bin because you think they're one-year wonders, here's good news: You can bring 'em back again and again, using this simple method. After the big, beautiful flowers fade, clip off the blooms, remove each

Here's to YOU!

It never seems to fail: You're rushing to a dentist appointment or a business meeting, and you have to stop for gas. You don't want to show up with eau de gasoline on your hands (and, of course, there's no full-service station in sight). But you're in luck—that is, if you keep a few plastic grocery bags in the trunk. Just pop one over each hand before you get to pumpin'!

bulb from its container, and put it in a brown paper bag with the leaves and stem intact. (As with in-ground bulbs, as the greenery withers away, it provides the necessary food to produce next year's flowers.) Put the bag in a spot that will stay cool, dark, and dry all through the spring and summer. In the fall, replant it from 6 to 10 weeks before you want it to bloom. The timing varies, depending on the variety, but the instructions that came with the bulb should include the schedule.

Kill slugs safely. Salt is a classic slug killer. But don't even think of pouring the stuff directly on the pests—if your aim is off, the salt could do more damage to your plants than the slugs could! Instead, pour a quarter inch or so of salt into a brown paper bag. Then pick up the slugs one by one (I use old tongs for this job), drop them into the sack, and give it a few good shakes. End of story.

Eliminate tree borers. You'll know these pests are hard at work if your tree appears weak, it has branches dying back, or you see holes in the bark, surrounded by what looks like gummy sawdust. Your first mission is to prune off and destroy any affected branches. Then water and fertilize the victim to speed up the recovery process. Next, set

Grocery Bags

about preventing the next generation of borers by trapping their mothers (clearwing moths that resemble wasps, with translucent wings, black bodies, and markings that are either red, orange, or yellow). Simply wrap brown paper bags around the tree's trunk—overlapping and taping them together as you go—and coat the paper with petroleum jelly or a commercial adhesive. Just remember to check your traps every week or so, and replace them with new ones as necessary. *Note:* This trick works just as well for trapping other tree pests, including ants that are farming aphids in the upper branches.

Head off pest problems. Many garden pests and disease organisms live—and multiply—in dead plant material of all kinds. So, whenever you go out to your garden, carry along a pair of clippers and a brown paper bag. The minute you spot a dead, damaged, or just plain odd-looking plant part, clip it off and drop it into the bag—before it has a chance to fall on the ground and become a bad-bug motel. If the stuff you've collected is healthy, toss it, bag and all, into the compost bin, or simply dig a hole in an out-of-the-way spot in your yard and bury the whole shebang (it'll break down and improve your soil in no time). But if there's any sign of pesky pests or dastardly diseases, don't take chances: Send it all off with the trash collector.

Discourage critters. Most wild animals, and even some roaming domestic ones, will flee from the sound of human voices. But you don't have to sit on your porch chatting day and night. Just turn on a battery-powered radio to an all-talk station, slide the radio inside a plastic grocery bag, and tie it closed. Then set the talking box among your at-risk plants. Chances are, the critters will scurry in a hurry. Just remember that our furry friends have ultra-sensitive ears, so it's fine to keep the volume turned down low. In fact, if you don't, the noise may also send neighbors scurrying— right to your doorstep!

Keep seedbeds cat free. It's a frustrating fact that for most outdoor cats, a bed of loose, freshly dug soil is the ultimate litter box. But it's simple to say "Not here, my dear!" Just cut open some brown paper bags and lay them in a single layer over your planting beds (or your newly sown lawn). Use stones to hold the paper in place. Within a couple of days, the soil will have settled enough that Fluffy won't find it tempting. Then you can pull up the bags and toss them into the compost bin.

Make luminaria. Is it fiesta time at your hacienda? Then brighten the scene with some classic Southwestern-style lights. Cut out decorative shapes from the sides of brown paper bags, and pour about 2 inches of sand into the bottom of each one. Insert a small candle (like a votive candle) in the center, and push it slightly into the sand. Set the filled sacks wherever you like—for instance, around your patio or along your sidewalk—and use long fireplace matches to light the candles.

Even when plastic grocery bags have a few holes or slits in them (say, from a run-in with the sharp corners of a cereal box), you can still put them to good use. Here's a trio of possibilities:

* Crumple them up and use them as packing material when you store Christmas decorations or other breakables.

* Decorate for a party by cutting colorful bags into streamers. Start at the open end, and stop when you get to within 2 inches of the bottom. Then hang the bags from cord that you've strung on the wall, from porch pillars, or between trees.

* Use them as waterproof stuffing for outdoor cushions, or for homemade pool and tub toys.

Clean up after your dog. When Fido does his duty—whether you're romping in your yard or strolling around the neighborhood—pick the stuff up with a plastic grocery bag. Then flip it inside out, tie it closed, and toss it in the trash can. (They also work great for dispensing with scooped-up, clumping cat litter.)

Make scarecrows. Are some of your fine-feathered friends inviting themselves to dinner in your newly planted garden (or newly seeded lawn)? Make a "Restaurant Closed" sign this way: Collect a bunch of plastic grocery bags—the more colorful, the better. Fill them with air, tie them shut, and fasten them securely to the top of stakes about 5 to 6 feet tall. Push the stakes into the ground throughout your gar-

Here's to
YOU!

It's no secret that commercial packing materials, like bubble wrap and foam peanuts, can cost a pretty penny. Fortunately, if relocation figures into your future, products from the Bags & Wraps aisle—both new and used—can help ease the strain on your budget. Not only are some of them (like grocery bags) absolutely free, but when you unpack at your new home, you can put all that protective stuff to good use. Here are some penny-pinching pointers I've picked up from various vagabond friends:

* Wrap breakables in paper or plastic bags.

* Crumble up bags, wax paper, or plastic wrap, and stuff the wads into the nooks and crannies inside of packing boxes.

* Use food-storage containers or cardboard tubes, or even boxes from aluminum foil, plastic wrap, or wax paper (either full or empty), to cushion your goods.

den (or your newly seeded lawn). I set mine in a random pattern, 10 to 15 feet apart. When the bags bob in the breeze, they look an awful lot like people bending over, and the birds don't like that one little bit!

Light your fire. Who needs smelly old chemical fire starters, when you can make your own for free? Just stuff a small (lunch-sized) brown paper bag with crumpled newspaper and a few candle nubbins. Then set it among the kindling in your outdoor fireplace or fire pit.

Plastic Wrap

Make a mini greenhouse. To give seeds or cuttings the humidity they need, insert a clean chopstick or Popsicle® stick into each corner of the flat and lay a sheet of plastic wrap on top. Take the cover off for an hour or so every day to get rid of excessive moisture and fend off mildew.

Make plant labels. Just cover empty seed packets with plastic wrap, and tape or tack them to whatever upright supports you can come by easily—for example, chopsticks, skewers, Popsicle® sticks, or paint stir-sticks. Then sink your colorful signs into the ground at appropriate spots in your garden.

Keep stored paint fresh. It's frustrating, all right: You need to touch up a few spots on the fence you painted last summer, so you pull the can of paint off the shelf in your workshop, open it up—and find that it's dried out. That won't happen again if you use this easy trick. When you've finished your project, stretch a sheet of plastic wrap over the open can, then put the lid on and tap it down gently with a hammer. That'll prevent the paint from drying out.

Keep a flower standing straight. One of the most effective floral "arrangements" of all is a single, perfect flower in a beautiful, narrow-necked vase—that is, except when that pretty posy wants to tilt and tip every which way. Fortunately, it's a snap to stop the swaying. After you've poured in the water and inserted the stem, just wad up a small piece of plastic wrap and stuff it into the vase at its narrowest point (most likely, you'll have to use a chopstick, pencil, or screwdriver to maneuver it in). The stem will stay on the up-and-up.

Have you ever stopped to think that there might be a medicinal use for plastic wrap? You haven't? Well, there is! In fact, there are several. Try these, for example:

Here's to **YOU!**

Get rid of a hangnail. At bedtime, apply hand cream to the nasty thing, wrap your fingertip with plastic wrap, and secure it with tape (any kind you have on hand will do). While you're snoozing, the wrap will act as a sort of mini greenhouse, retaining moisture and softening the wayward cuticle.

Treat psoriasis. Apply a topical steroid cream to the trouble spot, cover it with a piece of plastic wrap, and use adhesive tape to hold it in place. The wrap will seal in moisture, thereby enhancing the effect of the steroid. Plus, it will help stop the rash from spreading. (No wonder dermatologists often recommend this routine!)

Intensify liniment action. After you rub your (or your doctor's) choice of liniments into an aching joint or muscle, cover the area with plastic wrap. It'll increase the heating effect of the salve. *Note:* Give this treatment a test run on a small area first to make sure it doesn't burn your skin.

Like many of the products we take for granted today, plastic wrap first hit the supermarket shelves in the 1950s. Also, like many of our modern-day staples, this handy stuff was discovered years before it reached household consumers—and quite by accident. It happened in 1933, and the unintentional inventor was Ralph Wiley, a college student who worked part-time cleaning glassware in a Dow Chemical Company laboratory. One day, Ralph came across a vial covered with a green, greasy, foul-smelling film that, as hard as he tried, he could not scrub off. He nicknamed it "eonite" after an indestructible substance featured in the "Little Orphan Annie" comic strip. He told Dow's research scientists about his find, and they took the ball and ran with it. The result: a dark green, greasy film that they re-christened "Saran" (although its technical name is *polyvinylidene chloride*). Saran's early admirers included the U.S. military, which sprayed it on fighter planes to guard them from the ravages of salt-laden sea spray. And Detroit automakers used it to protect car upholstery.

Eventually, Dow managed to eliminate the green color and unpleasant odor, and transformed Saran from a sprayable liquid to a solid material. In 1953, it was approved for food packaging and three years later, as a contact food wrap. And thus, in 1956, Saran Wrap® was born.

Protect a book from the elements. Remember, it's a dirty world out there! When you head outdoors with a good book—whether you're taking it to the garden to use as reference, or you just plan to sit in the shade and read awhile—protect the covers with a sheet of plastic wrap.

Fix a kite. When a youngster's (or your own) kite has a run-in with a tree limb or fencepost, cover the tear with plastic wrap and tape it onto the paper. This temporary repair won't last forever, but it will at least buy you a little more flight time.

Plastic Wrap

Hold a screw in place. Do those little bits of hardware keep slipping and sliding right out from under your screwdriver? Stop those shenanigans by pushing the screw through a small piece of plastic wrap. Then insert the screwdriver into the groove on the screw head, and pull the wrap back over the tip of the screwdriver and hold it as you proceed as usual.

Repair the glass in a cold frame. Dang! The weather forecast calls for a sudden temperature drop tonight, while you've got a frame full of young plants, and a brand new hole in the glass—courtesy of a stone kicked up by your lawn mower. No problem! Simply tape plastic wrap over the hole or crack, and attach it with duct tape. (Of course, this same emergency fix-up works just as well for windows in your greenhouse or your home, sweet home.)

 # Trash Bags

Turn an old lampshade into a planter. Just turn the shade upside down and line it with a heavy-duty trash bag. Trim away any excess plastic, and staple the liner in place along the sides. Cut a few slits in the bottom for drainage, add some potting soil, and plant away! *Note:* This trick works just as well with wicker baskets, wooden boxes, or any other container that's not waterproof.

Weatherproof large pots. Freezing temperatures can cause clay and even some concrete containers to crack or flake. But if you have planters that are too heavy to move indoors, or you don't have the space to store them, try this simple trick: Remove as much potting mix as you can (soil that's left in the pot will expand as it freezes, thereby increasing the risk

A Bumper Crop—It's in the Bag!

Make that *on top of* the bag. If you're fixin' to grow heat-loving crops like squash, tomatoes, peppers, or corn, black plastic trash bags can the lead the way to a happy harvest. Here's all you need to do. First, get your planting beds ready in the fall, and cover them with a thick layer of leaves or straw. This will help keep the ground as warm as possible through the winter. Come spring, take off the mulch and replace it with black plastic trash bags to heat up the soil in preparation for planting. (For the exact timing, check the soil-temperature guidelines on the seed packet.) The next step depends on where you live:

* If summer gets steamy in your territory, take the plastic mulch off of your beds *before* you plant your seeds. Otherwise, later in the season, the soil will heat up too much. Once the plants are on their way, spread an organic mulch around them to keep the soil cool and the weeds out.

* In parts of the country where the soil needs all the warming help it can get, let the plastic stay on the ground. Just cut slits in it where you want to sow your seeds or set in your transplants. Be sure to anchor the sheet securely at planting time. If it shifts even a tad, it will cover the little seedlings and smother them in the blink of an eye.

of cracking). Then slip a black plastic trash bag over the pot to keep out moisture, help retain the sun's heat—and improve the planter's chances of surviving the winter.

Make planting bags. When planting time rolls around, do you always have more plants than containers to put them in? Well, there's no need to run out and buy more. Just fill dark-colored, heavy-duty trash bags with potting soil, compost, or a half-and-half mixture of compost and good garden soil. (Leave enough space so you can lay the filled bags on their sides and flatten them a little.) Tie the tops closed, set the sacks where you want them, and cut slashes in the bottom for drainage. Make more slits on top, and tuck in the annual flowers or vegetables of your choice. In the fall, toss the plants into your compost bin, and empty the bags onto planting beds, or use the material to fill low spots in your lawn.

Kill weeds. This is the easiest method I know of to create weed-free ground: In early summer, spread black plastic trash bags over any intruding weeds, and weight the cover down with rocks. The sun will cook the weeds to a crisp. In the fall, remove the plastic, and prepare your beds for spring planting.

"Babysit" your houseplants. Before you take off on a business trip or vacation, line your bathtub with trash bags and cover them with a big, wet towel. Set your plants on the towel, and just before you leave, water the plants thoroughly. Assuming the pots have drainage holes in their bottoms, your green pals should stay in fine fettle for two weeks or so.

Wash away spider mites. There's nothing these teeny terrors love more than houseplants. But they're no match for this lethal trick: Just set your mite-infested plants in the bathtub and turn on the shower—but first, cover each pot (but not the plant!) with a trash bag so the soil doesn't wash out in the process.

Force shrubs to bloom indoors. In early spring, just when plants are starting to show buds, clip off as many branches as you like, bring them inside, and put them in buckets of warm water. Into each pail, drop a cotton ball saturated with ammonia. Then put the branch-filled container into a giant trash bag and tie it tightly shut with twine or a twist tie. Before you know it, those baby buds will burst into bloom. (The process happens quickly, so check your branches every day or two—that way, you won't miss a minute of the big show!)

Kill small, sucking insects. If aphids, mealybugs, whiteflies, or spider mites are ganging up on your potted plants—indoors or out—you can send the bad bugs to the gas chamber with this simple trick: Just put a trash bag over the bug-infested plant, and blow cigarette smoke into the bag (or have a smoker friend do the honors). Then quickly seal the bag. Bingo: end of itty-bitty bugs!

Here's to
YOU!

Here's a painless way to battle clutter: Tie the handles of drawstring trash bags to coat hangers, and hang one in each closet in your house. Then, every time you come across a garment that you no longer wear, a toy that the kids no longer play with, or a gadget that you haven't used in ages, toss it in the bag. When you've got a bunch of filled bags, you're all set for your blockbuster garage sale—or a trip to the local thrift store. (Don't forget to ask for a receipt, so you can claim your tax deduction!)

Stop Colorado potato beetles. In addition to their namesake crop, these pesky pests target every other member of the *Solanaceae* family, which includes tomatoes, tomatillos, peppers, and eggplant. The time to stop 'em in their tracks is in the fall, when the adults have settled down in the soil for their long winter's nap, or in early spring, before they wake up. Here's all you need to do. Dig a trench about 8 inches deep around your target plants, with the sides as close to vertical as possible. Then line the trench with trash bags. When the beetles wake up in the spring, they're too weak to fly, so they have to walk to breakfast. When they reach the trench, they'll fall in and slide around on the plastic until birds come along and eat them up.

Say "sayonara" to slugs. And snails, too! First, dig a trench about 4 inches deep around your planting bed, and line it with strips cut from trash bags. Then pour about a $1/2$-inch layer of either salt or white vinegar into the bottom of your little moat. When the slimy squirts try to slither over to your plants, they'll fall into the trench and die.

Fend off fire ants. If you live in an area where these malevolent menaces ride the range (so to speak), you know that they love to build their nests in raised beds or big planters. To declare your territory closed to homesteading, just circle

Kitchen-Counter Compost

When winter winds are howling, it's no fun trudging outdoors to drop your kitchen scraps in the compost bin. So don't do it! Instead, do your composting indoors with my no-fail method.

1. In the fall, gather up some heavy-duty, black trash bags, and add a shovelful or two of finished compost or garden soil to each one. (This will jump-start the enzymes that break down the organic matter into "black gold.")

2. Fasten the bags tightly with twist ties, and keep them in your garage or basement, or on the back porch.

3. Every day or so, toss in your fruit or vegetable scraps, re-close the sack, and shake it a few times to blend the new material with the old.

Come spring, you'll have heaps of dark, earthy compost, all ready to mulch your planting beds with, or to dig into your soil.

your raised beds and planters with 6-inch-wide strips cut from a trash bag. Tack or tape the plastic in place, then coat it with any sticky substance, such as petroleum jelly, spray adhesive, or a commercial stick-um like Tanglefoot®. Just remember to keep the strips clear of "bridges" that the ants could scramble over, like twigs, leaves, or dead bugs.

Guard gardenias from grasshoppers. As you no doubt know if you live down South, these voracious villains invade gardens at night to munch on gardenia buds. But it's easy to call a halt to their dining pleasure. In late evening, cover each plant with a trash bag, then take it off in the morning, when the hoppers have gone home to bed.

Foil raccoons. Lay a 3-foot-wide strip of heavy-duty trash bags around your trash can, bird feeder, vegetable garden, or anything else you need to protect. Raccoons have hairless and very sensitive feet, and they don't like walking on slippery surfaces. So when they feel the slick plastic, they'll clear out in a hurry.

Improvise a windbreaker. When the temperature suddenly plummets, trash-bag "coats" can keep you warm. Cut a head-size hole in the bottom and two armholes in the sides. Then wear your protective gear under your regular coat.

Frolic in the snow. When a snowstorm turns your yard into a winter wonderland, but you have no sled or saucer, just wrap a heavy-duty trash bag around your fanny like a diaper, and slide, baby, slide down the nearest hill!

Do the hula. You'll be the hit of your next barbecue! Just cut the bottom off of a large, drawstring trash bag and cut vertical, inch-wide strips to within about 3 inches of the cord. Then put on your "grass skirt," and let the luau begin!

Here's to **YOU!**

For my money, there's no better summertime fun than a backyard barbecue. And there's no more irksome chore than cleaning the grill after your guests have gone home—that is, unless you use this ultra-easy method: After the rack has cooled, put it into a black plastic trash bag. (The color is crucial, because only a black bag will absorb enough intense heat from the sun.) Lay the bag on the ground, pour in enough ammonia to cover the rack, and close the bag tightly with a twist tie. Leave it lying in the sun for 2 or 3 hours, then turn it over, and leave it for another 2 or 3 hours. When you open the bag (carefully, so you don't splash ammonia on yourself), that rack will be clean as a whistle. Just rinse it with clear water, and dry it off. Then call up the gang and invite them over for another barbecue!

Deter birds. Even though birds are some of the best pest-control helpers you'll ever find, some of them can snatch more than their fair share of grass or vegetable seeds. Here's an easy way to stop that action: Starting at the open end of a trash bag, cut strips about an inch wide to within 3 inches or so of the bottom. Tape or staple the 3-inch band to your garden fence, or to posts that you've pounded into the ground in the area you want to protect. When a breeze comes up, the fringe will flap in the wind—making the startled birds scurry in a hurry!

Make waterproof stuffing. Calling all crafters! When you make pool or bathtub toys, or cushions for outdoor furniture, don't bother to buy special waterproof stuffing. Use trash bags instead. Just cut a trash bag into strips and use the pieces to fill up your creations.

Cover your outdoor gear. Catalogs and home centers sell fancy covers for patio furniture, barbecue grills, and other outdoor gear, but they can cost a pretty penny. So why shell out big bucks? Instead, when foul weather hovers on the horizon, put extra-large trash bags over anything that remains outside and needs protection from the elements.

Sleep dry. Do your children or grandchildren like to have backyard campouts? Help them rough it in comfort by spreading extra-large trash bags on the ground under their sleeping bags. This will keep 'em high and dry.

Protect your clothes. Use an extra-large trash bag as a waterproof smock for messy chores, indoors and out. Just cut a head-sized hole in the bottom and an armhole in each side, and slip the sack over your head. These handy garments also make great emergency rain slickers—I keep a few in my car's glove compartment for just that purpose.

Wax Paper

Protect tender seedlings. Drat! You've got flats of seedlings sitting on your deck, all ready to be planted, and the weatherman just predicted an unexpected frost tonight. Well, don't drag all those baby plants inside—just cover each flat with a long sheet of wax paper, and tuck the ends under the container. That waxy topper will give your future crops the protection they need from Jack Frost's capers.

Store leftover seeds. They'll stay fresh and be rarin' to grow next year if you follow this routine: Make an airtight, watertight packet by folding a piece of wax paper in half. Then fold two sides inward to form roughly ½-inch flaps, and tape

Wax Paper

41

them closed. Mix your seeds with an equal part of powdered milk, and pour them into the pouch. Fold over the top of the little bag and tape it closed. Label the outside using a permanent marker, and stash your plants-to-be in the refrigerator (not the freezer) until planting time.

When you reach the end of a roll of aluminum foil, plastic wrap, or wax paper, don't throw it away! Instead, add it to your yard-and-garden tool chest. Here are some of the dandy devices you can make from those humble cardboard tubes:

Anti-cutworm collars. Cut each tube into pieces about 5 inches long. Then sink one into the soil around each seedling, with about 2 inches of cardboard above ground and 3 inches below it.

Pest detectors. When you don't know what kind of bug is eating your plants, bait a tube by putting a spoonful of peanut butter and a few drops of olive oil inside it. Then set the roll in your garden in the late evening, and check it first thing each morning. After a couple of nights, you should find the culprit inside, and you can take the appropriate control measures.

Blade sheaths. Flatten a tube, close one end with duct tape, and bingo—you have a protective covering for a knife, shears, or a small pruning saw.

Seed-starting pots. Cut tube sections about 3 inches long, then wrap foil or plastic wrap around the outside of each piece to keep the cardboard from falling apart when it gets wet. Stand the little pots on a waterproof tray, then add seed-starting mix and sow your seeds. Come transplant time, remove the outer covering, and plant your seedlings, pots and all!

If you're like most folks, when you hear the name Thomas Edison, you think of things like electric lightbulbs, telegraphs, and phonographs. But this American icon is also credited with inventing wax paper in 1872, at the age of 25. The stuff was first used for wrapping candies. The manufacturing process is pretty simple: A triple coating of paraffin wax is pressed onto tissue paper. The wax fills up the pores and spreads across the surface of the paper. The result: a strong, moisture-resistant household standby.

Store dried flowers or crafting herbs. First, get a metal tin, like the ones that fancy cookies and candies come in. (You can buy one at the supermarket and have the pleasure of eating the contents, but you'll find dozens of terrific tins at your local thrift store for next to nothing.) Then simply layer your fragile treasures between sheets of crumpled wax paper, and snap on the lid. They'll stay safe and sound until you're ready to turn them into works of art.

Make kneeling pads. Tired of kneeling down to weed your garden—then standing up with dirty pants and sore knees? Here's a simple solution to that problem: Fold wax paper into squares that are three or four layers thick, and use them as kneeling pads. Or, if you're working with a small bed, run a triple-thick strip of wax paper along the entire length. The result: A tidy garden, clean pants, *and* more comfortable knees!

Make shoveling easier. Help save your achin' back by rubbing crumpled wax paper over the blade of your shovel to help it cut smoothly through the earthy crust. This simple trick works remarkably well.

Now that plastic, in one form or another, has become a food-storage superstar, wax paper doesn't command the huge share of the Bags & Wraps market that it once did. But it can still make your life a whole lot easier. Just take a gander at these time- and labor-saving feats:

Here's to **YOU!**

Protect stored candles. Simply wrap them in wax paper, and tuck them into a drawer to guard against scratches, scuffs, and dust.

Make clothes hangers glide smoothly. Rub wax paper over your closet rods—your duds will slide along like a dream.

Clean your iron. Wipe the sole plate with some wax paper, then heat the iron slightly and use a soft cloth to remove any excess wax.

Line a birdcage. Just cover the bottom with wax paper for a water-resistant *and* pet-safe "rug."

Save your sugar. Or any other dry ingredients for a recipe. Before you start measuring, fold a sheet of wax paper down the center, open it up, and lay it on the counter. Fill your measuring cup, and level it off with a knife, letting the excess fall onto the paper. Pick up the paper, refold it partway so the sugar (or what-have-you) migrates to the crease, and pour the stuff back into its canister.

Cut microwave cleaning time. Keep a sheet of wax paper on the oven's glass heating tray, and for added insurance, put another sheet on top of especially spill-prone foods like soups, chili, or spaghetti with marinara sauce.

Prevent rust on cast-iron pans. After you've washed and dried the pan, heat it slightly and rub wax paper over the surface. The wax will protect the metal, but it won't affect the flavor of food.

Preserve leaves and flowers. This makes a great rainy-day project for the budding nature lovers in your house! Arrange the leaves on a sheet of wax paper and lay another sheet on top. Insert your leaf "sandwich" between two sheets cut from a brown paper bag, then press the paper with a warm iron. Remove the outer layer, and trim the wax paper around the star attraction.

Protect seedlings from cutworms. No tender transplant is safe from these voracious villains. But they won't get the goods if you collar your baby plants this way: Fold a 10-inch piece of wax paper in half to make a two-layer strip. Then wrap it around the plant's stem so that about 2 inches of the collar extends below the soil surface, with 3 inches showing above. Remove the wrapping when the plant's stalk reaches about $\frac{1}{2}$ inch in diameter—at that stage, it's too thick for cutworms to damage.

Resurface a metal slide. Mother Nature takes her toll on anything that sits outdoors very long—including playground or swimming pool gear. To help things slide smoothly again, scrunch wax paper into a ball, and rub it over the surface. Better yet, have your child sit on a big sheet of wax paper and slide down the board a few times. It'll be slick and shiny as new!

Keep your car's antenna working. Attention, new-vehicle owners! Chances are, your car's antenna retracts automatically when you turn off the ignition, then glides back up when you start the engine again. At least, that's the way it's supposed to work. But when dirt builds up on the metal, it can stop the antenna in its tracks. To keep it moving smoothly (and your radio reception coming in loud and clear), rub the shaft with a piece of wax paper every now and then.

Baking Products

Baking Soda
Cooking Oil Spray
Cornmeal
Cornstarch
Flour
Food Coloring
Gelatin
Muffin Cups
Vegetable Oil

 # Baking Soda

Grow sweeter tomatoes. Once or twice during the growing season, lightly sprinkle baking soda on the soil around each plant. Your tomatoes will be so sweet, you'll want to eat 'em for dessert!

Feed your hydrangeas. Every couple of weeks, give your plants a drink of baking soda dissolved in water. (Roughly 2 teaspoons of soda per gallon of H_2O will do the job.) They'll respond by giving you the biggest, showiest blooms in town! And, by the way, begonias, clematis, dianthus, geraniums *(Pelargonium* spp.), and any other flowers that like alkaline soil will enjoy this treatment, too.

Test for acid soil. Put about a tablespoon of wet soil on a plate, and add a pinch of baking soda to it. If the soil fizzes, that means that it's extremely acidic—most likely below 5.0 on the pH scale—though how much below is anybody's guess. In this case, a more exact laboratory test is called for, because even most sour-soil lovers like azaleas and rhododendrons won't perform well if the pH is below 4.5.

Toughen up transplants. After you've hardened off flower or vegetable seedlings and just before you plant them in the garden, water them with a solution of 2 tablespoons of baking soda per gallon of water. This elixir will temporarily stop growth and increase the plants' strength, so they can face almost any obstacle Mother Nature throws their way.

Prevent black spot. Mix 3 teaspoons of baking soda with 1 teaspoon of mild dishwashing liquid in 1 gallon of water. Pour the solution into a handheld sprayer bottle, and spray your roses to the point of runoff every three weeks during the growing season. There'll be no more singin' the black spot blues! Be sure to use only mild, unscented dishwashing liquid. Avoid harsh detergents or any soap that contains antibacterial agents—they can do a *lot* more harm to your roses than the black spot will!

Foil soilborne fungi. This potent potion works on fungal diseases in both lawns and gardens. To make it, pour 1 gallon of water into a pot and stir in ½ cup of baking soda and 4 crushed garlic bulbs. Bring the water to a boil, then turn off the heat and let the mixture cool to room temperature. Strain the liquid into a watering can, and soak the ground in the problem areas (removing any dead grass first). Go *very* slowly, so the elixir penetrates deep into the soil. Then dump the strained-out garlic bits onto the soil and work them gently into the ground.

Cure potato blight. In addition to spuds, tomatoes and celery are targets of this dreaded fungus. The minute you notice the first symptoms (dark lesions on leaves, leafstalks, or stems), start spraying your plants every seven days with this formula: 1 tablespoon of baking soda and 1 tablespoon of light horticultural oil (available at garden centers) mixed in 1 gallon of water. Pour the solution into a handheld mist sprayer, and apply it to your plants to the point of runoff.

Here's to YOU!

If your cat is anything like mine, she won't go near any body of water that's bigger than her drinking bowl. So what do you do when she gets to the point where she really could use a good bathing? Just do what I do: Rub a little baking powder into her fur, and then brush it out. Presto—a clean *and* happy (or, at least, content) kitty!

Although a great many common supermarket products were discovered by chance, baking soda reached the shelves by way of a contest. Let me explain. In the 1760s, bakers began using potash, a material extracted from wood ashes, as a leavening agent in bread. (Before that, they had to hand-knead dough for long periods to get the right amount of air mixed in evenly.) Over time, wood became scarce in Europe; so in 1783, the French Academy of Sciences offered a reward to the first person who could develop a process for converting sea salt ($NaCl$) to soda ash (Na_2CO_3), which they reckoned would be a good substitute for potash. Enter Nicolas LeBlanc, a French surgeon and chemist. The project took him a while, but in 1791, he combined salt with sulfuric acid, coal, and limestone, and the resulting reaction produced the sought-after soda ash. Bakers tried the stuff and found its leavening powers to be every bit as good as those of potash. By that time, the Academy had disbanded, so M. LeBlanc received no prize for his efforts; but the French government did award him sole rights to the process for the next 15 years. Soon thereafter, the formula was tweaked a little to produce sodium bicarbonate (Na_2CO_2), which bakers declared to be superior to soda ash.

Fast-forward to 1846, when a Massachusetts farmer named John Dwight and a Connecticut physician named Austin Church established a factory in New York to manufacture baking soda. Both the brand name and logo for this hardworking product were inspired by a business that belonged to Dr. Church's son, John: the Vulcan Spice Mill. As you may recall from ancient history, Vulcan was the Roman god of forge and fire, and he is commonly represented by a muscular arm wielding a hammer—the symbol that still appears on every box of Arm & Hammer® baking soda today.

Baking Soda

Fend off powdery mildew. Mix 2 tablespoons of baking soda and 1 tablespoon of pure liquid soap in 2 quarts of water, and pour the solution into a handheld sprayer bottle. Spray your susceptible plants with this brew beginning in early spring, after they've begun to leaf out, but before temperatures routinely reach into the 80°F range. Coat the leaves thoroughly on both the top and bottom surfaces. Repeat the procedure once a week for two or three weeks, or as long as days are warm and nights are cool and humid (prime mildew weather). *Note:* This fungal disease attacks a great many plants, but prime targets include roses, asters, bee balms, and garden phlox *(Phlox paniculata)*. The good news, though, is that powdery mildew rarely causes serious damage—it just *looks* as ugly as sin.

Get rid of moss. First soak the area with a good soapy water solution (about ¼ cup of soap per gallon of water will do the trick), then pour baking soda directly onto the moss. Just make sure you take careful aim with both soap and soda, or you'll polish off "good" plants along with the "bad." *Note:* This is only a temporary fix. Because moss thrives in damp, shady spots with acidic soil, the only permanent solution is to increase the light level, improve drainage, and raise your soil's pH.

Kill hard-to-reach weeds. Like the ones that drive you crazy when they keep sprouting from cracks in your driveway and walkways. Just pour baking soda onto the concrete and sweep it into the cracks. (It's the heavy jolt of sodium that makes the weeds bow down and knuckle under.)

Keep a kiddy pool spotless. Just like any other outdoor equipment, a wading pool can pick up a lot of dirt. So wash it periodically with a solution made of 1 gallon of hot water and 4 cups of baking soda. It's powerful enough to clean up any soil Mother Nature can offer up—but safe enough to use when you've got tiny tots or inquisitive pets around.

A Medicine Chest in a Box

That was how my Grandma Putt used to refer to baking soda—and her description is just as accurate today as it was way back then. Here are just a handful of the ways good old sodium bicarbonate can keep you feeling *and* looking your best.

PROBLEM	SOLUTION
Bee stings	Get the stinger out. Then make a thick paste of lukewarm water and baking soda, and apply it to the area.
Canker sores	Rinse your mouth with a solution of $1/2$ teaspoon of baking soda in half a glass of warm water. Repeat every few hours, as necessary, until the sores are gone.
Hives or rashes	Soak in a warm bath with 3 or 4 tablespoons of baking soda added to it.
Insect bites	Dissolve 1 teaspoon of baking soda in a cup of water. Dip a clean, soft cloth into the solution, and hold it on the bites for 20 minutes or so.
Perspiration	Dust a little baking soda on your underarm skin to absorb the moisture and eliminate odors.
Pimples	Mix equal parts of baking soda and wheat germ with enough water to make a paste. Rub it onto the zits, wait about 10 minutes, rinse with warm water, and pat dry.
Tired, achy feet	Soak your sore tootsies in a basin of hot water with about $1/4$ cup of baking soda mixed in.
Tired, stiff muscles	Soak in a tub of warm water with $1/2$ cup of baking soda added to it. (This simple treatment will also make your skin feel smoother and softer.)
Trouble quitting smoking	With each meal, drink a glass of water with 2 tablespoons of baking soda mixed in it. (Do not use this method if you have an ulcer or are on a low-sodium diet.)

Clean outdoor surfaces. Lawn and patio furniture, as well as concrete patios or walkways, will come out as clean as a whistle when you wash them down with a solution made from 2 cups of baking soda mixed in 1 gallon of warm water.

De-grease your driveway. Or any other concrete surface, for that matter. Just pour some baking soda right from its familiar orange box onto the oil stain, and scrub it away.

Scour your barbecue grill. Mix ¼ cup of baking soda with ¼ cup of water to form a paste. Apply it with a wire brush, let it sit for 15 minutes, and wipe it off with a soft, dry cloth. Then, to remove any residue, warm the grill over hot coals for at least 15 minutes before you cook any food on it. (It wouldn't hurt you to consume the soda—but that's probably *not* the taste you want on your steak!)

Remove road tar. Whether the stuff is on your bicycle or your car, here's good news: Although it looks awful, it's a snap to get off—without damaging the paint. Just make a paste of 3 parts baking soda to 1 part water, and wipe it onto the spots with a damp cloth. Let it dry for 5 minutes or so, then rinse with clear water.

Put out fires. Baking soda is the key ingredient in many commercial fire extinguishers—but it works just as well straight out of the box to quell small fires, indoors and out. I keep buckets of soda in my garage and workshop, and right by the side of my barbecue. Then anytime flames leap up, relief is close at hand.

Maintain your pool's pH. Most swimming pools (and spas, too) require water that's somewhere between 7.2 and 7.8 on the pH scale. H_2O that's either too acid or too alkaline can damage plumbing and electrical equipment, as well as the pool's surface. And do you know what the experts recommend using when you need to raise the alkalinity? You guessed it— good old baking soda. The testing kit that came with your pool will tell you the exact amount to use, but here's the general rule of thumb: To raise the total alkalinity by 10 parts per million (ppm), add 1½ pounds of baking soda for every 10,000 gallons of water.

Melt ice—safely. Salt and most commercial deicing products can damage both plants and outdoor surfaces like concrete and wood. So the next time Old Man Winter hands you an icy walk or stairway, sprinkle it with a generous amount of baking soda. It'll melt the ice without harming anything else. Then, to provide better traction, top the soda off with some sand or clay cat litter.

MARVELOUS MiX

Quack-Up Slug Cookies

Slugs driving you crazy? Well, if you can lay your hands on some quack grass, these "baked goods" will save the day.

1 part dried quack grass blades, finely chopped
1 part wheat bran*
1 tbsp. of baking soda
1 can of beer

Mix the quack grass, bran, and baking soda in a bowl, then slowly add the beer, stirring until the mixture has the consistency of cookie dough. Run the dough through a meat grinder, or chop it into small bits (roughly 1/8 to 1/4 inch thick). Let the "cookies" air-dry overnight, and sprinkle them on the ground among your plants. The slugs will think it's time to party when they get a yeasty whiff of the tasty treats. But after a couple of bites, they'll have a killer of a hangover!

*If you don't find wheat bran in your supermarket's Baking Products aisle, check the health-food and cereals sections.

Baking Soda

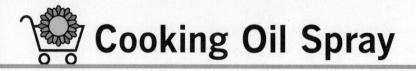

Cooking Oil Spray

Discourage swallows. Barn and cliff swallows can be a lot of fun to watch—but not when they set up housekeeping where you'd rather they didn't, like in the eaves of your house or under your front porch. To say a gentle "Please build else-where," first remove any nesting material from the spot (as long as it hasn't already been filled with eggs, that is!). Then coat the cubbyhole's surface with cooking oil spray. When the birds try to rebuild the nest, the new material will slide right out.

Make digging easier. Just give your shovel, trowel, or spading fork a spritz of cooking oil spray every now and then. Those blades'll glide through the soil!

Lighten your snow load. That pile of white flakes will all but float off of your shovel if you give the blade a shot of cooking oil spray before you get to work on your sidewalk or driveway.

Prune smoothly. Heading out to prune your trees or shrubs? First, shoot a little cooking oil spray into the working parts of your shears or loppers. They'll glide through their work, and your hands will say "Thank you!"

Clean your grill. There's no way to make that job fun—but this simple trick will help you get it done in a jiffy: Before you light the coals, coat the rack with cooking oil spray. Later, when the grill is cool enough to touch, simply wipe it clean.

De-squeak hinges. They're annoying, all right, but indoors or out, there's a fast, easy solution: Just give the noisy things a shot of cooking oil spray. Ahhh—blessed silence!

Lose the Labels

Dang! You've just bought new deck furniture—or maybe a big, fancy grill—and you're itchin' to show it off at a barbecue tonight. There's just one problem: The labels and price tags refuse to budge. No problem! Just grab a can of cooking oil spray and proceed as follows:

* To remove adhesive labels and tags from plastic or metal surfaces, coat the tag thoroughly with cooking oil spray. Let it sit for 5 minutes or so, then slide it off with a plastic scraper or one of those numerous (but nonfunctional) credit cards that banks send you in the mail.

* To get a paper label unstuck from wooden furniture, saturate the paper with cooking oil spray, let it sit for 5 to 10 minutes, and gently peel it off.

Have a nonstick mower blade. Before you start mowing your lawn in spring, give the blade and the whole undercarriage of your lawn mower a good going-over with cooking oil spray. It'll keep grass from sticking to the metal and gumming up the works. Follow up once a month throughout the growing season.

Loosen a screw. Don't you hate it when you have to struggle... and struggle, to get a stubborn screw or bolt loose? Well, struggle no more! Instead, blast the blasted thing with cooking oil spray, wait a few minutes to let it penetrate, and then have at it. It should come right out.

Clean wooden lawn furniture. It never fails: The whole gang's on their way over for a barbecue, and you realize that the chairs and tables on your deck are looking pretty dingy. No problem! Just reach for the cooking oil spray, apply it to the wood, and buff your furniture clean with a soft, dry cloth.

Cooking Oil Spray

Cooking oil and all sorts of other household sprays come equipped with dandy garden helpers: tall, roomy lids. Here are some of the ways that I put them to work around my place (after I've given them a thorough cleaning, of course).

Container-plant sticky traps. When bad guy bugs are munching on your potted plants, indoors or out, coat lids with corn syrup, petroleum jelly, or spray adhesive and set them right-side up on the soil in the pot, or (depending on the size of the plant) nestle them among the branches. One lid coated with sticky stuff will be enough to de-bug a small to medium-sized plant; use two or three traps for larger ones. Choose your lid color by consulting "Color Them Gone," on page 17.

Organizing aids. Use them in your workshop or garden shed to corral pint-sized gear like nuts, bolts, nails, and screws.

Pest-control helpers. To keep rabbits, groundhogs, and chipmunks out of your flower beds, sink lids into the soil among your plants, and fill them with a mixture of 1 part blood meal to 2 parts water. This way, the blood meal won't vanish into the soil when it rains, thereby giving your plants an overdose of nitrogen.

Pot fillers. Toss 'em in the bottom of a large container when you're getting ready to fill it. You'll reduce the amount of soil you need—and therefore, the weight of the pot. They'll also help ensure that water drains out faster.

Seed-starting pots. Collect as many lids as you'll need, punch or drill drainage holes in the bottom of each one, and set them in a tray or shallow pan. Then fill each "pot" with starter mix to within about $1/2$ inch of the top, and plant your seeds.

Wading pool, sandbox, or bathtub toys. Lids are the perfect playtime accessory. Just give a few (or a lot) of them to anyone between the ages of about 2 and 6, and watch the fun begin!

Slide faster. When it's time to hit the slopes with a snow saucer or plastic toboggan, you sure don't want to settle for a leisurely ride down a snow-covered hill. And you don't have to—simply give the sled's bottom surface a thorough spritz of cooking oil spray, and then go hit that slippery slope!

Cast farther. And more smoothly, too. Take a can of cooking oil spray along with you on your next fishing trip. Spray it on your line, and it'll float across the water like a dream. (Later on, you can spray it on your grill when you cook your catch!)

Lubricate a bike chain. When your (or your youngster's) bicycle chain is a tad bit creaky, but you don't have any lubricating oil on hand, use cooking oil spray instead. Just spray it on and wipe off any excess with a clean, dry cloth.

Cornmeal

Clobber Colorado potato beetles. These villains—both adults and larvae—mainly plague members of the *Solanaceae* family, which includes the bugs' namesake crop, as well as tomatoes, tomatillos, peppers, and eggplant. (But every now and then, they vary from their favored menu and go after cabbage.) Fortunately, there's a simple way to head 'em off at the pass: Sprinkle cornmeal on the leaves of your plagued plants. When the larvae eat the stuff, it swells up inside them, and they burst.

Deter slugs and snails. Almost no plant is safe from these slimy thugs. But you can protect your green treasures by dusting cornmeal on the soil around each one. The slimers won't even try to slink over the gritty grains.

MARVELOUS MiX

Ant Ambrosia

Here's a formula that's lethal to ants, but won't harm kids or pets. (Fido will love it, though, so if you want the stuff to do its duty, keep it out of his reach!)

> **4–5 tbsp. of cornmeal**
> **3 tbsp. of bacon grease**
> **3 tbsp. of baking powder**
> **3 packages of baker's yeast**

Mix the cornmeal and bacon grease into a paste, then add the baking powder and yeast. Dab the gooey mix on the sides of jar lids, and set them out in your invaded territory. Ants will love it to death!

Clean up oil spills. When your car or your lawn mower leaves a messy, black splotch on your driveway (or your garage floor), get rid of it the easy way: Just cover the spot with equal parts of cornmeal and baking soda. Wait until the oil has been absorbed, and then sweep up any residue.

Super-charge soap. There's no doubt about it: Gardening can be dirty work (or play, depending on how you look at it). To get your hands deep-down clean, add a pinch or two of cornmeal to the soap suds as you lather up.

Make bird treats. Want to make chickadees, thrushes, titmice, and other songbirds throng to your yard? Then serve up plenty of these tasty treats: Mix equal parts of cornmeal and black oil sunflower seeds with room-temperature bacon grease until the mixture is doughy. Then add a tablespoon or so of sand or crushed eggshells for grit. Shape the dough into a ball, put it in a mesh onion bag, and hang it from a tree.

Cornmeal Conquers All

Disease-causing fungi, that is. Scientific studies have found that this supermarket super product can cure fungal diseases on just about every kind of plant—including roses, tomatoes, and even turfgrasses. Researchers at Texas A&M University, who discovered cornmeal's fungicidal powers, say the grain works for a simple reason: It contains a type of beneficial fungus (to be specific, a member of the *Trichoderma* family) that kills off foul fungi in the soil. There are two ways to use this miraculous medicine:

Right from the box. Work 2 pounds of cornmeal into the soil for every 100 square feet of lawn or garden area. Then water well to jump-start the fungicidal properties. One application per season usually does the trick, but feel free to repeat the process if you like. With cornmeal, there's no such thing as an overdose—in fact, it feeds your soil at the same time that it's fighting diseases. If you have a lot of ground to cover with your cornmeal, consider using horticultural cornmeal (sold as a livestock feed in farm-supply stores) instead of food-grade cornmeal from the supermarket. Both kinds work equally well, but the animal food costs less, and you can buy it in bulk.

As a spray (commonly called cornmeal juice). Put 1 cup of cornmeal in a panty hose foot or cheesecloth pouch, and soak it for 8 hours or so in 1 gallon of water. Then strain the liquid (but don't dilute it) and pour it into a handheld sprayer. Spray your susceptible plants from top to bottom, repeating the process after every rain.

Just be sure you don't confuse cornmeal with corn *gluten* meal, which is cornmeal that's been processed to increase its protein content. For some reason, it doesn't have much in the way of fungicidal properties. It does have its place in the garden, though—as a first-rate pre-emergent weed killer. (It's also a common ingredient in many supermarket dog foods, so don't be surprised if you see it listed on the label.)

Scrub extra-grimy hands. For those times when it seems there's more dirt on your hands than in the garden, try this simple cleanup trick: Mix cornmeal with enough apple cider vinegar to make a paste. Scrub your skin thoroughly, working the mixture into all the joints and crevices in your skin. Then rinse well, and dry off. If any dirt still lingers, repeat the procedure. (Unlike harsh chemical cleaners, this stuff won't harm your skin—and it'll make it softer and smoother.)

MARVELOUS MiX

Pileated Possibility

For many backyard bird-watchers, the giant pileated woodpecker, a shining black bird with a bold red crest, is the Holy Grail at the feeder. If you live near a wooded area (this bird's normal habitat), the makings of a come-hither invitation are waiting for you in the Baking Products aisle. What are they? Pecans! Pileateds can't get enough of these tasty nuts. In fact, all woodpeckers love 'em, and so do chickadees, nuthatches, and titmice. Here's an easy way to serve them:

> **1 cup of suet or fat scraps, chopped**
> **$1/2$ cup of pecans, finely chopped or crushed**
> **$1/2$ cup of pecans, halves or large pieces**

Using the back of a spoon, "cream" the crushed pecans into the fat. Or mix them in well, using your hands. Pour in the large pieces. Lift and stir, working carefully to avoid breaking the nuts into small pieces, until the pecans are evenly distributed throughout the fat mixture. Spread about $1/2$ cup of the mixture directly onto a tree or post, about 3 feet above the ground. Put the remainder in a wire suet cage, and attach it about 1 foot above your suet smear. Fasten it securely so that it won't move under this extra-large woodpecker's weight.

Perform fabric first-aid. When a burger or some other greasy food comes off of your barbecue grill—and right onto your clean clothes or tablecloth—just cover the spot with cornmeal. When it dries, brush it off, and most of the oil will go along with it. Then as soon as you can, launder the item as usual.

Preserve cut flowers. This easy-as-pie technique works with any kind of annual, perennial, or flowering shrub you can name. Here's all there is to it: Mix 3 parts white cornmeal to 1 part borax. Pour about an inch of the combo into a pan or bowl. Set your flowers on top, and gently cover them with more of the mixture. Wait three to five weeks, then brush away the covering and lift out the dried flowers. Because the preservative doesn't absorb moisture from the flowers, you can use the same batch again and again. Just store it in an airtight container.

Save the bluebirds. When a big snowstorm strikes, bluebirds depend on backyard feeders to provide life-saving nutrition. So do your part for your true-blue pals by serving up calorie-rich snacks. Here's one ultra-simple recipe: Put 2 cups of cornmeal, $\frac{1}{2}$ cup of chopped suet or fat scraps, and $\frac{1}{2}$ cup of peanut oil in a deep bowl. Combine them thoroughly using a spoon, your hands, or an electric mixer. Then stuff the dough into a suet feeder that has a perch, or crumble it into a low or mid-height tray feeder.

Cornstarch

Make seed tape. Pre-spaced seed tapes make planting a snap, but they can cost a pretty penny. What's more, your choice of varieties is fairly limited. So take a winter evening or two, and make your own. It's simple, inexpensive—and fun! (It's also a great way to get youngsters involved in gardening.) Here's all there is to it: First, dissolve 1 tablespoon of cornstarch in 1 cup of water over medium heat. Stir constantly, until the mix boils and turns translucent and gel-like. While it cools, cut several paper towels lengthwise into 1-inch-wide strips. Use a waterproof pen to write the name of the seed you're sowing on each strip. Spoon some of the cornstarch mix into a clean plastic squeeze bottle (one that held mustard, ketchup, or mayonnaise is perfect). Squeeze out small cornstarch dots along each paper-towel strip, spacing the dots according to the spacing guidelines on your seed packet. Then set a seed on top of each dot. Once the strips are dry, roll 'em up and store 'em in a plastic bag until planting time.

Clean glass. When your cold frame's glass cover or your greenhouse windows get really dirty, mix a pinch or two of cornstarch with a little ammonia and water, and clean that grime away. Rinse with clear water. The cornstarch acts as a mild abrasive. (This trick will also make your car windows crystal clear.)

Loosen a knot. I must admit that I have known a few folks who actually enjoy the challenge of untying a stubborn knot. But I'm not one of them, and I'm guessing that you're not, either—especially, for instance, when you're rushing to get your tomatoes tied to their stakes before a wind storm hits and you have to struggle with a tangled nest of twine. So stop wrestling and start sprinkling—cornmeal, that is. Just pour it on the knots, and they'll loosen right up!

"Lubricate" latex gloves. Don't you just hate struggling to get your hands into wet rubber gloves? (Not to mention the cold, icky feeling once you've got them on!) To make things easier, just coat the insides with cornstarch. It'll dry them out and make them slide on and off quite easily.

Remove oil stains. When you're filling your mower's (or your car's) oil tank, and some of the stuff winds up on your clothes, don't fret. Just cover the spot with cornstarch, wait 12 hours, brush it off, and launder as usual. Those duds will look as good as new. Well, at least as good as they looked before the oil spill occurred.

Identify four-footed pests. Rabbits robbing you blind? Or maybe it's raccoons. Here's how to find out for sure: Just sprinkle flour on the ground in the problem area. When the thug returns to the scene of the crime, he'll leave his footprints in the white stuff. If you don't recognize them by sight, get out your *Audubon Field Guide,* and match those prints. Then you're ready for action!

An Inside Story

Although cockroaches most often invade houses, they sometimes find their way into workshops and garden sheds. If that happens at your place, just mix equal parts of cornstarch and plaster of paris, and sprinkle the mixture into all the cracks and crevices you can find. The roaches will eat the stuff and it will solidify inside them. Case closed!

Cornstarch

Get out bloodstains. Cutting yourself is never fun, to say the least, whether the "culprit" is a stray piece of glass in a garden bed or a carving knife that slipped as you were cutting meat for your barbecue. What's more, even a minor cut can leave ugly bloodstains on your clothes or table linens. But those splotches won't turn into permanent stains if you use this old-time trick: Make a paste of roughly 3 parts cornstarch to 1 part cold water. (It should be about the consistency of toothpaste, so add more of either ingredient if you need to.) Cover the marks with the paste, rub it into the fabric, and spread the item out in a sunny spot to dry. Then brush off the residue. If any stain remains, repeat the process.

Prevent blisters. When you need to do some outdoor chores and you can't find your work gloves—or you simply don't like to wear them—do yourself a favor: Before you leave the house, rub a tablespoon or so of cornstarch on your palms. It'll absorb perspiration and prevent blisters from forming.

 # Flour

Outline planting beds. Stakes and string work just fine for marking off straight-sided beds and borders. But if you want a circle, crescent, or other curvy shape, "draw" it on the ground with flour. If you don't like the result, just brush the stuff away and try again. Practice makes perfect!

Say "So long" to spider mites. Mites can attack every kind of plant under the sun, from tiny violets to towering trees. Generally, they only pose real problems in gardens where their natural enemies (of whom they have zillions) have been wiped out by chemical pesticides. But if the good guys

There are few materials that are trickier (or more intimidating) to clean than papier-mâché—that is, unless you go about it this way: Wash the object with a sponge dipped in cold water (no soap). Then, while the surface is still damp, dust flour all over it, and polish it with a cotton flannel cloth. This method works like a charm on sculptures, decorative plates, trays, or anything else that's made of papier-mâché.

in your yard can't keep up with the invading throng, just mix 2 cups of flour and ¼ cup of buttermilk in 2 gallons of water. Then pour the mixture into a handheld mist sprayer, and douse your mite-plagued plants from top to bottom.

Repel ants. Although these tiny tykes rarely damage plants, they can make big nuisances of themselves at backyard barbecues and other outdoor events. Well, don't let the pesky pests ruin your fun! Just pour a line of flour around the off-limits area. They won't cross that border!

Poison ants. When the little rascals are kicking up such a fuss that you have no alternative, mix equal parts of flour, sugar, borax, and alum with enough water to make a batter. Pour it into shallow pans, and set them out where the ants congregate—but where children or pets can't get to the traps.

Clobber cabbageworms. And deter other pests, too. Simply mix 1 cup of flour and 2 tablespoons of cayenne pepper, and sprinkle the mixture on all your cabbage-family plants. The flour swells up inside the worms and makes them burst, while the hot pepper keeps other bugs away. As for high-risk targets, cabbageworms keep their dastardly deeds almost entirely in the family. But the cabbage

Flour

(a.k.a. *Brassica*) clan is a *big* one that includes, on the veggie side, broccoli, Brussels sprouts, cauliflower, collards, kale, kohlrabi, mustard, radishes, rutabagas, and turnips. Flower-garden cousins include sweet alyssum, stock, and wallflowers. And the one outsider that these gluttons go for (for whatever reason) are nasturtiums.

Deter whiteflies. These tiny sap-sucking insects can plague almost any annual or perennial flower, as well as many trees, shrubs, fruits, and vegetables (especially those in the squash and tomato families). And every windowsill or greenhouse plant is a high-risk target. The solution: Sprinkle flour and a pinch or two of black pepper onto the soil (or the potting mix) around your plants. For some reason, that combo sends a loud "Steer clear!" signal to whiteflies.

Eliminate rats. Mice can make plenty of mischief around your yard, all right, but their big cousins are downright dangerous. So if rats are starting to show up at your place, don't pull any punches. Hit 'em hard with this homemade poison: Mix equal parts of flour and powdered cement, and put it in a

Do Tell!

As most of us learned in history class, the process of growing wheat and milling it into flour goes back at least 6,000 years, to the time when the hunter-gatherers in Mesopotamia (now known as Iraq) decided it was easier to farm the land than to chase after dinner every night. But have you ever stopped to think how many edibles besides wheat and other grains, like rye and corn, are made into flour today? The list includes (but is not limited to, as the lawyers like to say) potatoes, acorns, mesquite, amaranth, bananas, and even nuts, such as almonds, cashews, and pistachios.

Got small children stuck indoors on a stormy day? Then make them some modeling clay that you can clean up in a snap if it winds up on your furniture. Here's the easy recipe: In a saucepan, mix 2 cups of flour, 4 tablespoons of cream of tartar, 2 tablespoons of vegetable oil, 1 cup of salt, a few drops of food coloring, and 2 cups of water. Stir over medium heat for 3 to 5 minutes, until the mixture forms a ball. When it cools, mix it with your hands, and hand it over to your young sculptors. Better yet, make a supply in advance and store it in an airtight container, so that you can produce it *pronto* whenever the need arises.

shallow container, like a big jar lid or disposable pie pan. Set it next to a pan of water in a place where the rats can find it easily, but children and pets can't get at it. The wretched rodents will eat the powder, then take a drink. The cement will harden inside their bellies, and that'll be all she wrote!

Polish brass and copper. This nontoxic formula works indoors or out—for instance, on trellises, gate or door hinges, or metal planters. Here's the recipe: Mix 1 tablespoon of flour, 1 tablespoon of salt, and 1 tablespoon of white vinegar into a thick paste. Apply a thick layer with a damp sponge, and gently wipe the metal. Let the polish dry for about an hour, rinse with warm water, and buff with a soft cloth.

Clean chrome. Whether it's on a classic car or a fancy new planting pot, you want that metal to shine like the silvery moon. And it will when you sprinkle a little white flour on a dry rag and polish in a circular motion. The chrome will be so shiny, you'll think you're looking in a mirror!

Calling All Birds!

As the Pillsbury® Doughboy used to say, "Nothin' says lovin' like somethin' from the oven." And your fine-feathered friends couldn't agree more. They'll flock to your yard from near and far if you add baked goods to your feeders every now and then. But the treats don't have to come from your own oven. Birds are just as happy with cakes, cookies, breads, and other goodies that you buy at the supermarket.

BAKED GOOD(S)	HOW TO SERVE
Bread	Break into medium-sized pieces and serve in a tray feeder or, in dry weather, directly on the ground.
Breakfast cereal	Serve in a tray feeder.
Cookies	Break into pieces and serve in a tray feeder or, in dry weather, directly on the ground.
Corn chips	Crush or crumble and serve in a tray feeder.
Corn tortillas	Crush or crumble and serve in a tray feeder.
Cornbread	Serve whole or broken into pieces in a tray feeder or, in dry weather, directly on the ground.
Doughnuts	Serve whole, in a hanging feeder.
English muffins	Break into medium-sized pieces and serve in a tray feeder or, in dry weather, directly on the ground.
Muffins	Break into medium-sized pieces and serve, crumbs and all, in a tray feeder.
Piecrust (baked)	Crumble into large pieces and serve in a tray feeder or, in dry weather, directly on the ground.
Quick bread with fruit	Break into medium-sized pieces and serve in a tray feeder or, in dry weather, directly on the ground.
Quick bread with fruit and nuts	Break into medium-sized pieces and serve in a tray feeder or, in dry weather, directly on the ground.
Quick bread with nuts	Break into medium-sized pieces and serve in a tray feeder or, in dry weather, directly on the ground.

Just break them into pieces and offer them up in a tray feeder or, in dry weather, directly on the ground. Here's the menu and a sampling of the diners you'll attract. Just two notes of caution: First, it's okay if the products are stale—but *not* moldy! And whatever you do, don't serve chocolate in *any* form. It's harmful to birds and highly toxic to dogs and cats, who might help themselves to the tasty treats.

BIRDS ATTRACTED
Blackbirds, cardinals, catbirds, crows, grackles, house sparrows, jays, magpies, mockingbirds, robins, starlings, thrashers
Blackbirds, chickadees, house sparrows, juncos, mockingbirds, sparrows
Carolina wrens, catbirds, chickadees, grackles, house sparrows, juncos, mockingbirds, robins, sparrows, thrashers
Blackbirds, cardinals, grackles, house sparrows, juncos, magpies, meadowlarks, sparrows, tanagers
Blackbirds, cardinals, grackles, house sparrows, juncos, magpies, meadowlarks, sparrows, tanagers
Blackbirds, Carolina wrens, juncos, magpies, meadowlarks, mocking-birds, robins, sparrows, tanagers, thrashers
Carolina wrens, chickadees, titmice
Blackbirds, cardinals, catbirds, crows, grackles, house sparrows, jays, magpies, mockingbirds, robins, sparrows, thrashers
Carolina wrens, catbirds, juncos, mockingbirds, robins, sparrows, thrashers
Nearly all feeder birds, except for buntings, goldfinches, house finches, siskins
Carolina wrens, catbirds, juncos, meadowlarks, mockingbirds, robins, tanagers, thrashers
Carolina wrens, catbirds, chickadees, grackles, jays, juncos, meadow-larks, mockingbirds, robins, tanagers, thrashers, titmice, woodpeckers
Blackbirds, catbirds, chickadees, jays, juncos, mockingbirds, sparrows, thrashers, titmice, woodpeckers

Flour

 # Food Coloring

Stain unfinished wood. Want to add real pizzazz to outdoor planters or furniture? Then try this easy—and ultra-nontoxic—technique. (It's great for anything that's made of unfinished wood, but white pine works best.) Mix 1 part food coloring to 5 or 6 parts water. Saturate the wood surface, wait about 5 minutes, and wipe it down with a soft cloth to remove any residual dye. Let it dry overnight, then wipe again. Tip: Just be sure to buy your coloring in 4-ounce jars, instead of tiny bottles, or you'll be paying a small fortune!

Tint cut flowers. There's nothing more elegant than a big bouquet of white flowers. But for those times when you want something a little more dramatic—and the only blooms you've got on hand are white or very pale in color—here's a trick that works like magic. Just mix the food coloring of your choice in warm water, and insert the freshly cut stems into the solution. Let them sit overnight, and by morning, they'll be sporting multi-toned designs. (The more color-

Here's to **YOU!**

If you make your own liquid cleaning formulas, you know that most of them are colorless. So are many of the garden tonics you'll find throughout this book. It goes without saying (I hope!) that you should always label the bottles. But do yourself a favor, and go one step further: Add a few drops of food coloring to each one. That way, you can tell your window cleaner from your weed killer at a glance!

ing you use, the darker the petals will be, so just experiment until you get the shade you want.)

Paint the snow. Here's a great way to keep your kids (or grandkids) busy: Put a teaspoon or so of food coloring in a spray or squeeze bottle filled with water, and they'll have a ball spraying designs in the snow. Of course, if the wintry air brings your creative side to the fore, you can "paint" to your heart's content, too. Or you can simply write a festive message welcoming guests to your holiday party!

 # Gelatin

Feed houseplants. Every time you water, use this solution: 1 gallon of water mixed with ¼ cup of beer, one crushed vitamin B$_1$ tablet, and ½ tablespoon each of unflavored gelatin powder, fish emulsion, ammonia, and instant tea granules. It'll get 'em up and growing in no time at all.

Prevent diseases. When you sow your seeds, lightly sprinkle flavored gelatin powder over the top of them with a salt shaker (or use one of the plastic containers that baking sprinkles come in). Any flavor will help fend off plant diseases, but lemon is best because it also repels some bugs.

Nurture transplants. As your young flower or vegetable seedlings grow, serve up flavored gelatin mix every couple of weeks. (Use the kind made with real sugar, *not* artificial sweeteners). Gently work a tablespoon or so of the powder into the soil, being careful not to disturb the roots. The gelatin itself helps the soil hold water, and the sugar feeds the microorganisms in the soil.

Watch Roots Grow

Here's a science project the kids are sure to love: Simply prepare a bowl of clear, unflavored gelatin according to the directions on the package. Then have the youngsters insert the vegetable or flower seeds of their choice. They'll be able to watch as the root structures develop.

Sow seeds. Rather, I should say squirt them. Here's the routine: Empty a packet of gelatin—either flavored or unflavored—into a bowl. Add warm water, little by little, stirring as you go, until you've got a thick slush. Mix in your seeds, and pour the goop into a plastic squirt bottle (a clean mustard or ketchup container is perfect). Then squeeze it onto your prepared garden bed or indoor seed-starting flat. Later on, when the seedlings emerge, you can thin them out to the right distance.

 # Muffin Cups

Make a shining fence. Are birds snatching your newly planted seeds? Are four-legged felons grabbing your vegetables? To send 'em all scurrying, shine light in their eyes with this almost instant fence. To make it, all you need are wooden or metal stakes, twine, and a few packages of foil muffin cups. First, pound the stakes into the soil at 3- to 4-foot intervals all around the plot. Then poke a hole about an inch in from the edge of each muffin cup, and thread the cups onto the twine. Run the twine between the stakes and presto—you've got a flashing foil fence!

Foil fruit-snatching birds. Here's a brilliant idea for keeping birds out of your fruit trees and berry bushes: Use foil muffin cups. Just poke a hole near the edge of each cup, and hang them from the branches, using twine or nylon fishing line. The light flashing off the foil will send the fliers elsewhere for snacks.

Make seed-starting pots to go. Some vegetables, including cucumbers, squash, beans, peas, and corn, hate like the dickens to have their roots disturbed. But that doesn't mean you have to sow the seeds directly in the garden. You can still give them a head start indoors—as long as you use pots that can go right into the ground at planting time. Garden centers sell biodegradable containers (what I call travelin' pots), but it's a snap to make your own. I've found that kids especially love this method: Simply fill paper muffin cups with seed-starting mix, put them into (you guessed it) a muffin tin, and plant your seeds following the guidelines on the seed packet. When the seedlings are ready for life in the great outdoors, pop them out of the tin and plant 'em in your garden, "pots" and all. The paper will break down in a flash, enriching your soil in the process.

Even after you've used paper muffin cups for their intended purpose, you can still put them to work in your garden. How? Just toss 'em into the compost bin, or simply bury them in the soil, clinging crumbs and all. The whole shebang will quickly decompose into plant-pleasing humus. (I hope it goes without saying that we're talking about the paper kind here—foil muffin cups will not break down, so either put them in your trash can or, much better yet, rinse them off and reuse them in one of the ways described above.)

Hold pest-deterring potions. When you're searching high and low for containers to hold blood meal, beer, grape juice, or other liquid repellents, grab a box of foil muffin cups. Sink 'em into the ground up to their rims near your vulnerable flowers or vegetables, and fill each one with the appropriate substance—for instance, grape juice or beer to trap slugs, or blood meal mixed with water to repel rabbits.

Vegetable Oil

Make food-grade pesticide. This ultra-simple formula kills aphids, spider mites, and whiteflies on contact. But it won't harm children, pets, or wildlife—in fact, it's so safe, they could drink it! Just mix ⅓ cup of vegetable oil and 1 teaspoon of baking soda. Then combine 2 teaspoons of this mixture with 1 cup of water in a handheld sprayer, take aim, and fire when ready.

Control mosquitoes. Does your yard have puddles of standing water that you can't drain? To keep them from turning into 'skeeter maternity wards, pour a thin layer of vegetable oil onto the surface of each one. The oil will smother any newly hatched eggs.

Trap earwigs. These insects rarely cause any real trouble in a garden, but sometimes their chomping can get out of hand. If that happens at your place, pour equal parts of vegetable oil and soy sauce in empty cat food or tuna fish cans. Set the traps out at night, and toss them (and their contents) in the trash early in the morning before butterflies or other good-guy bugs flit in for a drink.

Conquer rust. Just about any kind of flower, fruit, or vegetable can fall victim to rust. The disease is caused by many different kinds of closely related fungi, each of which zeroes in on a specific type of plant. So, for instance, bean rust can't infect corn, and rose rust can't infect snapdragons. Fortunately, it's easy to make a diagnosis, because in every case, the symptoms are the same. The first signs you'll see will be powdery orange spots, usually on the undersides of your plants' leaves. The treatment is the same, too: Remove all infected foliage immediately. Then nix any lingering fungus with this formula: Mix 6 tablespoons of vegetable oil and 2 tablespoons each of baking soda and kelp extract in 1 gallon of water. Pour the solution into a handheld sprayer bottle, and spray the foliage from top to bottom (be sure you get the undersides of the leaves). Repeat every week to 10 days during periods of damp or humid weather.

MARVELOUS MIX

Basic Oil Mixture

Scale insects and a whole lot of other pests that attack all kinds of flowers, vegetables, and fruits will go belly up when they strike oil—or rather, when oil strikes *them*!

1 cup of vegetable oil
1 tbsp. of Murphy® Oil Soap

Pour the oil and the oil soap into a plastic squeeze bottle, and store it at room temperature. To use it, put 1 tablespoon of the mixture in 2 cups of water in a handheld sprayer bottle, and spray your pest-ridden plants from top to bottom, to the point of runoff. (Shake the bottle now and then to make sure the oil and water stay mixed.)

Vegetable Oil

Here's to **YOU!**

In the Baking Products aisle of any supermarket, you'll find a mind-boggling array of vegetable oils—canola oil, corn oil, peanut oil, sesame oil... I could go on and on. The fact is that when it comes to solving most garden-variety problems, any kind of vegetable oil will work just fine. (I always buy the cheapest store brand I can find.) But there is one exception to that rule, and that is when the problems involve your hardworking (or hard-playing) body. At those times, nothing but a good-quality olive oil will do. Here are just a few ways olive oil can make life easier for you:

Dry, chapped skin. Cold, dry winter winds can be just as hard on your skin as the hot summer sun. When a session of snow shoveling leaves your face as red as Santa's hat—and sore, besides—try this remedy: Massage olive oil onto your face, wait about 10 minutes, then rinse with warm water and pat dry.

Sore muscles and stiff, achy joints. This bedtime remedy will bring quick relief. Mix 1 teaspoon of dry mustard and 1 teaspoon of powdered ginger with 2 tablespoons of olive oil, and rub a tiny dab on your inner arm. Wait 10 minutes. If the skin shows no sign of irritation, rub the rest of the mixture onto the troubled area until you feel a warm, tingling sensation. Then either put on an old T-shirt, or cover the area with a soft cotton cloth to protect your sheets. Then hop into bed. In the morning, wash off the residue with soap and water. Repeat as often as necessary.

Ailing muscles and joints—daytime version. A gentle rubdown with this recipe will ease your aches and pains fast! Mix 2 egg whites with $1/2$ cup of apple cider vinegar and $1/4$ cup of olive oil. Massage it into the painful areas, and wipe off the excess with a soft cotton cloth.

AISLE 2 • BAKING PRODUCTS

76

Maintain your gardening tools. There's nothing more frustrating than heading into your garden shed to grab a tool that you haven't used in a while, and finding out that it's covered with rust. Well, that won't happen if you perform this simple chore faithfully: After each use, clean your shovels, rakes, and other gear, and then lightly coat all of the metal surfaces with vegetable oil. They'll stay neat, clean, and ready for work.

Store tools. To further foil rust and corrosion, store your trowels and other hand tools in a bucket of oily sand. Just pour a quart of vegetable oil into a 5-gallon bucket filled with clean builder's sand, mix it in, and keep it in an out-of-the-way corner of your garden shed.

Lubricate hinges. Good grief—there goes that dang screeching again! When the hinges on your garden gate or shed are driving you crazy, apply vegetable oil to the moving parts. (I use a medicine dropper for this job.)

So Long, Sap!

There's simply no way to prune evergreen trees and shrubs without getting sticky sap all over your pruning shears—and usually, your hands, too. Fortunately, getting the stuff off is simple. You even have a choice of remedies, straight from the Baking Products aisle. Either solid shortening, cooking oil spray, or vegetable oil will do the trick. Just grab whichever one is handiest, and proceed as follows:

Tools. Dab or spray the metal with your chosen fat or oil as a cleaner, then wipe it off with a soft cloth.

Hands or arms. Apply the shortening, spray, or oil. Work it into your skin thoroughly, and rinse with clear water. Then wash it off with soap and water.

Vegetable Oil

Make oil lamps. Here's a great way to shine a little light on the subject: Pour vegetable oil into a metal or heat-proof glass or ceramic container, and insert a cotton wick (available at craft stores). Then set several of these around your deck or patio, and light the wicks to brighten up the night.

Pour concrete—neatly. Getting ready to make a new patio or walkway? Then this tip's for you: Brush vegetable oil onto your wooden frames before pouring the cement mix into them. You'll end up with cleaner forms and a neater finished product.

Drown hand-picked pests. One of the easiest ways to get rid of beetles, weevils, caterpillars, and other large insects is to pick them off of your plants by hand. (Not your bare hands, of course! Either wear good, thick gloves, or use an old pair of tongs—or better yet, both.) So what do you do with the bad bugs once they're in hand? Drop them into a bucket filled with a solution made from 2 tablespoons of vegetable oil and 1 tablespoon of dishwashing liquid per quart of water. *Note:* In this case, feel free to use whatever kind of dishwashing liquid you have on hand—mildness doesn't matter.

Cure brown patch on your lawn. When this foul fungal disease has attacked your turf, you'll see patches or rings of dead grass that may be either brown or yellow. The culprit is a fungus by the name of Rhizoctonia, and you can send it packing (at least temporarily) with this routine: Mix 1 tablespoon each of vegetable oil and baking soda per gallon of water, and pour the solution into a handheld sprayer bottle. Lightly mist your turf—*don't* apply the mix to the point of runoff! Then do whatever you need to do to correct the source of the problem, which may be poor drainage, excessive watering, or an overdose of nitrogen.

Beverages

BEER
COFFEE
COFFEE FILTERS
FRUIT JUICES
SODA POP
TEA
WINE & SPIRITS

 # Beer

Polish your indoor plants. Are your dracaenas, philodendrons, ficuses, or other houseplants looking a bit dingy? Just wash their leaves with a little beer once a week, and rinse well. The foliage will gleam!

Fertilize your houseplants. When it's feeding time, and you're fresh out of your regular brand of plant food, don't dash off to the garden center to buy more. Just give your potted pals a drink of beer instead (an amount that's equal to your normal feeding ration is fine). It's one of the best all-purpose fertilizers you could ever hope to find!

Super-charge geraniums. When you pot up your *Pelargoniums,* apply 1 tablespoon of Epsom salts for each 4 square inches of container size, and water it in with a solution of 1 cup of beer, $1/4$ cup of instant tea granules, and 2 teaspoons of baby shampoo per gallon of water. The plants will repay you with fantastic foliage and mounds of beautiful blooms.

Grow show-stopping clematis. If your "Queen of Climbers" isn't performing as well as you'd like her to, maybe that's her way of asking for, shall we say, less commonplace food. The answer: Pour 1 cup of beer and 2 tablespoons each of fish emulsion, ammonia, and baby shampoo into a 2-gallon sprinkling can, and fill the balance of the can with warm water. Serve Her Majesty this tonic every two weeks throughout the growing season, and watch her put on a regal show!

Give your herbs a drink. As a group, herbs are just about the most easygoing plants you could ask for, but even they enjoy the occasional bracing beverage. So every six weeks throughout the growing season, mix 1 can of beer, $1/2$ cup of Murphy® Oil Soap, 1 cup of ammonia, and $1/2$ cup of corn syrup in your 20 gallon hose-end sprayer. Then turn on the hose and spray your herbs from top to bottom. They'll love you for it!

Jump-start your vegetables. Want to grow more—and tastier—vegetables than you ever thought possible? Here's how: Before you plant your garden, saturate the soil with the following, mixed in your 20 gallon hose-end sprayer: 1 can of beer, 1 cup of regular cola, $\frac{1}{2}$ cup each of dishwashing liquid and antiseptic mouthwash, and $\frac{1}{4}$ teaspoon of instant tea granules. Wait two weeks before you start planting. (This recipe makes enough to cover 100 square feet of garden area.) *Note:* Anytime a recipe calls for dishwashing liquid, do not use detergent or any product that contains antibacterial agents.

Speed up composting. Building a new compost pile? If so, after you've added each 6- to 8-inch layer of organic matter, sprinkle a can of beer over the top of it. This will launch the breakdown process into high gear.

Solid food is just fine for a routine diet, but plants like some liquid refreshment every now and then, too. So whenever you change the water in your fish tank, or toss an over-the-hill floral arrangement onto the compost pile, don't send the used H_2O down the drain—serve it to a plant instead. That liquid is chock-full of health-giving nutrients. So is the water that you've used to cook eggs, vegetables, or pasta, or to rinse out glasses, bottles, or cans that held any of these refreshing beverages:

* Beer	* Juice	* Tea	* Wine
* Coffee	* Soda pop	* Whiskey	* Flavored water

Energize lawn fertilizer. Even super-premium lawn foods benefit from a good kick in the grass. Here's how to deliver it: Two days after you feed your lawn in the spring, and again in the fall, mix 1 can of beer and 1 cup of dishwashing liquid in a 20 gallon hose-end sprayer, and fill the balance of the jar with ammonia. Overspray your lawn to the point of runoff. Serve this tonic as early in the morning as you can. *Note:* Anytime a recipe calls for dishwashing liquid, do not use detergent or any product that contains antibacterial agents.

Perk up annuals. Even tough-as-nails flowers like cosmos, zinnias, and marigolds can knuckle under during the dog days of late summer. So when they, or any of your other annuals, seem

MARVELOUS MiX

All-Purpose Yard Fertilizer

If your normally pristine lawn suddenly becomes spotty or lighter in color, pay attention—it's begging for food! So give it a hearty meal of this down-home fertilizer, then stand back and watch it grow.

> 1 can of beer
> 1 can of regular cola (not diet)
> 1 cup of apple juice
> 1 cup of lemon-scented dishwashing liquid*
> 1 cup of ammonia
> 1 cup of all-purpose plant food (15-30-15 is good)

Mix these ingredients in a large bucket, then pour 1 quart of the mix into a 20 gallon hose-end sprayer. Apply it to everything in your yard to the point of runoff every three weeks during the growing season, and you'll see fantastic growing results!

*Do not use detergent or any product that contains antibacterial agents.

on the brink of exhaustion, mix $^1/_4$ cup of beer and 1 table-spoon each of corn syrup, baby shampoo, and 15-30-15 fertilizer in a watering can with 1 gallon of water. Then slowly dribble the solution onto the root zone of each plant.

Get more strawberries. For a bumper harvest, soak your plants' roots in this elixir before tucking them into their holes: Mix 1 can of beer, 2 tablespoons of dishwashing liquid, and $^1/_4$ cup of cold coffee in 2 gallons of water. Soak the bare roots in the solution for about 10 minutes. Save the solution to dribble around the berries after you're done planting. *Note:* Anytime a recipe calls for dishwashing liquid, do not use detergent or any product that contains antibacterial agents.

Freshen up your lawn. If your grass doesn't spring right back up after you step on it, that means just one thing: It needs a drink—now! To help the water go straight to the roots, put on your golf shoes or a pair of aerating lawn sandals, and take a stroll around your yard. Then follow up with this elixir: Mix 1 can of beer, 1 cup of baby shampoo, $^1/_2$ cup of ammonia, and $^1/_2$ cup of weak tea in your 20 gallon hose-end sprayer. Apply it to the point of runoff.

Nix nasty nematodes. You'll never see one of these nearly microscopic worms, but there's no mistaking their damage. Above ground you'll see sickly and stunted vegetable plants; when you dig one up, the roots will be covered with small galls that you can't break off. Root-knot nematodes hang out in sandy soil, where they invade the roots of tomato-family plants and many other vegetables. But here's a simple way to end their dirty tricks: Before you plant your garden, mix 1 can of beer and 1 cup of molasses in a bucket, pour this into your 20 gallon hose-end sprayer, and thoroughly soak the infested area. The wicked worms will be history!

Give It Some Air

Aeration is a classic technique for loosening up compacted soil, as well as solving minor thatch problems. But even healthy lawns can benefit from a regular airing-out. The process simply involves poking holes in the soil, so that air can reach the grass roots—followed quickly by food and water. You should perform this task on a regular basis, following this simple two-part strategy:

1. Every few weeks, strap on a pair of aerating lawn sandals, and stroll back and forth across your lawn. Or, simpler yet, wear traditional, spiked golf shoes whenever you mow the lawn or do other yard chores. Besides improving the health of your lawn, the spikes will give you more secure footing on the grass.

2. Once a month throughout the growing season, combine 1 cup of beer and 1 cup of dishwashing liquid in your 20 gallon hose-end sprayer, and fill the balance of the sprayer jar with warm water. Then spray your lawn to the point of runoff to help keep the soil nice and loose and fluffy. *Note:* Anytime a recipe calls for dishwashing liquid, do not use detergent or any product that contains antibacterial agents.

"Age" terra-cotta pots. Some folks love the look of a brand new, beautiful clay planter. Others prefer containers that have a little more experience under their belt—or at least look as though they had. If you fall into the latter camp, then this tip's for you. Mix $1/2$ can of beer, $1/2$ teaspoon of sugar, and 1 cup of moss on low speed in a blender. Then paint the mixture on the outside of your terra-cotta containers. In a week or so, that lovely moss and lichen will start the aging process.

Trap flea beetles. In early spring, just when the first flowers and vegetables are poking their shoots above ground, these teeny terrors hop out of nowhere and start chewing itty-bitty holes in every leaf in sight. A big crowd of the beetles can kill a seedling, but even in small numbers, they can spread incurable viruses to any plant. Fortunately, there's an easy way to stop the monsters dead in their tracks: Just set out shallow pans filled with cheap beer. Flea beetles *love* beer, so they'll zoom right in—but won't zoom out again!

 # Coffee

Water acid-loving plants. Some of the most beautiful flowering shrubs of all, like azaleas, camellias, and rhododendrons, prefer their soil on the acidic side. A few edibles—including strawberries, blueberries, and potatoes—do, too. So, do the sourpusses in your yard a big favor: Pour cold coffee right on the soil around them. They'll love you for it—and they'll show it by delivering bushels of blooms, berries, and tasty tubers!

Make insecticides more potent. You know how coffee (or rather, the caffeine in it) gives you a big jolt of energy in the morning? Well, it can do just the same for any of the bug-killing tonics in this book (or any other homemade insecticide, for that matter). All you need to do is substitute good old java for the water called for in the recipe.

Stain outdoor furniture. Or anything else that's made of wood. Just mix about a cup of ground coffee in 4 cups of water and simmer for about an hour, adding more water as it evaporates. Let the mixture cool, strain out the coffee, and mix in ½ teaspoon of alum (available in the spice section of your supermarket) as a fixative. Then paint it onto the wood surface and let it dry. Repeat the process until you reach the desired shade of brown.

Round & Round
Round & Round

For my money, when you toss coffee grounds into the trash, you're throwing away a garden-variety gold mine. Here's a Baker's half-dozen ways to use them in your yard and garden:

1. Add coffee grounds (filters and all) to the holes when you plant acid lovers, like blueberries and evergreens.

2. When any plant needs a nitrogen boost, work coffee grounds into the soil.

3. Throw coffee grounds and the paper filters onto your compost pile. They're a great source of high-nitrogen ingredients, i.e., "greens". *Note:* Once the grounds have been composted, they'll no longer raise the acid level of your soil, because compost generally has a neutral pH.

4. Make it easier to sow tiny seeds, like those of lettuce and carrots, by mixing them with dried coffee grounds.

5. Sprinkle dried coffee grounds around plants to repel slugs and cutworms.

6. Repel cabbage maggots by working a tablespoon or so of coffee grounds into the soil in each hole before you set in your cabbage-family transplants.

7. Make a nutritious and attractive mulch by combining coffee grounds with chopped leaves or nut shells. *Note:* Don't use the grounds alone, because they tend to cake together and form a crust.

Control mosquitoes. These villainous vampires will lay their eggs in any body of standing water—even tiny puddles. You may not be able to drain all of the micro-mini ponds in your yard, but you can see to it that they don't turn into skeeter maternity wards. How? Just pour old, cold coffee into the water. (Of course, good, fresh coffee will work just as well, but why waste it?) But forget the decaf—it's the caffeine that does the trick. Scientists have discovered that when mosquito larvae are exposed to caffeine, they get so confused that they can't tell which end is up, and they drown!

De-mustify your workshop. After a long, damp winter, even the best-kept shop or garden shed can start smelling a little musty. But you can fix that in a hurry. Simply grind up some coffee beans very fine, pour the ground coffee onto a plate, and set it on your workbench for a day or two. Then breathe in the fresh air!

MARVELOUS MiX

Potted Plant Picnic

As all you container-gardeners know, when you water potted plants, you have to keep the flow going until that H_2O starts coming out of the holes in the bottom of the pot. But as that water runs out, it carries some of the valuable soil nutrients along with it. That's why it's crucial to keep up a regular feeding program. Here's a meal that your container plants are sure to appreciate.

> 2 tbsp. of brewed black coffee
> 2 tbsp. of whiskey
> 1 tsp. of fish emulsion
> $1/2$ tsp. of gelatin powder
> $1/2$ tsp. of baby shampoo
> $1/2$ tsp. of ammonia
> 1 gal. of water

Mix these ingredients in a watering can, and water your potted plants with the mixture once a week to keep them happy, healthy, and full of flowers!

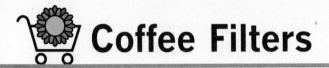

Coffee Filters

Start perennial seeds. Unlike most vegetable and annual flower seeds, which need warmth to germinate, many perennials won't sprout unless they get a period of chilly moisture. These cool customers will be identified as such on their seed packets, but some of the more common ones are anemones *(Anemone* spp.), bleeding hearts *(Dicentra* spp.), lady's mantle *(Alchemilla mollis),* monkshood *(Aconitum* spp.), phlox *(Phlox* spp.), and primroses *(Primula* spp.). Fortunately, providing the right kind of prenatal conditions is a snap. Just put a coffee filter inside a small, zippered plastic bag, pour 3 tablespoons of water on the filter, and space out your seeds. Then stash the bag in the fridge until the seeds sprout. (The length of time varies, depending on the kind of plant, so check your seed packet or a comprehensive gardening book.)

Hold soil in pots. Conventional wisdom used to claim that covering a drainage hole with pot shards would improve drainage, while keeping soil from washing out of the container. Well, now we know that this procedure can actually hinder drainage—and sometimes rob plants' roots of the growing space they need. So what's a container-gardener to do? Improvise by cutting pieces of coffee filter to put over the drainage holes. Water will flow out unhindered, but the soil won't leak out, and the plants' roots will have plenty of room to grow.

Strain tonics. When you whip up one of my terrific garden tonics, use a coffee filter to separate out the solid material. Then toss the solids, filter and all, into your compost bin. Or simply dig a small hole, and bury the whole shebang in a planting bed. Either way, that organic matter will soon decompose, enriching your soil in the process.

Coffee filters are handy things to have around the yard and garden, all right. But they can help make your life a whole lot easier in the kitchen, too. Here are just some of the feats they can perform—besides making a great cuppa joe, of course!

Here's to **YOU!**

Blot spills. Accidents happen—even when you're fresh out of paper towels. So absorb the mess with a coffee filter (or two or three).

De-cork your vino. When the cork crumbles and pieces wind up in the bottle, pour the wine through a coffee filter into a clean decanter.

Freshen your fridge. When you come home from vacation and discover a lot of, um, aromatic food that you forgot to pitch before you left, get rid of it *fast*. Then pull out six or eight coffee filters, and fill each one with 1/2 cup of baking soda. Set them on the shelves and in the produce bins and other compartments. The filters will help the soda absorb the odors faster.

Nuke food neatly. To prevent messy spills and splatters, use coffee filters to cover dishes when you put them into the microwave.

Protect your china. Separate stacked plates with flattened coffee filters to keep the rough bottoms from scratching the smooth tops.

Save your skillets. And other cast-iron pans, too. Put a coffee filter in the bottom of each one to absorb moisture and prevent rust from forming.

Weigh food. Before you set chopped ingredients on a food scale, put the pieces in a coffee filter. They'll be less likely to spill, and the featherweight paper won't affect the amount of each ingredient you need.

Coffee Filters

Recycle paint thinner. After you clean paintbrushes, there's still plenty of life left in the thinner. All you need to do is get rid of the colorful residue. Here's my favorite method: Layer two coffee filters over a clean jar, but don't pull them taut—keep them really loose. Pour the old thinner through them into the jar, and cap it tightly. Now you've got thinner to use another day. Just one word of caution: Although filtered thinner is fine for cleaning brushes, it will retain a little pigment, so don't use it to thin paint, stain, or varnish.

Round & Round Round & Round

If you buy your coffee in cans, then you get a great big bonus: some of the handiest garden helpers you could ever ask for. Here are just a few of the ways you can use these metal marvels:

Grow sweeter melons. Turn a can upside down, push it into the soil until the surface is a few inches off the ground, and set the melon on top of it. The fruit will be protected from rot and soilborne pests. Plus, the metal will absorb and hold heat—making the melon ripen faster and taste sweeter.

Irrigate deep down. Dig can-sized holes every few feet throughout your garden or flower beds. Then sink a can (with both ends removed) into each hole, and fill it up with gravel. Each time you water, fill the cans to the brim.

Spread grass seed or fertilizer. Punch holes in the bottom, and fill the can with whatever mix you need to spread. Then put on the plastic lid, and shake the can as you walk along.

Start your barbecue fire. Take off the bottom of the can, and punch holes in the sides. Then stand the can in the grill, fill it with charcoal briquettes (no need to add smelly lighter fluid), and light it up. When the coals are glowing, grab the hot can with a pair of tongs and set it in a safe place until the next time you barbecue.

Clean glass. It's time to set tender transplants outside, and you want to put them into your cold frame—but the glass is dirty and you're fresh out of paper towels. No problem! Coffee filters make perfect stand-ins. Of course, they work just as well on the windows of your house, on your camera lens, or, indoors, on mirrors and picture glass. Whatever you do, though, don't use filters to clean your eyeglasses (that is, unless the lenses are actually made of glass, which few are these days): Like any other paper product, coffee filters can leave tiny scratches on plastic.

Filter the air. Got some wood to saw for a garden fence? Or maybe you're sanding some furniture in your workshop. In a pinch, a coffee filter makes a fine stand-in for a dust mask. Just put it over your nose and mouth, secure it in place with a cord or a long rubber band, and (as the flight attendants say) breathe normally.

Serve hot dogs. Here's a terrific time- and work-saving idea for your next barbecue: As the franks come off the grill, skip the paper plates. Instead, wrap each dog-and-bun combo in a coffee filter. It's a holder and napkin in one convenient package. (This  trick also works great for tacos and messy sandwiches.)

Catch drips. Every kid knows that Popsicles® and ice cream bars are a big part of outdoor, summertime fun. And every grownup (at least the ones in charge of doing the laundry) knows how quickly those goodies can melt into sticky spots on T-shirts and sundresses. So don't take chances: Before you hand a frozen treat to a youngster (or even to a grownup), poke a hole in a coffee filter, and insert the stick. The result? No more messes!

 # Fruit Juices

Perk up your plants. You say that your green friends are healthy and pest-free, but somehow they just don't seem as, well, energetic and chipper as they ought to be? No problem! Just mix 1 cup of apple juice per 10 gallons of water in a handheld sprayer, and spray the solution on your lawn, flowers, shrubs, trees, fruits, and vegetables. Then stand back and watch 'em grow stronger, healthier, and much more productive!

Boost your blooms. If your annuals, perennials, and flowering shrubs just aren't churning out as many flowers as they usually do, the problem could be that their leaves are dirty. That film of dust and pollution prevents the sunlight from streaming through the leaf surface and releasing the nutrients that, in turn, provide the energy for flower production. The simple solution: Grab your 20 gallon hose-end sprayer and pour in 1 cup of apple juice, $1^1/_2$ cups of a sports drink that contains electrolytes, and $^1/_2$ cup of ammonia. Then overspray your flower beds to the point of runoff. This'll wash the dirt right off of those leaves, and enrich the soil at the same time. Before you know it, your flowers will be back to blooming like crazy!

Clean your houseplants. If your tap water has a lot of dissolved minerals in it, or if you mist-spray your plants with fertilizer, the leaves can start to look dull and drab. What to do? Wipe pineapple juice or any citrus juice onto the leaves with a clean, soft cotton cloth. They'll shine right up.

Hasten the harvest. When Old Man Winter is heading in fast, and your garden is still full of unripe vegetables, there's no time to waste! Pour 1 cup of apple juice, $^1/_2$ cup of ammonia, and $^1/_2$ cup of baby shampoo into your 20 gallon hose-end sprayer Then fill the balance of the jar with warm water, and spray your plants to the point of runoff. Your tomatoes, squash, cukes—and all of your other veggies—will hop on the fast track to ripeness in no time at all.

Trap Japanese beetles. These terrible terrors from the East have monumental appetites for roses and other flowering shrubs; but truth be told, the gluttons will gladly gobble up just about any plant they land on. Although they enjoy eating a variety of foods, they have one very favorite drink: grape juice. So invite the beetles over for a cocktail. Set a pan of soapy water on the ground about 25 feet from a plant that you want to protect. In the center of the pan, stand an opened can of grape juice with a piece of window screening over the top. The beetles will make a beeline for the juice, fall into the water, and that'll be all she wrote!

Kill slugs. These slimy menaces are famous for their love of beer, but believe it or not, they also go gaga for grape juice. All you need to do is bury shallow containers (like cans from cat food or tuna fish) up to their rims in the soil, and pour in about 1 inch of grape juice. The slugs will belly up to the bar, tumble in, and die happy.

Here's to YOU!

If gardening in hot, muggy weather lays you flat—or anytime you need a quick pick-me-up—treat yourself to this cooling energizer: Mix 1/2 cup of lemon juice, 1/2 cup of lime juice, and 5 or 6 drops of lemon extract in a bowl. If (but only if) you have hard water, add 1/2 cup of baking soda. Pour the solution into tepid bathwater, ease into the tub, and soak for as long as your little heart (or your achin' body) desires. When you get out, you'll be ready for action again!

Fruit Juices

93

Prevent dog spots on your lawn. That is, if they're arriving courtesy of your own pooch! Just add 2 tablespoons of tomato juice to his food twice a day. It'll neutralize the grass-killing acids in the urine that cause those ugly brown patches.

Remove rust from tools. When your gardening gear develops rust spots, don't throw in the trowel! You can make it look as good as new again with a paste made from 2 parts salt to 1 part lemon juice. Rub the paste onto the metal until the spots vanish, and rinse with clear water.

Entice hummingbirds. These guys throng to anything that's in the orange and red color range—including orange juice. Just add several drops of OJ to the sugar water in your nectar feeder, and you'll have hovering-room-only crowds every day—guaranteed!

MARVELOUS MiX

Oriole Cookies

Orioles of all kinds love the sweet taste of these treats. And you'll love the sweet songs the birds sing as they flock to your feeder to grab the goodies.

> 2 cups of cornmeal, regular grind
> 1/2 cup of orange juice
> 1 cup of suet or fat scraps, chopped

Put the cornmeal in a bowl, and pour the orange juice over it, stirring to moisten the cornmeal as you do so. Mix in the suet, mold the dough into balls, and wrap each one in plastic netting (like a mesh produce bag). Poke a stick into the ball to serve as a perch. Then attach a hook to the netting, and hang the treat from a highly visible tree branch or your bird feeder.

Soda Pop

Put your garden to bed. Your flowers and vegetables will wake up
rarin' to grow in the spring if you give them some extra
TLC in the fall. Here's all there is to it: At the end of the
growing season, cover all of your garden beds with a thick
layer of organic mulch. Then serve up
this nightcap: Mix 1 can of regular
cola (not diet), 1 cup of dishwashing
liquid, and ¼ cup of ammonia in a
20 gallon hose-end sprayer, and fill
the balance of the jar with warm water.
Apply it until the mulch is saturated.
Note: Anytime a recipe calls for dishwashing liquid, do not use detergent or
any product that contains antibacterial agents.

Feed your compost. Eventually, any pile of organic matter will
break down into a rich, plant-pleasing supply of "black
gold." But the process will happen a whole lot faster if
you spray the pile once a month with a mix of 1 can of
regular cola (not diet), 1 can of beer, and 1 cup of dishwashing liquid (see *note* above) mixed in your 20 gallon
hose-end sprayer.

Clean concrete. When your patio or walkway is so dirty that you
can't stand it a minute longer, don't bother with some
expensive "miracle" cleaner. Instead, just mix equal parts
of regular cola (not diet) and whole milk, and pour the
solution onto the grubby surface. Scrub with a stiff brush
or broom, rinse with the garden hose, and presto—a
spanking clean outdoor floor! Of course, this fabulous formula will work just as well on indoor surfaces like the
floor of your basement or garage, or the trendy concrete
counters in your kitchen.

It happens to all of us occasionally: We're puttering around in the garden, lose track of the time, and wind up with a nasty sunburn. That's the time to reach for one of these cooling skin soothers. Any one of them will beat the heat and help ease the pain fast!

Here's to **YOU!**

* Splash on some cold club soda.

* Pour some gin into a spray bottle, and spritz your sore body.

* Soak cotton pads in cold, strong black tea, and apply them to your skin every 10 to 15 minutes until the burning sensation subsides.

* Pour white wine into a handheld sprayer bottle and apply it directly to your burned body parts. Don't rub! When the liquid has evaporated, apply a moisturizing lotion.

Decompose grass clippings. Simply by leaving the clippings on your freshly mowed lawn, you can cut the amount of fertilizer you need by as much as 25 percent—and help prevent thatch at the same time! And that valuable organic matter will break down more quickly if you spray it twice a year with this timely tonic: Mix 1 can of regular cola (not diet), 1 can of beer, 1 cup of ammonia, and 1 cup of dishwashing liquid (see *note* on page 95) in a bucket, and pour the solution into a 20 gallon hose-end sprayer. Then spray your lawn to the point of runoff. Those grass clippings will almost dissolve right before your very eyes!

Remove rust from chrome. Is the chrome on your bicycle (or maybe your vintage car) starting to break out in rust spots? Don't panic! Just crumple up a piece of aluminum foil, dip it in cola, and rub the spots away.

Clean an oil spill from your lawn. Fill your 20 gallon hose-end sprayer jar with regular cola (not diet), and spray the oily area with mild pressure until the sprayer jar is empty. Then fill 'er up and go at it again. Repeat the process until you've doused that petro-puddle with a full gallon of cola. After that, remove the sprayer and saturate the site with clear water. You may still see some damage to your lawn, but if you give it normal TLC, it should come back like a champ.

I know this trick sounds too good to be true, but it isn't. The secret to its success is that an ingredient in the cola helps to break down the oil, and the sugar activates microbes that kick the soil and grass roots into recovery mode. (That's why it's crucial to avoid the artificially sweetened, diet stuff.)

De-grease your clothes. When you're working on a lawn mower or other motorized outdoor gear, it's all but impossible to avoid getting a little—or even a lot of—grease on yourself. Fortunately, it's a snap to get your duds clean and sharp-looking again. Simply launder them as usual, adding a can of cola to the regular wash cycle.

Clean your barbecue grill. Got burned-on burgers and steak all over the grill rack? No problem! Wait until the rack cools down, then put it into any container that's big enough to hold it (like a laundry sink or even your bathtub), and pour in enough cola to cover it. Let it sit for an hour or so, and wipe it clean.

What a Grape Idea!

Are birds plucking up your vegetable seeds as soon as you plant them? Then just sprinkle some grape Kool-Aid® mix (straight from the packet) on the soil over the seeds. Birds dislike it so much that they'll go elsewhere for lunch!

Soda Pop

A Soda Pop Timeline

It's no secret that Americans *love* soda pop (a.k.a. "pop" or just plain "soda"). And to prove it, in 2006, we spent a whopping $68.1 billion on carbonated soft drinks. According to *Beverage Digest,* that works out to be 828 servings (8 ounces per serving) for every man, woman, and child in the U.S.A. And just how did flavored fizzy water come to achieve this superstar status? Here's a rundown of some of the more illustrious events in the history of soda pop.

IN THE YEAR	THIS HAPPENED
1767	Joseph Priestly (the chemist who discovered oxygen) developed a process for making carbonated water.
1807	Benjamin Silliman, a Yale University chemistry professor, first bottled and sold seltzer water in New Haven, Connecticut.
1832	John Matthews of New York City popularized the drink by inventing the first compact soda-water machine and dispenser unit.
1838	Eugene Roussell added a "soda fountain" to his Philadelphia perfume shop, and combined carbonated water with fruit syrups to produce the first flavored sodas, including cherry, lemon, and orange.
1876	Charles Hires introduced his root beer to the public at the Philadelphia Centennial Exhibition.
1885	Charles Alderton invented Dr Pepper® and introduced it to customers at Morrison's Old Corner Drug Store in Waco, Texas.
1886	John Pemberton concocted the formula for Coca-Cola® and first sold it to the public at Jacob's Pharmacy in Atlanta, Georgia.
1893	Caleb Bradham developed a beverage called "Brad's drink," which he served to customers at his pharmacy in New Bern, North Carolina. Five years later, in 1898, Mr. Bradham changed the name to Pepsi-Cola®.

IN THE YEAR	THIS HAPPENED
1907	John McLaughlin of Toronto, Ontario, patented a light-colored ginger ale that he called Canada Dry Pale Dry Ginger Ale®. (Dark versions had been created in Ireland in the early 1850s.)
1929	Charles Leiper Grigg of St. Louis began manufacturing "Bib-Label Lithiated Lemon-Lime Soda," which he soon re-christened 7 UP®.
1962	The first no-calorie soft drink, Diet-Rite® Cola, hit the supermarket shelves, distributed by the R.C. Cola Company. It was quickly followed by TaB® in 1963 and Diet Pepsi® in 1965.

Clean stainless steel. This gleaming metal isn't just for kitchen gear anymore—it's showing up outdoors on everything from plant containers to lawn furniture. And you can keep your trendy treasures spotless with this classic routine: Simply rub them down with a clean, soft cloth saturated with club soda. (Or, if you prefer, pour the soda into a handheld sprayer and apply it to the steel surface, then wipe it off.)

De-bug your windshield. When you're cruisin' down the highway at 55 miles an hour (or more), the bug bodies pile up fast and stick on hard. But club soda will take them off in a jiffy. Just pour the bubbly stuff into a handheld sprayer, apply it to the splatters, and wipe them off with paper towels, old panty hose, or a clean, soft cloth.

Clean your car's battery terminals. These essential auto parts seem to collect corrosion in the blink of an eye. Here's an all-but-effortless way to remove it. Just pour soda pop over the terminals, let it sit for 5 minutes or so (until the deposits begin to dissolve), and wipe off the residue with a damp sponge. The stuff that does the trick is carbonic acid, a key ingredient in nearly all carbonated soft drinks.

Remove fresh blood spots. Whoops! You pricked your finger on a rose thorn, and the blood spurted onto your favorite shirt. Don't worry—if you act fast, you can still wear it to your barbecue tonight. Just blot the spots immediately, then pour on cold club soda. Repeat as often as necessary until the stain is gone for good.

Super-charge your plants. Soda pop is a power lunch for every green, growing thing in your yard. That's because it supplies a jolt of carbon dioxide, which plants need to convert the sun's energy into food. To serve the pop, surround your plants with a 3-inch layer of chunky mulch like bark chips, gravel, or cocoa bean hulls. Then twice a week during the growing season, pour a can of soda pop right through the mulch. Any flavor will do, as long as it's good and fizzy.

Here's to **YOU!**

Ouch! You're sound asleep when, out of nowhere, a painful leg cramp jolts you wide awake. Well, don't just lie there losing that valuable shut-eye. Instead, hobble into the kitchen, pour an 8-ounce glass of tonic water, and drink it down. The quinine in the fizzy mixer could be enough to uncramp your muscles. If you don't care for the taste of plain tonic, jazz it up with a squirt of orange juice, a wedge of lime—or even a shot of gin!

Loosen rusted-on nuts and bolts. After a long search, you've found the perfect handle for your garden gate. There's just one problem: You can't get the old one off because the hardware holding it in place has rusted solid. Well, you *could* send out a call for the strongest handyman in town. Or you could simply soak a rag in soda pop, wrap it around the stubborn nut or bolt, and let it sit for several minutes. Then go at it with your wrench again; it should come right out. If it doesn't, repeat the process.

Keep cut flowers perky. You put a lot of hard work into your flower garden, so when you cut blooms to bring indoors, help them stay fresher longer with this simple trick: Fill your vases with 1 cup of soda pop and $1/4$ teaspoon of bleach for every 3 cups of warm water (about 110°F). The sugar will make the flowers last longer (so don't even think of using a diet version!), and the bleach will keep algae from growing in the water. Just one more note: If your bouquet is in a clear vase, use a colorless soda pop, like 7 UP® or Sprite®.

 # Tea

Make seeds germinate better. And faster, too! Before you sow any kind of flower or vegetable seeds, soak them in the refrigerator for 24 hours in a solution made of 1 quart of weak tea and 1 teaspoon each of baby shampoo and Epsom salts. Then drain off the liquid, and plant your seeds according to the directions on the packet.

Prevent damping-off. This foul fungal disease is Public Enemy No. 1 for indoor seedlings. To protect your brood, use a sterile, soilless potting mix that's made especially for starting seeds, provide good air circulation—and as soon as your seedlings appear above the soil surface, "immunize" them this way: Mix 4 teaspoons of chamomile tea and 1 teaspoon of dishwashing liquid (see *note* on page 102) in 1 quart of boiling water, and let the mixture steep for at least an hour. When it's cooled to room temperature, pour it into a handheld sprayer, and mist-spray your baby plants.

Energize your seeds. Once you've sown your seeds, give them an extra-strong send-off with this elixir: Mix 1 teaspoon each of whiskey, ammonia, and dishwashing liquid in 1 quart of weak tea. Pour the solution into a handheld sprayer bottle, shake it gently, and mist-spray the surface of your newly planted seedbeds or containers. *Note:* Anytime a recipe calls for dishwashing liquid, do not use detergent or any product that contains antibacterial agents.

Rev up bare-root perennials. When you order your perennials through the mail, they generally arrive with their roots as dry as a bone and as bare as a new baby's bottom. In fact, you may even think the plants are dead. But looks can be deceiving—once they're in the ground, they'll be up and

MARVELOUS MiX

Moss-Buster Brew

If the moss growing in your yard is driving you to drink (or simply increasing your consumption), I have good news and bad news. First, the bad news: Moss thrives in damp, shady spots with acid soil, so to get rid of it for good, you'll need to raise the pH of your soil to neutral or slightly above, improve drainage to the level of excellence, and find a way to let in more sunshine. The good news is that you can bid moss a short-term farewell by applying this timely tonic.

1 cup of chamomile tea
1 cup of antiseptic mouthwash
1 cup of Murphy® Oil Soap

Mix these ingredients in a bucket, pour the mixture into a 20 gallon hose-end sprayer, and apply it to your lawn and beds to the point of runoff every two weeks to keep the moss at bay.

growing strong in no time at all. And this simple maneuver will help them grow even stronger faster: Before you set your plants into the ground, soak them for 24 hours in a solution made from $1/4$ cup of brewed tea, 1 tablespoon of dishwashing liquid, and 1 tablespoon of Epsom salts mixed with 1 gallon of water. *Note:* Anytime a recipe calls for dishwashing liquid, do not use detergent or any product that contains antibacterial agents.

Boost herb production. No matter how you intend to use your herbs, they will give you more leaves and flowers to work with if you feed the plants with a mix of 1 cup of tea and $1/2$ teaspoon each of hydrogen peroxide, ammonia, and whiskey (any kind will do) in 1 gallon of warm water. Serve up this solution every six weeks during the growing season, and you'll reap a bumper harvest!

Winterize your houseplants. Houseplants need lots of humidity for good growth. So in the winter, when the heat is on and the air is dry, mist-spray your leafy plants at least every other day early in the morning. Use weak tea water, which you can make by soaking a used tea bag and 1 teaspoon of dishwashing liquid (see *note* above) in a gallon of warm water until the mix is light brown. Follow this schedule in summer, too, if your home dries out because of air conditioning.

Start roses out right. In a watering can, mix 1 tablespoon of dishwashing liquid (see *note* above), 1 tablespoon of hydrogen peroxide, 1 teaspoon of whiskey, and 1 teaspoon of Vitamin B_1 Plant Starter in $1/2$ gallon of warm tea. Then pour the liquid all around the root zone of each newly planted (or transplanted) rosebush. Before you know it, everything will be comin' up roses!

Tea

Whatever you do, don't throw your used tea bags or loose tea leaves in the trash—or even the compost bin! Instead, tuck them into the mulch at the base of your roses or acid-soil-loving plants like azaleas and rhododendrons. They'll be pleased as punch, and they'll reward you with beautiful blooms!

Keep ants outdoors. When the little nuisances forget where they belong and start marching into your house, brew up a batch of strong mint tea and spray it on their pathways. They'll turn right around and head back out to the garden.

Repel cabbage maggots. These ugly little worms attack every member of the cabbage family—and what a colossal clan it is! Besides the head of the household, the relatives include broccoli, Brussels sprouts, cauliflower, collards, kale, kohlrabi, mustard, radishes, rutabagas, and turnips. Grandma Putt had a simple way to protect them. At spring planting time, she'd put a tea bag into each hole before she set in her transplants. Loose tea leaves work just as well; simply work a tablespoon or so of leaves into the soil in the bottom of each hole.

Prevent fungal diseases. During periods of cool, damp weather (prime time for many foul fungi), mix 1 cup of chamomile tea, 1 teaspoon of dishwashing liquid, 1/2 teaspoon of vegetable oil, and 1/2 teaspoon of peppermint oil in 1 gallon of warm water. Pour the solution into a handheld sprayer. Mist-spray your plants (annuals, perennials, herbs, and vegetables) every week or so when temperatures are below 75°F. *Note:* Anytime a recipe calls for dishwashing liquid, do not use detergent or any product that contains antibacterial agents.

Clean a cloudy vase Drat! You've got a big, beautiful bouquet of flowers, but your favorite glass vase is as hazy as an LA morning. Don't worry—to clear it up in a flash, mix 1 cup of cool black tea with $\frac{1}{3}$ cup of lemon juice, pour the solution into the vase, and let it sit for a few hours. Then wipe the inside surface with a soft brush or cloth, and rinse with clear water.

Here's to
YOU!

If you've always thought of tea as just a nice, soothing beverage, then think again—it's actually a medicinal powerhouse. Here are just some of the ways tea can improve your health and well-being:

Clear up cold sores. Several times a day, hold a warm tea bag on the sores for about 15 minutes. Repeat until they disappear. This same trick will also heal painful boils.

Ease sore-throat pain. Mix 1 part hot tea with 1 part warm lemon juice, add a generous amount of honey (enough so that it coats your throat going down), and drink to your good health!

Fend off a cold. Or at least lessen its severity. Tests indicate that tea's antioxidants may rev up your immune system and help it fight back when trouble strikes.

Heal a plantar wart. Just hold a hot, wet tea bag on it for 15 minutes every day. It'll be gone before you know it.

Soothe sore, puffy eyes. Squeeze most of the moisture out of two damp, cooled tea bags, lie down in a comfortable spot, put one bag over each eye, and relax for half an hour or so. (To keep the tea from staining your skin, you can wrap each bag in tissue first.)

Tea

Fight brown patch. This fungal disease causes irregular, brownish patches of turf, with a grayish color on the grass at the outer edge of the brown patch. You may also notice filmy, white tufts covering the grass during the morning dew. Your mission: In a large bucket, mix 1 tablespoon of instant tea granules, 1 tablespoon of baking soda, and 1 tablespoon of all-season horticultural oil or dormant oil (available at garden centers) in 1 gallon of warm water. Pour the solution into a handheld sprayer and lightly spritz the affected grass. Do *not* apply it to the point of runoff! Repeat in two to three weeks, if necessary.

Patch bare spots in your lawn. You've pulled some weeds out of your lawn, but now, instead of unwanted greenery, you've got little bald patches in the turf. Well, you won't have them for long if you try this simple trick: Set a moist tea bag on each spot, and sprinkle grass seed right on top. As the bag decomposes, it'll provide both moisture and fertilizer, and before you know it, fresh, green grass blades will be springing up all over.

 # Wine & Spirits

Start woody plants out right. After you've planted a new tree or shrub, treat it to a drink of my Tree and Shrub Transplanting Tonic. To make it, mix $1/3$ cup of hydrogen peroxide, $1/4$ cup of whiskey (any kind will do), $1/4$ cup of baby shampoo, 4 tablespoons of instant tea granules, and 2 tablespoons of fish emulsion in 1 gallon of warm water. Then after you've filled the planting hole and watered thoroughly, slowly dribble about a quart of this mixture onto the soil so that it reaches the roots. This will help that young plant get off to a healthy, happy, and stress-free start!

Energize seeds. Once you've sown flower or vegetable seeds, indoors or out, give them an energy boost with this elixir: Mix 1 teaspoon each of whiskey (any kind will do), ammonia, and dishwashing liquid in 1 quart of weak tea. Pour the solution into a handheld sprayer bottle. Shake it gently, and mist the surface of your newly planted seedbeds or flats. *Note:* Anytime a recipe calls for dishwashing liquid, do not use detergent or any product that contains antibacterial agents.

Give shrubs a spring tonic. When Old Man Winter has finally flown the coop, serve your shrubs this tasty cocktail: Put 2 gallons of water in a watering can, and mix in 4 tablespoons of whiskey, 4 tablespoons of instant tea granules, and 2 tablespoons of dishwashing liquid (see *note* above). The pour the solution slowly onto the root zone of each shrub. (This recipe makes enough for one large plant.)

Feed your food crops. Vegetable plants really work up an appetite churning out all that good stuff for us, and even the most well-balanced diet needs a little kick every now and then. Here's a great one: Every three weeks during the growing season, mix 1/2 cup of fish emulsion; 2 tablespoons each of whiskey, instant tea granules, and Epsom salts; and 1 tablespoon of baby shampoo in a 20 gallon hose-end sprayer. Then apply it to all your veggies to the point of runoff. It'll turn them into lean, mean, growing machines!

Dye Easter eggs. Yikes! It's your turn to host your family's annual outdoor Easter egg hunt, and the preparations are taking you right down to the wire—but you just ran out of dye with a dozen more eggs to color. There's no time to rush out for another coloring kit. So what do you do? Use red wine instead. It'll color the shells a pretty shade of purple. Just set your hard-boiled eggs into a bowl, pour in enough red wine to cover them, and put them in the refrigerator. Let them sit until they reach the desired intensity, and then hand them over to the Easter Bunny.

MARVELOUS MIX

Robust Rose Tonic

Hybrid tea roses have a well-deserved reputation as the prima donnas of the plant kingdom. But this fabulous formula will keep them happy, healthy, and churning out blooms galore, all summer long!

> 2 tbsp. of instant tea granules
> 1 tbsp. of dry red wine
> 1/2 tbsp. of fish emulsion
> 1 tsp. of baking powder
> 1 tsp. of iron (available at garden centers)
> 1 gal. of warm water

Mix these ingredients in a bucket and treat each rosebush to a quart of the mixture every three weeks during the growing season.

Leave your houseplants lush. Ferns, philodendrons, and other foliage plants will stay at their green, leafy best if you feed them every two weeks with this elixir: $1/2$ tablespoon each of bourbon, ammonia, and hydrogen peroxide; $1/4$ teaspoon of instant tea granules; and 1 crushed multivitamin-plus-iron tablet—all mixed in 1 gallon of warm water. *Note:* For flowering houseplants, like Christmas cactus, cyclamen, and Persian violets, use vodka instead of bourbon.

Pep up tired soil. Don't bother changing the soil for your potted perennials every year. Instead, just add one shot of bourbon, Scotch, vodka, or gin plus 1 ounce of dishwashing liquid per gallon of water. Use this formula to replace plain water when you mix up your favorite plant food, and it'll liven things up like nobody's business! *Note:* Anytime a recipe calls for dishwashing liquid, do not use detergent or any product that contains antibacterial agents.

Kill stubborn weeds. When you've got tough customers that just won't take "no" for an answer, call out the big guns. Mix 2 tablespoons each of gin, vinegar, and dishwashing liquid (see *note* above) in 1 quart of hot water. Pour the solution into a handheld sprayer bottle, and blast those weeds to you-know-where. Just be careful not to get any on plants you want to keep! By the way, if you don't have gin on hand, feel free to substitute vodka.

Keep cut flowers fresher. They'll stay a whole lot fresher a whole lot longer if you add a shot of vodka to the water in the vase. *Nostrovia!*

Condiments & Flavorings

CAYENNE PEPPER

CONDIMENTS

DRIED HERBS & SPICES

EXTRACTS & OILS

HOT PEPPER SAUCE

SALT

VINEGAR

Cayenne Pepper

Say "Nuts!" to squirrels. If the little rascals insist on robbing your bird feeder blind, mix ground cayenne pepper with the seed (1 to 2 tablespoons of cayenne per quart of seed will do the trick). Birds don't mind the hot pepper one bit, but squirrels can't stand it. Fill your feeders immediately, or store the treated seed in an airtight container (to preserve the pepper's potency) until you're ready to use it.

Protect your tulips. If the squirrels are gunnin' for these beautiful bulbs, try this tactic. Mix 3 tablespoons of ground cayenne pepper with 2 cups of hot water in a bottle, and shake well. Let it sit overnight, then strain off the liquid and mix it in a handheld sprayer bottle with 1 tablespoon each of hot sauce, ammonia, and baby shampoo. Start spraying the stems when flowers appear, and continue as long as new buds are forming.

Defend your cole crops. Cabbage pests on the rampage? Mix 2 tablespoons of ground cayenne pepper with 1 cup of flour, and dust the resulting mixture on all your cabbage-family plants. Cabbage worms and loopers will eat the mixture and die; other bad guys will simply go elsewhere when they smell (or taste) the pepper.

Kill leaf-eating insects. No matter what kind of bad bugs are munching on your flower and vegetable plants, this potent spray will polish them off. To make it, combine 4 to 6 garlic cloves, 1 small onion, and 1 teaspoon of ground cayenne pepper in a blender with 1 quart of water, and liquefy the mix. Let it sit overnight, then strain out the solids and add 3 drops of baby shampoo. Pour the solution into a handheld sprayer bottle, and fire when you see the whites of their eyes (so to speak).

Repel Japanese beetles. These voracious villains are famous for their love of roses, but they don't stop with America's National Flower—they'll gleefully gobble up every kind of leaf or blossom in sight. But this ultra-hot toddy will say a loud, strong "Go away!" to any beetle that starts to sink its choppers into your plants. To make it, put $1/2$ cup of whole, dried cayenne peppers and $1/2$ cup of whole, dried jalapeño peppers in a pan with 1 gallon of water. Bring it to a boil, and let it simmer for half an hour. (Keep the pan covered, or the peppery steam will make you cry a river of tears!) Let the mixture cool, strain out the solids, pour the liquid into a handheld sprayer bottle, and apply it to your plants to the point of runoff. To ensure continued protection, reapply the mixture after every rain.

MARVELOUS MIX

Dead Bug Brew

When you want to keep all kinds of live bugs from dining on your flowering plants, serve them this mulligan stew made with their dead kin.

> **$1/2$ cup of dead insects (the more variety, the merrier!)**
> **1 tbsp. of ground cayenne pepper**
> **1 tbsp. of dishwashing liquid***
> **2 cups of water**

Put the ingredients in an old blender (one you'll *never* use again for food preparation) and puree the heck out of 'em. Strain out the pulp, and dilute the remaining brew at a rate of $1/4$ cup of brew per 1 cup of water. Apply it to your plants with a handheld sprayer to the point of runoff. *Note:* Use this formula on ornamental plants only—not on edible crops!

*Do not use detergent or any product that contains antibacterial agents.

Are your feet extra-sensitive to the cold? Then do what I do: Before you head outdoors in the wintertime, put on a pair of thin socks. Then grab a thicker, warmer pair, and shake about $\frac{1}{2}$ teaspoon of ground cayenne pepper into each sock. Slip these over the thinner ones, and you're good to go. Your feet will stay toasty warm, even when everyone else has footsicles!

Keep animals out of flower beds. This is one of the simplest good-riddance tricks you'll ever find: Just sprinkle ground cayenne pepper around the off-limits area. It won't harm plants, pets, or wildlife; but critters dislike the smell, so they'll take one whiff and get outta Dodge!

Deter deer. When the brown-eyed bruisers just won't leave your trees and shrubs alone, this is the remedy to reach for. It's become a classic, and for good reason: It works like a charm! Put 2 tablespoons of ground cayenne pepper, 2 tablespoons of hot pepper sauce, 2 eggs, and 2 cloves of garlic in a blender with 2 cups of water. Puree, and let the mixture sit for two days. Then either pour it around your deer-plagued plants, or apply it with a handheld sprayer.

Seal pruning wounds. After you prune trees or shrubs, paint the cut ends of the branches with a mixture of $\frac{1}{2}$ cup of interior latex paint, $\frac{1}{2}$ cup of antiseptic mouthwash, and 1 teaspoon of cayenne pepper. This will help keep insects and disease germs from moving into the tender tissue and doing their dirty work.

Condiments

Clean your anti-slug fence. Encircling a planting bed with copper stripping is a foolproof way to fend off slugs and snails—that is, until the metal becomes dirty and tarnished. When that happens, the chemicals in the copper can no longer react with the pests' slime to deliver the fatal blow: a jolt of static electricity. But there's an easy way to remove the crud. Just pull up the strips, coat them with a thin layer of ketchup, and let them sit for 5 to 30 minutes (depending on the amount of dirt). When the tarnish has vanished, rinse the copper strips with clear water, dry them thoroughly, and put them back on garden guard duty.

Keep wooden tool handles shipshape. Just rub them every now and again with a mixture of 2 parts mayonnaise to 1 part lemon juice on a soft cloth. The wood will stay smooth, clean, and free of cracks.

Remove gunk. Mayonnaise will get grease, tar, sap, or pine pitch off your tools, your car, your hands, or just about anything else. Simply rub on the mayo, let it sit for a few minutes, and wipe it off.

For reasons I've never figured out, any kind of pickle juice makes gardenias all but stand up and cheer. So if you grow these gorgeous shrubs—indoors or out—do yourself a favor: Every time you polish off the last pickle in a jar, pour the juice onto the soil at the base of your gardenia plants. They'll return the favor by producing mountains of snowy-white, sweet-smelling blooms.

Hooray-for-Horseradish Tonic

This tangy tonic is instant death to some of the vilest villains in gardendom, including blister beetles, aphids, Colorado potato beetles, whiteflies, and any caterpillar that ever crept down the pike.

2 cups of dried cayenne peppers, finely chopped
2 tbsp. of bottled, pure horseradish*
3 qts. of water

Bring the water to a boil, add the peppers and horseradish, and let the mixture steep for an hour or so. Let it cool to room temperature, then strain out the solids. Pour the liquid into a handheld sprayer, and blast those bugs to you-know-where!

*Not mixed with mustard, mayonnaise, or any other ingredients.

Spruce up your houseplants. When the leaves of your dracaena, ficus, and other foliage plants start looking drab and dingy, reach for the mayonnaise. Mix the mayo with enough water to form a thick paste, apply it to the leaves with a soft cloth, and wipe off any excess. Those leaves will be so shiny, you'll be able to see yourself in them— well, almost.

Delete crayon marks from wood. Yikes! Your barbecue guests are due any minute now, and your young Georgia O'Keefe is creating a masterpiece on your wooden patio table. Don't panic—and don't even rush indoors for a table-cloth. Just grab the mayonnaise instead. Then rub it onto the marks, let it sit for a minute or so, and wipe the table clean with a damp cloth. (Of course, this trick works just as well on indoor furniture, no matter what kind of wood it's made of.)

Condiments

Winterize your tools. Drat! It's time to put your garden gear away for the winter, and you're fresh out of oil to guard against rust. No problem—use mayonnaise instead! Just wash the tools, dry them, and rub mayo onto all the metal parts, using a soft cloth. Rub off any excess before you hang the tools up on the wall or wrap them in newspaper for winter.

Trap earwigs. These evil-looking bugs rarely cause any real trouble in a garden. Sometimes, though, their chomping can get out of hand. If that happens at your place, pour equal parts of soy sauce and vegetable oil in empty cat food or tuna cans. Set out the traps at night, and toss them (and their contents) out early in the morning before butterflies or other good-guy bugs can flit in for a fatal drink.

Dried Herbs & Spices

Scrub scale. Scale insects form tiny bumps on stems as they suck the life-giving sap from flowers, trees, shrubs, fruit plants, and sometimes even vegetables. You can suffocate many of the pests by spraying your plants in the fall with a good horticultural oil. Any survivors will wake up in the spring and start moving around; that's the time to hit them with this super-simple spray. To make it, put 1/4 cup of dried chives in a bowl, pour 2 cups of boiling water over them, and let them sit for an hour. Strain out the chives, mix 1 part of the liquid with 2 parts water, and add a few drops of dishwashing liquid. Pour the solution into a handheld sprayer, shake, and apply it to your plants to the point of runoff. Then say "So long, scale!" *Note:* Anytime a recipe calls for dishwashing liquid, do not use detergent or any product that contains antibacterial agents.

Clobber mealybugs. When these tiny terrors gang up on your houseplants, don't pull any punches. Mix about $1/4$ teaspoon of ground cloves with $1/4$ cup of rubbing alcohol, and let it steep overnight. In the morning, dab the mix onto each bug with a cotton swab. They'll never know what hit 'em!

Make ants scram. If you've got an ant invasion on your hands, help is as close as your spice rack—or the supermarket spice section. Just sprinkle cream of tartar, paprika, red chili powder, or dried peppermint around the problem areas. Ants find them all disgusting and will avoid them like the plague.

Keep ants out of a hummingbird feeder. There's nothing more frustrating than seeing a line of ants marching up to your nectar feeder. To end those shenanigans fast, mix 1 tablespoon of ground cloves with 1 cup of white vinegar in a handheld sprayer bottle, and spray it all along the ant trail leading up to the "chuck wagon."

Keep bugs at bay. Here's one of the simplest ways around to repel all kinds of destructive insects: Lightly dust your flower and vegetable plants with garlic powder every week or two (and after every rain).

Round & Round Round & Round

When you finish all the spice in a jar, don't throw the little thing away! With those perforated tops, they make perfect dispensers for lettuce, carrot, and other tiny seeds that can drive you crazy when you try to sow them by hand. Spice jars are also just the right size for storing leftover seeds. Just put 1 part seed to 1 part powdered milk in the jar, screw the lid on tight, and put it in the refrigerator (not the freezer) until planting time rolls around.

Time for Tea

Herbal tea is a time-tested remedy for almost anything that ails ya'. And nothing could be easier to make. Just put 1 to 2 teaspoons of dried herbs into a ceramic teapot or mug that you've already pre-heated by pouring boiling water into it and then dumping it out. In a pan or teakettle, bring 1 cup of water to a boil, and pour it over the herbs. Let it steep for 3 to 5 minutes, then strain it into a fresh cup or mug. Add honey to taste, if you'd like, and drink to your good health and long life!

As to what kind of herbs to use, here's a look at some of these old-time "wonder drugs" that come straight from the Dried Herbs & Spices section of your supermarket. *Note:* If you're pregnant, on medication of any kind (even aspirin), or suffering from high blood pressure, diabetes, or any other chronic condition, check with your doctor before you dose yourself with any of these herbs.

HEALING HERB	HOW IT HELPS
Basil	Fights colds and flu infections, sharpens mental alertness, eases migraines, relieves stress, helps cure depression, and stimulates the flow of milk in nursing mothers.
Bay	Contains chemicals that fight tooth decay and ease the pain of headaches and stomachaches.
Dill	Soothes upset stomachs, eases muscle spasms, freshens breath, and stimulates the flow of milk in nursing mothers.
Garlic	Kills bacteria, clears lung congestion, lowers blood sugar and cholesterol levels, boosts circulation, and acts as an antihistamine.
Ginger	Fights nausea, cures motion sickness, eases pain from diarrhea and gas, stimulates the appetite, subdues menstrual cramps and migraines, promotes sweating to break a fever, and kills germs.
Parsley	Freshens breath, rids the body of excess water (thus easing bloating during menstruation and menopause), and relieves gas pains.

HEALING HERB	HOW IT HELPS
Rosemary	Stimulates memory, boosts energy, and helps to relieve the blues.
Sage	Restores vitality and strength, fights fevers, and soothes mucous membrane tissue—thereby curing mouth ulcers, sore gums and throats, and even laryngitis.
Tarragon	Stimulates the appetite, relieves colic and rheumatism, may help lower blood pressure, and helps restore regularity to menstrual cycles.
Thyme	Fights germs that cause sore throats, colds, and congestion.

Fend off foul fungi. Protect your plants from powdery mildew and other fungal diseases with this easy formula: Mix 2 tablespoons of cinnamon powder with 2 cups of rubbing alcohol. Shake well, and let the mixture sit overnight. Filter out the sediment, and pour the liquid into a handheld sprayer bottle. Spray your plants every week during early spring, and during damp spells throughout the growing season.

Prevent damping-off in seedlings. Use the cinnamon formula described above (see "Fend off foul fungi"), but substitute hot water for the alcohol, which can dry the tiny tykes out. Apply it to the young plants when the first bits of green appear above the soil surface.

Annihilate aphids. These pesky, pear-shaped pests start showing up near the end of spring, and begin draining the juices out of every kind of plant you can name. If the vile villains have invaded your garden, fight back with this libation. Mix $1/2$ cup of parsley flakes and 2 tablespoons of minced garlic in 3 cups of water, and boil it down to 2 cups. Strain and cool, then pour the tea into a 20 gallon hose-end sprayer, and drench your plants until the aphids are history.

Dried Herbs & Spices

Protect your houseplants. From dogs and cats, that is—and vice versa, because many common houseplants are toxic to our four-footed friends. The simple secret: Just shove a few cinnamon sticks into the soil in each pot. Felines and canines both seem to dislike the aroma, so they'll steer clear.

Deodorize a vase. Rats! You've plucked a few picture-perfect roses from your garden, but when you started to put them in your favorite narrow-necked vase, you made an unpleasant discovery: It's still carrying a foul scent left by flowers you forgot to throw out before you went on vacation. No problem! First, put your roses in a temporary container, then soak your vase overnight in a solution made from 1 teaspoon of dry mustard per 4 cups of warm water. Then rinse well, add fresh water, and insert your ravishing roses.

MARVELOUS MiX

"Hit the Trail" Mix

This spicy concoction will make any pesky critter hightail it away from your garden.

- 4 tbsp. of dry mustard
- 3 tbsp. of cayenne pepper
- 2 tbsp. of chili powder
- 2 tbsp. of cloves
- 1 tbsp. of hot sauce
- 2 qts. of warm water

Mix all of these ingredients together in a watering can, and sprinkle the solution around the perimeter of your flower or vegetable garden—or anyplace else you don't want four-legged visitors venturing.

Repel slugs and snails. Are these slimy mollusks buggin' your flowers? Just sprinkle powdered ginger on the soil around your plants. The voracious villains will more than keep their distance. (Of course, you will have to replace your spicy "fence" after every rain.)

Make groundhogs go away. These pudgy rascals are cute, all right, but a single groundhog can demolish a flower garden or vegetable garden faster than you can say "Punxsutawney Phil." Fortunately, as much as they love all kinds of plants, they hate one spicy aroma: ground pepper. Just sprinkle it on the ground around the wood-chucks' targets. Either red or black pepper will send 'em heading elsewhere for dinner.

Extracts & Oils

Make an instant insecticide. Need a potent weapon *right now*? This one will kill some of the peskiest pests around, including aphids, leafhoppers, cabbage worms, and even mosquitoes. Just mix 1 tablespoon of garlic oil and 3 drops of dishwashing liquid with a quart of water in a handheld sprayer bottle, and blast away your pest problems. *Note:* Anytime a recipe calls for dishwashing liquid, do not use detergent or any product that contains antibacterial agents.

Protect container plants. Just like people, pets vary in their tastes. Some dogs and cats aren't bothered at all by citrusy aromas (or even flavors). If that's the case at your house— or if you grow highly toxic plants like angels' trumpets (*Brugmansia* spp.), philodendrons, dieffenbachia, or azal-eas—don't take any chances. Rub chili oil (an ultra-hot oil used in Asian stir-fries) onto any leaves that are within your pet's reach. You can use either a cotton ball or a soft cloth for this job, but be sure to wear rubber gloves to avoid burning your skin. *Note:* If your pal does get a taste of the oil, he may sneeze and drool a little, but there will be no permanent harm done.

Say "No" to pets. The ones who want to cavort in your garden, that is. Just spray the perimeter of the beds with a solution of 2 tablespoons of orange or lemon extract or oil per gallon of water, using a handheld sprayer bottle. Most dogs and cats hate the smell of citrus and will stay away.

Deter cucumber beetles. In addition to dining on their namesake crop and its relatives, these menaces attack many other vegetables and ornamental plants. What's more, as they feed, cuke beetles also spread three of the worst diseases that can strike any garden: bacterial wilt, fusarium wilt, and cucumber mosaic virus. But you can protect your harvest by mixing 2 tablespoons of artificial vanilla extract per quart of water in a handheld sprayer bottle, and spraying your plants thoroughly from top to bottom.

If you grow cucumbers and you have children or grandchildren who help you out in the garden, this trick has your name written all over it. All you need is a small-necked glass bottle—preferably a square one with straight sides, like the kind that many flavored oils come in. When one of your cukes is still tiny, slip it into the bottle, being careful not to tear it from the vine. Then shade it with newspaper so the fruit doesn't bake in the sun.

When the cuke gets big enough to rate oohs and aahs—but not so big that it breaks the bottle—cut it from the vine, take it indoors, and put it center stage on the coffee table.

Protect container plants, take 2. To keep Fido and Fluffy out of your big pots and planters, soak cotton balls in orange or lemon extract or oil, and tuck them into the soil just deep enough to keep them from blowing away. One of these homemade repellents will work for a small pot; for larger containers, use two or three cotton balls.

Make mice move on. Mice really like the tasty bark of trees and shrubs. And they really hate the cool scent of mint. To put this powerful tool to work in your yard, just mix 2 tablespoons of peppermint oil or extract in a gallon of warm water. Pour the solution into a handheld sprayer bottle, and thoroughly spritz the crown and lower stems of your trees and shrubs. To protect container plants, simply saturate a cotton ball in the extract, and tuck it into the pot at the base of the plant. (For large specimens, use two or three cotton balls.)

Bash beetles and weevils. A soap spray will kill any insect you can name, but when you use it on hard-bodied bugs, you need to add some extra firepower. And you can't find a more powerful kicker ingredient than peppermint oil. It cut rights through a bug's waxy shell, so the soap can get in and work its fatal magic. Here's the fabulous formula: Mix 2 tablespoons of dishwashing liquid in 1 gallon of warm water, then stir in 2 teaspoons of peppermint oil (*not* extract). Pour the solution into a handheld sprayer bottle, take aim, and fire! Those bugs will never know what hit 'em! *Note:* Anytime a recipe calls for dishwashing liquid, do not use detergent or any product that contains antibacterial agents.

Repel squash bugs. These pests find their targets by scent. So put them off the trail by masking the aroma they're zeroing in on: a bitter compound in the leaves of cucurbit-family plants. How? Just spray the leaves with a half-and-half solution of water and artificial vanilla extract.

Here's to
YOU!

Herbs and spices are not the only healthcare workers in the Condiments & Flavorings aisle. Extracts and flavored oils deserve a place in the medicine cabinet, too. Just take a look at what feats these extracts and natural wonders can perform for you:

Ease the pain of a minor burn. Gently dab a little artificial vanilla extract onto the painful area.

Disguise the taste of a fizzy antacid remedy. Add a few drops of your favorite flavored extract to the mixture.

Relieve dry, itchy skin. Apply a teaspoon or so of sesame oil to your face and neck, and scrub gently with a warm, damp washcloth. Rinse with warm water, and pat dry.

Get rid of head lice. (It's a growing problem in schools.) Wash the child's hair as usual, adding 2 teaspoons of coconut oil to the shampoo (coconut oil is lethal to lice). Lather thoroughly, rinse, and repeat. This second time, though, wrap the child's head in a towel, and leave it on for half an hour. Remove the towel, and comb the hair with a nit comb. Finally, wash the hair again, and rinse well.

Remove calluses from your hands. (Like the ones that develop in your palms if you use a cane, crutches, or a walker.) Mix 1 tablespoon of avocado oil and 1 to 2 tablespoons of cornmeal until it forms a paste with a meal-like texture. Take the mixture in the palm of your hand, and rub both hands together, working the gritty stuff into the calluses and around your fingers. Repeat once or twice a week, and before you know it, your skin will be soft and smooth again.

Deodorize your tool shed. Or your workshop, garage, or car. Simply soak a few cotton balls in artificial vanilla extract, and set them around the room. Or, if the object of your nose's displeasure is your car's interior, tuck the cotton balls under the front seat.

Mask paint odors. Even when you're painting outdoors, the aroma can be unpleasant, to say the least. But you won't even notice it if you use this old-time painters' trick: Pour half of a small bottle of artificial vanilla extract into 1 gallon of paint, and mix it in well.

Hot Pepper Sauce

Keep raccoons out of your garbage can. There's nothing these masked marauders love more than your leftovers—that is, unless you heat up those vittles. To do that, dip a large wad of paper towels in ammonia, douse it thoroughly with hot pepper sauce, and toss the wad into the trash can. The rascals will dine elsewhere.

Protect your trees. To mice, voles, and rabbits, there's no tastier winter snack than the bark on young trees and shrubs. But this super-heated repellent will say, loud and clear, "Take your choppers elsewhere!" Mix 2 tablespoons of hot pepper sauce, 2 tablespoons of cayenne pepper, and 1 tablespoon of dishwashing liquid in 1 quart of warm water, and pour the solution into a handheld sprayer bottle. In the late fall, drench the trunks of all your young trees and shrubs to a height of about 18 inches. If the weather is wet, repeat the treatment every few weeks to keep the scent fresh. *Note:* Anytime a recipe calls for dishwashing liquid, do not use detergent or any product that contains antibacterial agents.

Hit-'Em-Hard Houseplant Tonic

No matter what kind of insects are ganging up on your indoor plants, this intensive treatment will send the little buggers to the local pest cemetery.

1/4 cup of gin or vodka
2 tbsp. of baby shampoo
2 tsp. of hot pepper sauce
1 qt. of warm water

Mix these ingredients in a handheld sprayer bottle. Then put your plant in your bathtub or kitchen sink (cover the soil with aluminum foil or plastic wrap to keep it in the pot). Rinse the plant thoroughly with clear water. Then apply this tonic to the point of runoff, being careful to drench all stems and both sides of the leaves, as well as the leaf nodes (the point where a leaf meets the stem—a favorite hiding spot for many small insects). Let the plant sit for 15 to 20 minutes, then rinse thoroughly again with clear water. You'll kiss your pest problems goodbye!

Chase moles. The little pests will pack up and head outta town (or at least out of your yard) when they get a taste of this potent potion: In a bucket, mix 2 tablespoons of hot pepper sauce, 1 tablespoon of dishwashing liquid, and 1 teaspoon of chili powder in 1 quart of water. Then pour some of the mix every few feet in newly burrowed tunnels. The little guys will get a surprise they won't soon forget!

Banish bad bugs. There's nothing more frustrating than putting a lot of time and effort into your vegetable garden, only to have it feasted upon by any and all bugs that walk, crawl, or fly by. Well, here's a way to keep those pesky pests at the proper distance—treat 'em to a little heat! It's simple, too. Just mix 1 cup of hot pepper sauce and 2 tablespoons of baby shampoo in 1 gallon of water. Pour the solution into a handheld sprayer bottle, then apply it to your troubled plants to the point of runoff. It'll get rid of any unwanted diners and keep them from coming back.

Discourage deer. When the Bambi bunch is munching on the bark of your trees, you need an extra-strong coat of armor—like this super-spicy potion. To make it, mix $1/4$ cup of hot pepper sauce and $1/4$ cup of ground cayenne pepper in 1 cup of vegetable oil, then rub the solution into the bark using a stiff brush or a cloth. (Be sure to wear rubber gloves to avoid burning your skin.) Reapply the fiery "paint" every couple of weeks during rainy or snowy periods, and every month or so when the weather's dry.

 # Salt

Weed in tight places. To rout stubborn weeds from between the stones in your driveway or patio, upend a salt shaker and sprinkle away. Just be sure to aim *away* from any plants that you want to leave standing, or they'll shrivel up right along with the weeds!

De-worm your vegetables. Some of the most annoying garden pests of all are those little green worms that hide out in broccoli, cabbage, and lettuce leaves. They're perfectly harmless to the plants (and you, too), but you sure don't want to cook them or toss them into a salad by mistake! Here's the simple good-riddance method I learned from Grandma Putt: Put your freshly harvested crops in a big bowl of cold water, and add a couple teaspoons of salt to it. Within minutes, any stowaways will float to the surface, and you can pour them and the salty water down the drain.

Pour weeds away. If you live in gusty territory, or you're not too sure about your aim, use this weed-killing method instead of sprinkling salt: Add $1/4$ cup of salt to 1 gallon of boiling water, and pour it over the unwanted plants.

Kill poison ivy. And poison oak, too. If either of these ultra-wicked weeds has moved into your yard, call out the heavy artillery. Drench the plants with a solution made from 3 pounds of salt and 1 teaspoon of dishwashing liquid per gallon of water. Repeat as often as necessary until the nasty stuff is history. *Note:* Anytime a recipe calls for dishwashing liquid, do not use detergent or any product that contains antibacterial agents.

Keep up your slug defenses. If you use a copper barrier to keep slugs out of planting beds, here's a sobering fact that you need to remember: Once verdigris builds up on copper, the metal loses its slug-killing power. Fortunately, it's easy to keep that mini-fence clean and potent. Just mix salt with enough vinegar to make a gritty paste, rub it onto the metal with your fingers or a sponge, and work it in with a fine (00) steel-wool pad. Rinse well with clear water.

Here's to YOU!

Sweating is your body's natural, healthy response to hot, humid weather. But heavy sweating can quickly lead to dehydration. So when you're working in your garden on a steamy summer day, be prepared: Keep your cool by drinking plenty of water, with $1/2$ teaspoon of salt added to every quart. And start downing those fluids before you feel thirsty, because your body needs water before your brain knows it.

It Works, But...

Salt is famous as a potent slug killer. But never simply pour the stuff on the slimy pests—if your aim is off, the salt could do more damage to your plants than the slugs could! Instead, use one of these no-risk methods of slugicide:

* Pour a quarter inch or so of salt into a paper bag or coffee can. Then pick up the slugs (I use old tongs for this job), drop them into the container, and give it a few good shakes.

* Dig a trench about 4 inches deep around your planting bed. Line it with strips from plastic garbage bags, and pour a $^1/_2$-inch layer of salt in the bottom of your little moat. When the slimy squirts try to slither over to your plants, they'll fall into the trench and die. (*Note:* If you have some old lengths of gutter on hand, you can use those instead of the plastic. In this case, dig your ditch deep enough so that the gutters' rims just reach the soil surface.)

* Bury some shallow cat food or tuna cans up to their rims. Then slice some cabbage leaves into thin strips, put them into the cans, and fill each one with salt water (about 1 teaspoon of salt per can of water). The slugs and snails will home in on the cabbage, fall into the drink, and drown.

Prevent cabbage worms. In the spring, when you set your cabbage, broccoli, and cauliflower transplants into your garden, dust the plants' leaves with a mixture of 1 tablespoon of salt per cup of rye flour. Repeat the process two weeks later. This will discourage cabbage butterflies—the worms' mothers—from setting down on the plants to lay their eggs. Even if some larvae do appear, you're still covered: The worms will eat the flour, which they can't digest, and they'll die.

Get rid of ants. Whether they're farming aphids on your plants or simply making nuisances of themselves at a barbecue, just sprinkle salt on their trails. They'll scurry in a hurry!

Salt

The Salt of the Earth

Today when you walk into any supermarket, you see aisle after aisle crammed with special remedies for every health problem under the sun (not to mention the hundreds of prescription drugs tucked behind the counter in the pharmacy section). But when my Grandma Putt was a young woman, most of those miracle medicines didn't even exist. Instead, people healed their wounds and cured their ills with the same tried-and-true products their ancestors had used for centuries. One of the superstars was salt—and you can put its healing powers to work for you.

PROBLEM	SOLUTION
Athlete's foot	Toss about 1/2 cup of salt into a basin filled with warm water, and mix it well. Then soak your feet for 5 to 10 minutes. The briny solution will kill the trouble-causing fungus, and also soften your skin so that any antifungal medication you use can penetrate better.
Headache	Heat a few tablespoons of salt in a dry pan until it's hot, but not too hot to touch. Pour the salt into a thin dishtowel, and fold it up into a packet. Then hold it to the back of your head (yes, even though you feel the throbbing in the front), and rub. The dry heat should draw the pain right out.
Heat exhaustion	Mix 1 teaspoon of salt in a glass of water, and sip it slowly.
Itchy skin caused by poison ivy, insect bites, food-allergy rashes, or post-sunburn peeling	Mix 1/2 cup of salt in a tub of warm water, and soak for as long as you like.
Muscle aches and pains	Soak in a bathtub of hot water (as hot as you can stand it) with a handful each of sea salt and dry mustard mixed in it.

PROBLEM	SOLUTION
Sore throat (minor)	Mix 1 teaspoon of salt in about 2 cups of warm water. Then tip your head back and gargle that pain away!
Sore throat (major)	Put 1 teaspoon of salt, 1 crushed garlic clove, and a tiny pinch of cayenne pepper in a glass, fill it with warm water, and stir. Gargle with the solution, and repeat as needed. If your throat doesn't feel better in a day or so, call your doctor.
Stuffy nose	Dissolve $1/4$ teaspoon of salt and $1/4$ teaspoon of baking soda in 1 cup of warm water. Use a medicine dropper to spritz the liquid into one nostril while you gently pinch the other nostril shut. Inhale, then repeat for the other nostril. Use whenever you need some air.
Sunburn or other minor burns	Mix 1 to 2 teaspoons of salt in a glass of ice-cold milk, and sponge the solution onto your skin once or twice a day (or as needed) until the pain is gone. If the burn is severe, or shows signs of becoming infected, see a doctor immediately.
Tired feet	Soak your hardworking (or hard-playing) dogs in $1/2$ cup of salt mixed in a basin of water, heated to the temperature of your choice.
Tooth pain, swollen gums, or abscessed teeth	Mix 1 teaspoon of salt in an 8-ounce glass of warm water. Take a mouthful of saltwater at a time, and swish it around for 10 to 30 seconds, directing it toward the painful area as much as possible. Proceed until you've finished the glass, and repeat as needed throughout the day. (If you're on a low-sodium diet, use Epsom salts instead of table salt.)
Uncomfortable new dentures or braces	Gargle with a solution of 1 to 2 teaspoons of salt in a glass of warm water. If your mouth is still tender after a few days of this treatment, call your dentist or orthodontist.

Salt

Do Tell!

I think it's safe to say that there's hardly a kitchen in the country that doesn't have salt in it. But how much do you really know about this ultra-common supermarket product? Here are some fabulous factoids you can toss around at your next barbecue to impress your family and friends:

✳ Early Roman soldiers received part of their earnings in the form of special salt rations. They were known as *salarium argentum,* and that's where we got our English word *salary.*

✳ The term "worth his salt" came from ancient Greece, where salt was traded for slaves.

✳ The United States is the world leader in salt production, to the tune of about 44 million tons a year.

✳ Only about 6 percent of the salt consumed in the U.S. is used to season food. Depending on whose statistics you read, anywhere from 17 to 25 percent of it is used for de-icing roads.

✳ Salt plays a role in roughly 14,000 industrial processes, including the manufacture of products ranging from synthetic fibers and dyes to plastics, cosmetics, and medicines.

De-grime your hands. Sometimes, after a day of working hard in the garden, it almost seems like there's more dirt on your hands than there is in the ground! Don't worry. Simply add about a teaspoon of salt to the soap lather as you wash up, and your paws'll come out as clean as a whistle.

Remove rust from tools. You've found some beautiful, vintage shovels and spades at a local flea market, and you just couldn't resist taking them home. Unfortunately, the blades have picked up more than their fair share of rust over the years, and now you're wondering whether you can ever get it off. Sure you can! Here's how: Make a paste from 2 parts salt and 1 part lemon juice. Rub the paste onto the metal until the spots vanish, rinse with clear water, and dry thoroughly.

Clean bottles. Some of my Grandma Putt's favorite vases were actually beautiful bottles that were perfect for showing off one or two fabulous flowers. Grandma had a neat trick for keeping these containers crystal clear, in spite of their hard-to-reach "shoulders." Here's her method: Pour $1/2$ teaspoon or so of salt into the bottle, and plug the top with a cork or a wad of paper towel. Shake, rattle, and roll the bottle until it's spotless, then rinse well with clear water.

Maintain white wicker. To a lot of people, nothing shouts "summertime!" like a big, old-fashioned porch filled with white wicker furniture. If you're one of those folks, you'll appreciate this tip. To keep your treasures as white as snow without painting, mix $1/4$ cup of salt in 1 gallon of warm water. Dip a stiff brush into the solution, give the furniture a good scrubbing, and let it dry in the sun. Then, to return moisture to the reeds, rub them down with a soft cloth dipped in a half-and-half mixture of turpentine and boiled linseed oil (available at hardware stores).

Clean concrete surfaces. If you have a concrete patio, driveway, or workshop floor, you know how fast it can go from spotless to downright grungy-looking. That's why I always keep a supply of this super-powered cleanser on hand. To make it, mix 2 cups of rock salt with 6 cups of sifted sawdust and $1^{1}/2$ cups of mineral oil. Store the mixture in a plastic garbage can with a tight lid. When the need arises, just dip it out with a scoop, sprinkle it on the floor, and sweep it up—along with a whole lot of dust and dirt.

 # Vinegar

Give seeds a rousing send-off. Before you plant flower, herb, or vegetable seeds—indoors or out—soak them overnight in a solution made from 1 cup of white vinegar and 1 tablespoon of baby shampoo in 2 cups of warm water. Those seeds will all but jump out of their shells!

Make azaleas bloom better. And also other acid-soil lovers like gardenias, rhododendrons, hydrangeas, and camellias. Just water them every week or so with a solution of 3 tablespoons of white vinegar per gallon of water. Just one word of caution: Discontinue this routine when the plants come into bloom; at that time, the vinegar could harm the plant or shorten the life of the flowers.

MARVELOUS MIX

Extra-Strength Weed Killer

This potent formula is tailor-made for tackling the toughest weeds in your yard—like those deep-rooted perennials that just keep on coming back...and coming back...and coming back!

> 1 qt. of water
> 5 tbsp. of white vinegar
> 2 tbsp. of salt

Bring the water to a boil, then stir in the vinegar and salt. While the liquid is still boiling (or as close to it as possible), pour it directly on the weeds. *Note:* Keep this potion well away from any plants that you want to save, or it will kill them right along with the weeds.

Test for alkaline soil. Put a tablespoon of dried garden soil on a plate and add a few drops of vinegar to it. If the soil fizzes, that means it's extremely alkaline—most likely above 7.5 on the pH scale—though how much above is anybody's guess. In this case, a more exact laboratory test is called for, because very few garden plants will tolerate soil with a pH that's above 7.5.

Kill slugs the easy way. There are a lot of ways to eliminate these slimy pests, but this is one of the surest and simplest: Shortly after dark, when the pests come out to feed, fill a handheld sprayer bottle with white vinegar, head out to the garden, and let 'em have it. Or pour the tangy stuff into squirt guns, put a bounty on the slugs' heads, and send a posse of youngsters out to do the job for you.

Trap slugs and snails. If a-hunting you'd rather not go, bury shallow containers like cat food cans or old cake pans at ground level in your garden. Then pour in a mixture of 1 teaspoon of brown sugar per cup of apple cider vinegar. The malevolent mollusks will belly up the bar, fall in, and drown.

Fight foul fungi. Fungal diseases can strike flowers or vegetables at any time during the growing season, but they're most likely to visit during periods of wet or humid weather. And the spores multiply like crazy when the air is stagnant. So here's your simple two-part battle plan: Provide excellent air circulation for your plants (thin them out if you need to), and spray them once a week during the growing season with a solution of 3 tablespoons of apple cider vinegar per gallon of water. Use a handheld sprayer, and be sure to do the job in the morning so that your plants have plenty of time to dry off before nightfall. Just remember: Fungal spores *love* dark, damp gardens!

Vinegar

Pickle bark beetles. These tiny pests zero in on woody plants that are diseased, dead, or under stress; but once they're in the neighborhood, they sometimes attack healthy trees and shrubs, too. The larvae chew through and just under the bark, cutting off the flow of nutrients in the process. Once they've tunneled into a plant, no insecticide can reach them. But you can catch the adults on the fly simply by setting jars of white vinegar among your troubled woodies. The beetles will dive right in—and they won't get out alive. *Note:* Only white distilled vinegar will work for this trick because apparently its odor is the same as a tree's distress signal.

MARVELOUS MIX

Time-to-Fly Spray

You know how even beneficial bugs can drive you crazy when they're buzzing at your windows all evening long? It would make St. Francis himself say, "Enough is enough!" Well, here's a spray that he just might use. It will make the little guys go elsewhere for fun and games, but it won't hurt them one bit. (In fact, it will save many of them from ending up as splatters on the glass.)

> 1/4 cup of vinegar (any kind will do)
> 8 tbsp. of essential oil of bay*
> 3 cups of water

Pour the vinegar, oil, and water into a handheld sprayer bottle. Tighten the cap, and shake until the ingredients are well blended. To keep the bugs from flying at your closed windows, use the potion to clean the outside of the glass in your usual way. If the little guys are bouncing off the screens, thoroughly spray the mesh, too. Just make sure you spray from the inside out so that you don't wind up with puddles on the floor!

*Available at craft-supply and herbal-products stores.

The Drink of Death

Although codling moths are most famous for ruining apple harvests from coast to coast, they also target crabapple, pear, quince, and sometimes plum and walnut trees. The good news is that, regardless of the fruit they're after, my "Drink of Death" traps will make sure they don't get their wish. I make a bunch of them in spring, just as the apple blossoms are beginning to open. All you need are some 1-gallon plastic milk jugs and a solution that's made of 1 part molasses to 1 part apple cider vinegar. Pour 1 to 2 inches of solution into each jug, tie a cord around the handle, and hang the trap from a branch. The moths will belly up (or rather, in) for a drink, and that'll be all she wrote! *Note:* Bees like sweet stuff too, so if some of these good guys are poking around your traps, cover the opening with $1/8$- to $1/4$-inch mesh screen.

Kiss weeds goodbye. White vinegar, applied straight from a handheld sprayer, is a nightmare come true for shallow-rooted weeds. For best results, pull off the plant's green tops, then point your sprayer downward and saturate the crown. And be extra-careful not to spritz any plants you want to keep, because the vinegar will kill them, too. (This trick is especially helpful for those impossible-to-get-at spots like cracks in a concrete driveway, or narrow spaces between stone or brick pavers.)

Turn off tomcats. When wandering male felines are leaving your garden smelling anything *but* flowery, relief is as close as your kitchen cupboard. Fill a handheld sprayer bottle with white vinegar, and regularly spritz the places where the boys are making their mark. The scent will confuse and repel the rascals. Don't spray your plants, though— straight vinegar could kill them. Instead, take aim at your garden fence or a patch of weeds, or saturate pieces of board and set them around the problem areas.

Vinegar

Eliminate skunk odor. You say Pepé Le Pew came to visit and left a fragrant calling card behind? Don't fret. Just mix 1 cup of white vinegar and 1 tablespoon of dishwashing liquid with $2\frac{1}{2}$ gallons of water. Then thoroughly saturate walls, stairs, outdoor furniture, or anything else that reeks of eau de skunk. *Note:* Use this formula only on inanimate objects. In Chapter 8, you'll find odor-removal remedies for both humans and pets.

Trap fruit flies. Yuck! You harvested bushels of vegetables to put by for the winter and piled them on your porch while you got your canning gear ready. And now there are clouds of fruit flies feasting on your bounty. Well, they won't dine for long if you try this simple trick: Mix $\frac{1}{4}$ cup of apple cider vinegar and 1 teaspoon of dishwashing liquid in 2 cups of water, and pour the solution into a jar. Then set the jar next to your plagued produce. The fruit flies will be drawn to the vinegar, dip into the water for a taste, and drown (thanks to the soap, which will coat their tiny bodies). Replace the solution every couple of days to keep the vinegar scent fresh and (of course) to clear out the dead bugs.

Put out fire blight. This bacterial disease strikes apples and pears, and it spreads like (yes) wildfire in warm, moist weather. First, reddish, water-soaked lesions appear on the bark of limbs and branches, and on warm days, an orangey-brown liquid oozes out. Infected shoots look as though they've been scorched. Branch tips wilt and turn under at the ends, like a shepherd's crook. Your mission: At the first sign of trouble, prune off all the infected branches at least 12 inches below the wilted section. Then, remove all suckers and water sprouts, where more bacteria could be lurking. After each cut, to avoid spreading the disease, dip your shears or saw in a solution of 1 part bleach to 4 parts water. Finally, spray the tree from top to bottom with a solution of 4 parts vinegar to 6 parts water. Then spray again two weeks later.

Revive a drooping bouquet. First, cut $\frac{1}{4}$ inch or so off the bottom of each flower stem. Then put the flowers into a clean vase with fresh water, and add 2 tablespoons of white vinegar and 1 tablespoon of sugar to each quart of water. Those posies'll perk up in no time at all!

Clean a water-stained vase. Over time, hard water can leave ugly marks on glass—and you sure don't want ugly marks detracting from your big, beautiful floral bouquets! So try this old-time trick: Soak paper towels in white vinegar, and press them against the inside surfaces of the vase. Let everything sit for an hour or so, then remove the towels and wipe the spots away with a clean, soft cloth.

Here's to YOU!

Are you looking for a really effective insect repellent that doesn't contain toxic chemicals? Look no further! Here's a formula that bugs hate, but is safe enough to use on kids. What's more, it's a snap to make. Just put $\frac{1}{2}$ cup each of fresh mint, lavender, thyme, and rose-scented geraniums in a bowl. Heat 1 cup of white vinegar just to the boiling point, and pour it over the herbs. Cover the bowl, and let the herbs steep until the vinegar has cooled to room temperature. Then strain out the solids and pour the liquid into a handheld sprayer bottle. Spritz all your exposed skin with the potion before you head outdoors, and reapply it every couple of hours. Annoying bugs will bug you no more! *Note:* Store your repellent in the refrigerator, where it will keep for about two months.

Prep metal furniture for painting. Simply rub it down with a solution of 1 part white vinegar to 4 parts water. (Wear rubber gloves when you perform this maneuver, because the oil from your hands will hinder the paint's stick-ability.) Than spray or brush on the paint—no primer necessary.

Prep old concrete, too. Getting ready to paint a patio or garage floor? Clean it first, using white vinegar. Just wipe it on with a rag or sponge mop—there's no need to rinse.

Keep your car windows frost-free. When you have to leave your vehicle outdoors on a cold winter night, spray the windows with a solution made of 3 parts of vinegar to 1 part of water. When you walk out the next morning, your windows will be footloose and frost-free!

Do Tell!

Nobody knows exactly when vinegar was discovered, but it was at least 10,000 years ago—most likely, historians figure, when some winemaker's vat was prematurely opened to the air, and instead of maturing into a delicious alcoholic beverage, the fruit "morphed" into a not-so-tasty, but much more versatile fluid. Ever since then, vinegar has played an impressive role in history. Caesar's soldiers drank it as a fortifying beverage, while Helen of Troy bathed in it to relax. Hippocrates, the father of medicine, prescribed it to his patients for numerous ailments. But one of my favorite pieces of vinegar lore comes from Titus Livius, a historian who lived around the time of Christ (long before the days of steam shovels and backhoes). He wrote that when people needed to move huge boulders, they built fires to heat the rocks, then drenched them with vinegar. This caused the stones to crack into smaller pieces that could be easily hauled away.

Remove rust. The good news is that you finally found your favorite trowel that's been missing for months. The bad news is that it was lying under a bush in your yard, and now it's covered with a thick layer of rust. Don't despair! Just soak the blade overnight in full-strength white vinegar. The rust will dissolve like magic.

Stain outdoor furniture. Or anything else that's made of wood. Simply mix white vinegar with water-based ink in the color of your choice. (The more ink you add, the darker the stain will be, so the amount is your call.) Apply the mixture to the wood surface with a rag or a paintbrush. Wipe off any excess with a clean, soft cloth.

Clean brick or stone. Keep a patio or walkway looking its very best by mopping it regularly with a solution made from 1 cup of white vinegar in a bucket of warm water. Of course, how often you need to do this chore depends on how much traffic the surface gets and how pristine you want it to look.

Get burn marks off of brick. No matter how careful you are, accidents will happen. When you wind up with burn marks on your brick patio or hearth—perhaps courtesy of a toppled candle or a dropped piece of kindling—reach for the white vinegar. Sponge it onto the spots and rinse with clear water. Bingo: clean bricks once again!

Clean off bird poop. If your fine-feathered friends' aim is a little too good, clean up the mess in a hurry. Just fill a handheld sprayer bottle with apple cider vinegar and douse the spot, or hit it with a little vinegar on a rag. The droppings will wipe right off.

Vinegar

The Dairy Case

BUTTERMILK
EGGS & EGGSHELLS
MILK
POWDERED MILK

Buttermilk

Repel cabbageworms. If you love buttermilk as much as I do, then here's a little secret you ought to know: Cabbageworms *hate* the stuff. So every time you empty a carton, rinse it out and pour the milky liquid onto your cabbage-family plants. Even well-watered down, it'll still send the 'pillars packin' pronto!

Make rabbits run. Got bunnies feasting on your flowers and woody plants? This old-time trick will send them scurrying. Mix 1 gallon of buttermilk with 2 cups of soot from your chimney or wood stove. Boil it for 20 minutes, then pour it into a handheld sprayer bottle and spray your ornamental plants. (Don't use this stuff on anything you intend to eat!) Stir the mixture every now and then to keep it from clogging the sprayer's pump.

Move mites out of fruit trees. Spider mites are so tiny that you can hardly see them, but they can do big damage to your apple, pear, plum, or other fruit trees. This formula will stop the action—fast. Just mix 5 pounds of white flour, 1 pint of buttermilk, and 25 gallons of water. Keep the potion in a tightly closed garbage can. Stir before use, and spray your trees once a week with a handheld sprayer until the mites are history.

Grow a no-maintenance lawn. Are there damp, shady spots in your yard where nothing grows well except moss? Instead of waging a constant struggle to get rid of it, encourage those mossy patches to grow into a soft, green, cushiony—and utterly care-free—carpet. Simply scoop up 1 cup of moss and whirl it in an old blender with 1 pint of buttermilk and 1 teaspoon of corn syrup. Then, using a paintbrush, dab the mixture onto the ground in places that

MARVELOUS MiX

So Long, Suckers! Spray

When spider mites, aphids, or mealybugs are draining the juices from your flower or vegetable plants, give 'em a drink that'll stop 'em in their tracks.

   ¼ cup of buttermilk
   2 cups of white flour
   2 gallons of water

Mix all of the ingredients in a bucket. Then pour the mixture into a handheld sprayer bottle and douse your pest-plagued plants from top to bottom. The little buggers will never know what hit 'em!

could use a touch o' the green—for instance, along the base of a stone wall, among the roots of a big old shade tree, or between stones in a pathway. While your moss is getting started, keep it covered with lightweight plastic mesh (available at garden centers), so birds and squirrels can't dig it up. Even after your no-care "lawn" has matured, hang onto that netting and toss it over the moss in the autumn to catch falling leaves. Then you can simply lift them off and whisk them away to your compost pile. Not only will that save you the trouble of raking, but it will also be much easier on the moss.

Keep moss healthy. To a lot of folks, nothing says "old-time charm" like a little soft, cushiony moss growing on stone walls or planters, or in the space between stepping stones. And you couldn't ask for a lower-maintenance plant. Just spray the moss with buttermilk to the point of runoff several times a year, and it'll stay green and chipper as can be.

Eggs & Eggshells

Feed your cucurbits. Getting ready to plant squash or cucumbers? Then here's an old-time trick you should know about: Mound up your soil into hills, according to the directions on your seed packet, and bury a hard-boiled egg 6 to 8 inches deep in the center of each hill (gently crack the shell first). Then plant three pairs of seeds in a circle around it. As the egg decomposes, it'll provide time-released nutrients for your growing plants.

Make your soil sweeter. If you need to make your soil more alkaline, the classic prescription is to add ground limestone (a.k.a. lime). That's a great quick fix, but here's a better idea: Add the right kind organic matter, like ground eggshells, instead. You'll get longer-lasting results and improve the structure of your soil, besides.

Green up your compost. Eggshells are rich in nitrogen, which makes them a top-notch "green" ingredient for making compost. So every time you cook eggs, rinse off the shells and toss 'em onto the pile or into the bin.

Prevent blossom-end rot. This nasty condition attacks squash, tomatoes, peppers, and watermelon. You'll know it's struck if the bottom end of the fruit suddenly collapses and rots. It's caused by a calcium deficiency in the ground, and soil that's alternately wet and dry. To help fend it off, apply an organic mulch to keep the ground moisture constant, and each time you water, scratch ground eggshells into the soil around each plant. Or, if you'd prefer, soak the shells in water overnight, and then water your plants with the calcium-rich "tea" that results from the soaking.

Start seeds indoors. My Grandma Putt used to start seeds in eggshells, and I still do. The routine couldn't be simpler. Every time you break an egg, carefully remove only the top third or so. I use a special egg-cutting tool that's like a pair of scissors, except with a circular opening where the pointy blades should be. Put the opening over the top of the egg, squeeze the handles, and presto! A sharp blade slices right through the shell. Rinse the shell carefully and poke a hole in the bottom, using a pushpin or a small nail. Set the shell into an empty egg carton, and put it aside until you have another egg, then repeat the process. At seed-starting time, fill the shells with starter mix and plant your seeds. When it's time to move the seedlings into bigger pots or straight into the garden, plant the whole shebang. Just crack each shell gently as you set it into its hole, so that the roots won't have to struggle to get out.

End your fly frustrations. Sick and tired of swatting at flies all summer long? Then simply beat 1 egg yolk with 1 tablespoon of molasses and a pinch of black pepper. Pour the mixture into jar lids or shallow cans (like cat food or tuna fish cans), and set them around your house. The flies will fly in for a three-point landing, and they won't take off again.

Here's to **YOU!**

To treat a sty or cyst on the eye, doctors often prescribe a hot compress, applied three or four times a day. And you'll find just what the doctor ordered in your refrigerator: an egg. Pull one out and hard-boil it. Wrap the hot egg in a washcloth, and lay it against your sore eye for 10 minutes. When it's time for your next egg-laying session (sorry, I couldn't resist), put that same piece of "hen fruit" back in a pot of water, reheat it, and then reapply.

Whether the eggs you buy come in pressed-paper, plastic, or polystyrene cartons, don't toss those containers out! Just look at some of the ways you can put them to work around your own green scene:

Start seeds. Fill paper cartons with starter mix, and plant your seeds according to the packet directions. At transplant time, cut the sections apart and put 'em right in the ground.

Pre-sprout spuds. Potato eyes are more likely to sprout if you start them indoors, and paper egg cartons make perfect starter pots. Just cut your seed potatoes into pieces (make sure each one has at least one eye), and tuck a chunk into each section of the carton. Fill them with sterilized potting soil, and keep it moist. When green shoots start to appear, cut the sections of the carton apart and plant them in your garden.

Overwinter summer-blooming bulbs. Are your winters too cold for bulbs like gladiolus, dahlias, and tuberous begonias to survive outdoors? Then here's a terrific storage solution: In late fall, dig up and clean the bulbs, put one bulb into each section of a paper egg carton, and close the top. Write the name and color of the bulbs on the outside cover. Stack your cartons in a dry place, like an insulated garage or basement, where the temperature will stay between 40° and 50°F.

Cool your sunburn. Separate the top and bottom halves of a plastic egg carton and pour milk into each egg-shaped compartment. Pop both sections into the freezer. Then whenever you need relief from sunburn or heat rash, pull out a mini "milksicle" and rub it over the affected skin.

Start your fire. Just put a charcoal briquette into each section of a paper egg carton, set it in the bottom of your grill, and light it. There's no muss, no fuss—and no odor!

Make ice. When you need to make a whole lot of ice for a barbecue (or even an indoor get-together), you can use clean plastic or polystyrene egg cartons as auxiliary trays.

Deter deer. Are big, brown-eyed bruisers making mincemeat out of your flower garden? Here's a super-simple way to lay out a big unwelcome mat: Just dissolve 2 well-beaten eggs and 2 teaspoons of beef broth in 1 gallon of water. Let the mixture sit for two days, or until it smells really potent. Then pour it into a handheld sprayer bottle, and spritz the plants on the edge of your flower garden. (Just don't use this odiferous stuff on anything that you intend to eat!)

Repel ants. Whether the mischief-makers are spoiling the fun at your barbecue or moving into your tool shed (or your kitchen cupboards), I know an easy way to put an end to their high jinks: Set dishes of crushed eggshells around the off-limits areas. I've never figured out why this trick works—but it does!

Put it to 'possums. These strange-looking creatures are actually excellent pest-control workers. They eat grubs, snails, snakes, and beetles by the bucketful, along with other bad-guy bugs, gophers, mice, and rats. But they do have one annoying habit: They love to take sample bites out of your tomatoes, corn, and other vegetables, then leave 'em to rot on the vine. If the rascals are coming to your place to snack on your snails and grubs and staying on to make bigger mischief, close the restaurant with this odiferous elixir: Mix 2 eggs, 2 cloves of garlic, 2 tablespoons of ground cayenne pepper, and 2 tablespoons of ammonia in 2 cups of hot water. Let the mixture sit for three or four days. Then paint it on fences, trellises, and wherever else the varmints are venturing.

Clean small-necked vases. It's a frustrating fact of life that some of the most attractive flower vases have necks that are smaller than a human hand (at least an adult hand). So how can you get the dang things clean? It's simple! Just grind up a few dried eggshells, pour them into the vessel, and add water. Then hold your hand over the opening, or stick a cork in it, and shake until the dirt vanishes.

Do Tell!

We all know about the custom of the bridegroom carrying his bride over the threshold on their wedding day. But in France, they do things a little bit differently. There, a bride breaks an egg on the threshold of her new home before stepping in—thereby ensuring good luck and healthy babies. (Seems to me like a pretty messy way to start out a marriage!) Here are a few more fascinating facts that you might not know about eggs:

✻ At last count, there were roughly 280 million laying hens in the United States, and each year, these hardworking gals produce a combined total of some 60 billion eggs.

✻ A hen starts laying eggs at 19 weeks of age and, on average, lays from 300 to 325 eggs each year.

✻ To produce a single egg, a hen labors for 24 to 26 hours, and requires 5 ounces of food and 10 ounces of water. Then half an hour later, she starts the process all over again.

✻ A mother hen rolls each of her eggs over about 50 times a day. This prevents the yolk from sticking to the sides of the shell.

✻ The older a hen gets, the larger the eggs she lays. The biggest chicken egg on record had a double yolk and double shell, and tipped the scales at 1 pound! (This mama didn't divulge her age.)

✻ Nutritionists tell us that eggs contain the highest quality protein of any food, along with 13 essential vitamins and minerals. In fact, as a source of human nutrition, they rank second only to mother's milk.

Remove coffee stains. After your last barbecue, you were trying to tidy up the deck and drink a cup of coffee at the same time. And now you've got a big, brown java spot on your favorite apron. Well, don't cry over spilt coffee. Instead, break an egg and mix the yolk with about a tablespoon of lukewarm water. Rub the mixture into the spot, and launder as usual. The result? End of stain! By the way, this method also gets coffee stains out of carpet—rub the egg/water mix into the spot, then rinse with clear water.

Rout out root-knot nematodes. These nasty Nellies tunnel into the roots of tomatoes and many other vegetables that are growing in sandy soil. You'll know they're on the scene if your plants are sickly and stunted, and their roots are covered with little galls that you can't break off. Your battle plan: Call out the enemy! To do that, just dig plenty of eggshells into the soil. They contain chitin, which is what nematode eggs are covered with. Chitin eaters from near and far will show up and start to feast. When they finish the free food you've given them, they'll start in on the nematode eggs with a vengeance! (If you buy fresh or frozen unpeeled shrimp, work the peels into your soil, too—they're another potent source of chitin.)

 **Milk**

Treat plant viruses. Any flower or vegetable plant can come down with a virus. While there are many viral diseases, the symptoms are the same: stunted plants with leaves that are puckered or distorted, and mottled in shades of yellow and light green. There is no cure. In advanced cases, you'll need to pull or dig up the victims and destroy them. If you reach the scene early, though, just pull off the mottled leaves and get rid of them. Then regardless of which tack you've taken, spray every nearby plant with a mix of 1 part milk to 3 parts water. Repeat every few days throughout the growing season.

Help houseplants breathe better. Just like anything else in the house, the leaves of indoor plants can pick up their fair share of dust and even greasy film. But this dirty covering doesn't simply look unattractive—it also blocks some of the light the plants need to produce food. So do your green pals a favor: Once a week or so, gently wipe their leaves with a solution made from equal parts of milk and water.

Give Your Plants a Flu Shot

Anyplace you've got sap-sucking insects like aphids, thrips, and flea beetles at work, your plants face the threat of viruses. There is no cure for a viral disease, but there is a product that may prevent an outbreak. What is this wonder drug? Good old moo juice! Scientists have proven that milk helps protect plants against these nasty little organisms. You can put milk's germ-fighting power to work in three ways:

1. Every time you empty a carton of milk, cream, or buttermilk, fill the container with water, shake it, and pour the contents onto one of your flower or vegetable plants. (This is excellent preventive medicine, even when your garden is an insect-free zone.)

2. If sap-suckers are already on the scene, take stronger action. Mix 2 tablespoons of milk in 1 gallon of water. Pour the solution into a handheld sprayer bottle, and spray your plants' foliage every two or three weeks throughout the growing season.

3. Whenever you're working with insect-plagued plants, keep a bowl handy that's filled with a half-and-half mixture of milk and water. Then every few minutes, dip your hands and tools into the liquid to keep the little buggers from spreading.

Milk

Black out black spot. If you grow roses, you're probably all too familiar with this ugly fungal disease. But here's something you may not know: Milk contains a beneficial fungus that fends off the black spot fungus. Here's how you can put this miraculous vaccine to work in your garden: About a month before the last expected frost in your area, fill a clean, hand-held sprayer with skim milk, and apply it generously to your rosebushes, including the stems and both sides of all the leaves. Be sure you do the job in the morning, so the foliage has time to dry before nightfall. (Like all foul fungi, black spot loves moist, dark places.) Repeat the process every five to seven days for the next six weeks. Follow this routine, and you'll have spot-free roses all summer long!

Prevent powdery mildew. Sooner or later, this disease shows up in just about every flower or vegetable garden, but highest-risk targets include roses, asters, and garden phlox *(Phlox paniculata)*. The fungus goes on the rampage anytime days are warm and nights are cool and humid—most commonly in late summer or early fall. It first appears as a grayish white powder on leaves, buds, or stems. Eventually, plant parts become distorted and drop off. The good news is that although powdery mildew looks as ugly as sin, it rarely causes serious damage. At the first sign of trouble, simply clip off and destroy the affected plant parts, then spray the victim from top to bottom with a 50-50 mix of milk and water. Repeat once a week for the rest of the growing season, and your mildew miseries will be history.

Feed outdoor ferns. These elegant, feathery plants lend an old-time charm to any shade garden. To keep them in tip-top shape, mix 2 cups of milk and 2 tablespoons of Epsom salts in a 20 gallon hose-end sprayer, and spray the plants to the point of runoff every two weeks during the growing season.

Grow healthy tomatoes. Are you reluctant to grow tomatoes this year because your past crops have fallen victim to so many diseases? Well, don't give up! This time, when you set out your transplants, add my Tomato Blight Buster (see page 159) to their planting holes. Then, in the early part of the summer, give your plants a booster shot made from 1 part skim milk and 9 parts water. Apply it with a handheld sprayer to the point of runoff, and it'll do a bang-up job of discouraging diseases from getting started!

MARVELOUS MIX

Aphid-Free Tree Tonic

Some ants just can't get enough of the sticky honeydew that aphids produce. And the little rascals have a clever way to ensure themselves a steady supply of the sweet stuff: They turn trees into ranches, where they actually tend herds of the tiny sap-suckers. Throughout this book, you'll find plenty of ways to get the cowboys outta Dodge. And this lethal weapon will send the aphids running to the bad-bug stockyard—pronto.

> 3 tbsp. of skim milk
> 3 tbsp. of garlic-and-onion juice*
> 2 tbsp. of baby shampoo
> 1 tsp. of hot pepper sauce
> 1 gal. of water

Mix all of these ingredients in a bucket, and pour the solution into a 20 gallon hose-end sprayer. Then spray your tree every 10 days until the aphids are lyin' 6 feet under Boot Hill.

*To make garlic-and-onion juice, puree 2 cloves of garlic, 2 medium onions, and 3 cups of water in a blender. Strain out the solids, and pour the remaining liquid into a jar. Store it in the refrigerator, and use it whenever it's called for in a tonic recipe. Bury the solids around plants in your garden to repel aphids and other pesky pests.

Milk

Repel whiteflies. These pests are so tiny (just $\frac{1}{20}$ to $\frac{1}{16}$ inch long) that you can barely see them with the naked eye. But they can do big damage to annual and perennial flowers, vegetables (especially the squash and tomato families), and even trees and shrubs. There's a simple way to keep them at bay. Just spray your plants to the point of runoff with a mixture of 1 cup of sour milk, 2 tablespoons of flour, and 1 quart of warm water. Reapply the potion after every rain, and make sure you get the underside of every leaf. (To make sour milk, put 1 tablespoon of vinegar in a measuring cup, and pour in fresh milk to the 1-cup line.)

Trap aphids. Are these tiny insects draining the life out of your flower and vegetable plants? Well, don't just stand there! Grab a handheld sprayer, fill the bottle with skim milk, and spray your plagued plants from top to bottom. As the milk dries, the soft-bodied pests will be stuck in the residue. Later, get out the garden hose, and rinse off the dried milk and the itty-bitty bodies.

Keep cole crops caterpillar-free. Mix about 1 tablespoon of lemon juice in 1 cup of milk. Then once a week throughout the growing season, put about a tablespoon of the mixture into the center of each of your cabbage plants, as well as other brassica-family members, including broccoli, Brussels sprouts, cauliflower, and kale. The potion will fend off both cabbageworms and cabbage loopers.

Head off cutworm problems. These larvae are the worst enemies a flower or vegetable seedling ever had. To put a big dent in the population, trap the egg-laying, night-flying moths with this old-time trick: Fill a wide, flat pan with milk, and set it in your garden. Beside it, place a lighted lantern that shines on the milk. The moths will zero in on the glowing target, fall into the milk, and drown.

Not so long ago, almost no one bought milk at the supermarket. Instead, a milkman delivered it right to your doorstep—in glass bottles. Once in a while (being of a certain age), I find myself wishing those days were back again. But then I think to myself, "What on earth would I do without plastic milk jugs?" Here are some of the more imaginative ways I use them in my garden—and you can, too!

Protect young plants. For keeping out chilly winds and fending off hungry bugs, you can't beat plastic milk jugs. Just cut the bottoms off, and sink one a couple of inches into the ground around each flower or vegetable plant. On cold nights, keep the cap on the jug, but take it off on warm days to let air in. (Depending on the size of the plant, you can use a quart, half-gallon, or 1-gallon jug.)

Harvest faster. Cut a large hole opposite the handle of a half-gallon or 1-gallon jug. Loop the handle through your belt or a rope tied around your waist, and just like that, you'll have both hands free for plucking berries, cherries, or small vegetables.

Water deeply. Soaker hoses and in-ground irrigation systems are not the only ways to provide the kind of slow, deep moisture that plants need. To make your own delivery system, gather up some 1-gallon milk jugs and use a large nail to poke small holes in the sides, about an inch above the bottom. Set the jugs all around the root zones of your plants, and fill each container with water. It will seep into the soil at a slow, easy pace. When the jugs are empty, move them to another spot in your garden and continue the process, or tuck 'em away until it's time to serve up the next round of drinks.

Make a sprinkling can. Poke a dozen or so holes just below the spout of a 1-gallon jug, on the side opposite the handle. Fill the bottle with water, screw on the cap, and sprinkle away to your heart's content.

Milk

A First-Aid Kit in a Jug

Or maybe in a wax paper carton. No matter what kind of container your milk comes in, moo juice is one of the best first responders around when it comes to treating aches, pains, and minor injuries. Here's a sampling of ways you can put its healing powers to work. *Note:* After you've used any of these treatments, be sure to rinse your skin with cool water—otherwise, before you know it, you'll be smelling like sour milk!

PROBLEM	TREATMENT
Eczema	Mix equal amounts of whole milk and water in a bowl, and saturate a soft, cotton cloth with the solution. Apply it to the affected area for about 3 minutes. Repeat 2 to 4 more times in quick succession. Perform the procedure as needed throughout the day.
Minor burns	Soak a clean, soft cloth in milk, and lay the compress on the burned skin, hold it there for 20 minutes or so, then rinse the milk off with cool water. Repeat the process every 2 to 4 hours, until the pain and redness subside. *Note:* Be sure to use whole milk or (better yet) half and half—it's the fat content that soothes the burn and helps it heal faster. (If the burn is severe, hightail it to the emergency room!)
Pepper in your eye	Flush it out with a few drops of milk.
Poison ivy	Dip a clean, soft cloth in milk, and gently wash the affected skin.
Rough, sore hands	Rub a little warm milk into your skin each night.
Sore, swollen eyelids	Soak two cotton pads in ice-cold, whole milk, put one over each eye, and lie down for 5 to 10 minutes.
Sunburn	Mix 1 to 2 teaspoons of salt in a glass of ice-cold milk, and sponge the solution onto your skin once or twice a day until the pain is gone.

Wash up. The next time you come in from the garden with your hands dirty, irritated, and sporting stains from grass, berry juice, and who knows what else, try this old-time trick: Mix some milk with enough uncooked oatmeal to make a coarse paste. Rub it thoroughly into your grubby paws, and rinse them with clear water. Besides removing the stains and dirt, the oats-and-milk mixture will soothe and soften your skin.

Banish berry stains. Double drat! Your raspberry bushes are covered with plump, ripe, juicy berries. And now, after a berry-picking session, your shirt is sporting a crop of red and purple spots. Don't worry—there's a simple solution. Pour salt on the spots (after you've changed your shirt, of course!). Then put the shirt into a pan of milk, and let it soak until the marks vanish. *Note:* This same trick removes any kind of fruit or wine stains from clothes or table linens.

Clean concrete. Got a walkway, driveway, or patio that's looking pretty grimy? To clean it up, make a half-and-half solution of whole milk and regular cola (not diet), pour it on the dirty surface, and scrub with a stiff brush. Rinse it clean with the garden hose.

Keep oilcloth spotless. My Grandma Putt often used pieces of oilcloth to cover tables, especially outdoor ones at picnic time. Like many of the things she took for granted, this vintage textile is back in vogue. If you have some at your house, keep it clean the way Grandma did: Wash it once a month with a solution made from equal parts of skim milk and water. Then once every three months or so, rub the surface with boiled linseed oil on a soft, cotton cloth, and polish it with a scrap of silk. (You can buy boiled linseed oil at your local hardware store. As for the silk, if you don't have a worn-out blouse on hand, check the rag-bag section of your favorite thrift store.)

Milk

Remove ink stains. Yikes! You went out to your yard to draw up your new garden plan, and when you were finished, you stuck the pen in the back pocket of your jeans—and now they've got a nice, big, embarrassing ink splotch on the rear end. No problem! Just dampen a sponge with milk, dab the stain until it's gone, and launder as usual. (Be patient, though—it may take a while to get all of the ink out.)

Ease muscle aches. When a long day in the garden leaves you tired, stiff, and sore all over, sink into a tub full of hot water and a milky toddy for the body. To make it, combine 2 cups of milk, 1 cup of salt, 1 cup of honey, and ¼ cup of baking soda in a large bowl. Fill your bathtub with water, pour in the mixture, and then add ½ cup of baby oil (and, if you'd like, a few drops of your favorite fragrance). Sink in, relax, and say "Ahhh...."

Maintain leather car upholstery. If the seats of your fancy auto are covered in genuine leather, it goes without saying that you want them to stay soft and free of cracks. And they will if you perform this routine chore: Several times a year, wipe the leather with milk, then polish it with a clean, soft cotton cloth. This is also the way to keep leather-upholstered furniture looking showroom-new.

 # Powdered Milk

Store seeds. When your spring planting's all done, and you've got some leftover flower or vegetable seeds, don't let 'em go to waste! Instead, mix the seeds with an equal amount of powdered milk in a glass jar with a tight-fitting lid, and put it in the refrigerator (not the freezer). Next spring, they'll be fresh and rarin' to grow. (I hope it goes without saying

MARVELOUS MIX

Tomato Blight Buster

To ward off many common tomato diseases, I use this mix on all of my newly transplanted tomato seedlings—and you should, too!

> **3 cups of compost**
> **$1/2$ cup of powdered nonfat milk**
> **$1/2$ cup of Epsom salts**
> **1 tbsp. of baking soda**

Mix these ingredients in a bucket, then sprinkle a handful of the mixture into each planting hole. For additional disease defense, sprinkle a little more powdered milk on top of the soil after planting, and repeat every few weeks throughout the growing season.

that you should use a different jar for each kind of seed—that is, unless you're planning to grow a crazy-quilt flower garden or a bed of mixed greens. In that case, feel free to mix and mingle to your heart's content!)

Paint your fence. Or your tool shed, patio furniture—or even your whole house, if the siding is wood. How? With the same method clever folks have been using for centuries! To make an astoundingly durable paint, mix 3 cups of powdered milk per cup of water. (Add more milk or more water, as needed, until you get the consistency of latex paint.) If you want a color other than basic white, add food coloring or water-based pigment (available at art-supply stores) until you get an eye-pleasing shade. Then brush the stuff on as you would any other paint. Let the first coat dry for at least 24 hours before applying a second coat. Let that one dry for three days before using any painted furniture (or before adding a third coat of paint, if desired).

Powdered Milk

As we're leaving the dairy aisle, let's not forget about the sturdy plastic containers that cottage cheese, margarine, sour cream, and yogurt come in. For my money, they are some of the handiest garden helpers you could ever hope to find. Here's a roundup of ways you can put them to work at your place:

Start seeds indoors. Simply poke drainage holes in the bottoms, fill 'em up with seed-starter mix, and put them in a tray that has no holes. Then plant your seeds!

Make anti-cutworm collars. Cut the bottoms off of small containers, and sink them into the soil around your seedlings so that the plastic extends about 2 inches below the ground and 3 inches above.

Trap flying insects. Fill plastic margarine tubs with soapy water, and set them on the ground near your plants. As long as you choose the right color, the bugs will zero in on the target, fall in, and drown. In most cases, you'll want to use yellow tubs; but some insects are drawn to other colors. You'll find the "menu" in Chapter 1 (see "Color Them Gone," on page 17).

Capture slugs. Sink plastic margarine tubs into the soil up to their rims, and fill them with grape juice, cheap beer, or any of the other baits you'll find throughout this book. The slimy so-and-sos will slither in for a drink and then drown.

Keep twine untangled. Get a clean cottage cheese or yogurt container, poke a hole in the cover, and feed the end of the twine through the hole. Drop the rest of the ball into the container, and replace the lid. If you want to be able to just yank at the twine, put a stone in the bottom of the container before you insert the ball.

Get organized. Whether they're single-serving sizes or the extra-large, 64-ounce versions (or any size in between), dairy product containers provide perfect, airtight storage for everything from my Marvelous Mixes to plant labels and leftover seeds.

Fend off foul fungi. This potent potion is a godsend for preventing fungal diseases of all kinds on both ornamental *and* edible plants. And it's so safe, you could mix it in cookie dough! To make it, mix ½ cup of powdered milk, ½ cup of molasses, and 1 teaspoon of baking soda into a paste. Place the mixture into an old panty hose toe or a cheesecloth pouch, and put it into a container filled with 1 gallon of warm water. Let the "tea bag" steep for several hours. Strain the liquid, pour it into a handheld sprayer bottle, and apply it to your plants every week during the growing season.

Nourish seedlings. Getting ready to start flowers or vegetables indoors? Get them off to a healthy start by sprinkling powdered milk over the seeds when you put them in their flats. Then cover them with starter mix to the depth noted on the seed packet. When the seedlings emerge, the milk powder will provide a gentle dose of calcium, which all plants need for good growth.

Get rid of mice. When the tiny terrors are driving you crazy, indoors or out, use one of my favorite weapons. Just mix equal parts of flour and plaster of paris, and spoon the powder into jar lids or other shallow containers. Add a pinch or two of powdered hot cocoa or powdered chocolate milk mix to each one, and stir it in. Then set out the bait where *only* mice can get to it (not children or pets), and put a saucer of water nearby. The mice, being bonafide chocoholics, will gobble up the bait and rinse it down with a swig of water. That will activate the plaster of paris, which will form a big, hard lump inside the critters' tummies. End of story!

First Aid & Health Supplies

ADHESIVE TAPE & GAUZE

ALCOHOL (RUBBING)

ASPIRIN

CASTOR OIL

EPSOM SALTS

HYDROGEN PEROXIDE

PETROLEUM JELLY

VITAMINS

Adhesive Tape & Gauze

Remove a tick. Rats! You were working away in your garden when, bam!—a tick latched onto you. Now you're in the bathroom searching high and low for your tweezers, but they're nowhere to be found. Well, don't waste any more time looking—and whatever you do, don't touch the tick with your bare fingers! Instead, cover the foul thing with a strip of adhesive tape, then pull it off with a smooth motion. The little bugger should come right out. (If you're fresh out of tape, use the sticky part of an adhesive bandage.) Then drop the critter into a jar of rubbing alcohol to kill it instantly. Whatever you do, don't use the old-time trick of dabbing the tick with alcohol—or anything else—before you pull it out. The experts now say that can cause the tiny terror to regurgitate germs into your skin.

Stop ants in their tracks. Are the little rascals marching up the legs of your picnic table? No problem! Just wrap some adhesive tape, sticky side out, around each leg. It'll end their fun fast!

Get a grip on your trowel. Or any other tool with a handle that gets slippery when your hands sweat. Just wrap adhesive tape around it. Overlap the tape by about half its width, and use as many layers as it takes to get a firm, comfortable grip.

Make a hat fit better. Problem: You need to do some garden work on a hot, sunny day, but the only sun hat you can find is a couple of sizes too big. Simple solution: Wrap adhesive tape around the sweatband until the layer is thick enough to take up the slack. Besides making that chapeau fit better, the tape will also absorb perspiration.

Avoid pricked fingers. Do you need to work with a prickly plant like a cactus or a thorny rose? Before you put your gloves on, wrap a layer or two of adhesive tape around each finger. That way, even if the stickers penetrate the gloves, they won't jab your skin.

Label your seed flats. When you sow seeds indoors, it's easy to lose track of what kind of plant you put where. So mark each container with a mini banner. Just double a strip of $1/2$-inch-wide tape around one end of a toothpick, and write the plant's name and the sowing date on the tape. Stick the little "flagpole" into the soil, and bingo—no more mystery seedlings!

Take a Powder

Athlete's foot powder, that is. This odiferous health-care product can fend off much more than the foul fungi that make your tootsies cracked and sore—it can also help protect your garden from pests and diseases. Here are just a few examples of how you can put that strong aroma to work:

Repel ants. Just sprinkle the powder around the ants' target. They'll keep their distance for sure.

Deter deer. Pour athlete's foot powder onto cotton cloths and hang them on your fence, or in the branches of your trees and shrubs, to keep deer away.

Critter-proof spring bulbs. Before planting spring-flowering bulbs, dust them with the powder. It'll keep squirrels, chipmunks, and other four-legged pests from digging them up and eating them for dinner.

Protect bulbs in storage. When you dig up gladiolus, dahlias, and other tender bulbs in the fall, dust them with athlete's foot powder before stashing them away. It'll fend off insects and diseases that could sneak in over the winter.

Strain garden tonics. Anytime you whip up a Marvelous Mix that contains solid ingredients, strain the potion through a piece of gauze. Then pour the liquid into a sprayer jar or watering can, and toss the solids—gauze and all—onto the compost pile.

Stake your plants. All kinds of flowers and vegetables, from tomato and cucumber vines to tall delphiniums and floppy peonies, need help staying on the up and up. And when it's time to tie those plants to stakes or trellises, you'll find one of the best fasteners right in the First Aid aisle. What is it? Rolled gauze. It's soft enough for the most tender stems, but strong enough to support even the biggest perennials. *Note:* If you prefer your plant ties to be garden-variety green, dye the gauze in a solution made from food coloring and warm water. (The more coloring you use, the darker the material will be, so just experiment until you get the shade of green you want.)

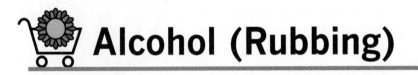

Alcohol (Rubbing)

Make an instant insecticide. When there's no time to fumble with fancy formulas, whip up this potent potion. It's instant death to almost any bad bug in the book. Just mix 1 cup of rubbing alcohol with 1 teaspoon of vegetable oil in 1 quart of water. Pour the mixture into a handheld sprayer bottle, take aim, and give each pest a direct hit.

Battle big bugs on a big scale. When the insect population is too large to tackle with a handheld sprayer (for instance, beetles that are gobbling up your roses, or ticks that are hanging out on your shrubs), use the same ingredients, but increase the quantities. Mix 4 cups of rubbing alcohol and 1 tablespoon of vegetable oil with 1 gallon of water in a medium-sized bucket. Then pour the solution into your 6 gallon hose-end sprayer jar, and spray your plants from top to bottom—making sure you get under all the leaves.

Cure black spot. Believe it or not, when this foul fungus attacks your roses, you can actually remove the ugly blotches from the leaves—that is, if you reach the scene when spots first begin to pop out. Here's how: Chop 15 tomato leaves and 2 small onions into fine pieces, and steep them overnight in ¼ cup of rubbing alcohol. Then use a small, sponge-type paintbrush to apply the mix to both the tops and bottoms of any infected rose leaves. To get rid of the fungus for good, use the cornmeal cure described in Chapter 2 (see "Cornmeal Conquers All," on page 59).

Rub out mealybugs and scale. Both of these sap-sucking pests are most famous for the damage they do in sunrooms and home greenhouses. But they also target a wide range of outdoor plants, including annual and perennial flowers, trees, shrubs, and sometimes even vegetables. Your best response: If the plant is small, or if you  catch the invasion in its early stages, go head to head with the little pests. Just dab each one with a cotton swab dipped in rubbing alcohol, and it'll bite the dust instantly.

Pickle hand-picked pests. The most effective (and least toxic) way to deal with larger insect pests, such as slugs, snails, beetles, weevils, and caterpillars, is to simply pluck them off your plagued plants and drown them in a bucket of water with a cup or so of rubbing alcohol added to it. If you'd prefer a less hands-on method, hold a bowl of alcohol-laced water under the bug-infested plant, and jostle the leaves; the pests will tumble into the drink and drown.

Words to the Wise

Before we get very far into the First Aid aisle, let me pass along a couple of reminders about alcohol:

* Do not confuse isopropyl (rubbing) alcohol, which you can buy at the supermarket, with denatured alcohol, which you can buy in hardware stores. Denatured alcohol is ethanol (the same stuff that's used in alcoholic beverages). By law, it must contain toxic and foul-tasting chemicals that make it unfit for drinking—and those chemicals are not things you want to use on plants, or on your own (or your pet's) skin.

* Rubbing alcohol, on the other hand, is perfectly safe for skin contact, and for most plants. Some plants, however, are super-sensitive to alcohol; so before you use it, either straight or in a Marvelous Mix, test it on a few leaves first. Then wait 24 hours and check for damage. If you act too quickly, you could end up killing the victim right along with the villains!

Say "scram" to spiders. Miss Muffet to the contrary, spiders (especially the ground-dwelling kinds) are terrific garden helpers who eat bad bugs by the bucket load. But that doesn't mean you want Charlotte and her pals spinning their webs in your window frames—indoors or out. The simple solution: Just pour some rubbing alcohol into a handheld sprayer bottle, and spritz the windowsills. The super spinners will set up housekeeping elsewhere.

Remove moss from underfoot. Many people (including yours truly) consider moss to be one of Mother Nature's most delightful creations: a soft, green carpet that thrives with no care whatsoever, even in the shadiest spots where nothing else will grow. But even the most devoted moss lovers draw the line when the slippery stuff moves onto walkways and stepping stones, where it becomes an accident waiting to happen. Fortunately, there's an easy removal

Alcohol (Rubbing)

method that's as close as your medicine chest (or the First Aid aisle at the supermarket). Just spray the green invader with a solution of 2 tablespoons of rubbing alcohol per pint of water, then rinse it away using the garden hose.

Kill weeds. Yikes! It's spring, and young weedlings are poppin' up all over the place! They're in flower beds, in the vegetable garden—even in the cracks in your driveway. Don't panic—and don't rush out and buy a toxic herbicide. Instead, just mix 3 tablespoons of alcohol and 1 pint of water in a hand-held sprayer bottle. Then fire away. *Note:* If any of the weeds are especially reluctant to bite the dust, or if you want to be extra-sure of getting them on the first try, increase the quantity of alcohol as much as you like. Just be sure to aim carefully to avoid killing any plants you want to keep.

MARVELOUS MIX

Homegrown Daisy Spray

If you grow painted daisies (*Tanacetum coccineum*), you've got the makings of one powerful pesticide. It'll deal a death blow to lilac borers and just about any other bad bug you can think of. And the recipe couldn't be any simpler to make.

> **1/8 cup of rubbing alcohol**
> **1 cup of packed, fresh painted daisy flower heads***

Pour the alcohol over the flower heads, and let it sit overnight. Strain out the flowers, then store the extract in a sealed, labeled container. When you need it, mix the extract with 3 quarts of water, and pour the solution into a handheld sprayer bottle. Then take aim, and let 'er rip!

*If you don't grow painted daisies, look for them in the florist section of your local supermarket or, in the summertime, at your local farmer's markets.

Soothe poison ivy. A run in with this vile weed is never fun—to put it mildly! But if you act fast, you can lessen the effects of the rash, or even head it off entirely. All you need to do is swab the affected skin with rubbing alcohol, which will cut through the plant's toxic oil and dilute it. Then wash the area with soap and water.

Clean grimy glass. Of course, wooden surfaces aren't the only ones that suffer from Old Man Winter's shenanigans. The outsides of windows pick up more than their fair share of grungy dirt, too. So as soon as the wild spring weather calms down, whip up a batch of this homemade miracle cleaner: Mix 2 cups of rubbing alcohol and 1 table-spoon each of ammonia and dishwashing liquid in 2 quarts of water. Then pour the solution into a handheld sprayer bottle, and go to town. This super-duper concoction will beat commercial, streak-less glass-cleaning products hands down!

Pre-wash painted wood. Over the course of a long, messy winter, painted decks and porches can pick up a *lot* of dirt and grime. So before you tackle that spring cleaning chore, wipe the wood surface down with a soft cloth or mop that's been dipped in alcohol. It'll dissolve the greasy dirt, so the detergent can really get in there and do its job.

Get pine pitch off metal. Big, stately pine trees may give a yard a certain old-time, homey look. But they sure make a mess when the sap drips all over metal lawn furniture (not to mention your car). Fortunately, it's a cinch to get the goo off. Just dampen a soft, cotton cloth with alcohol, and buff the sticky stuff away. *Note:* This same simple routine will keep chrome spotless, whether it's on a clas-sic car, a classic bicycle, or your barbecue grill (or even your kitchen appliances).

To the Rescue!

For some of your most vexing household cleaning tasks, you'll find the best—and simplest—solution right in the First Aid & Health Supplies aisle at your local supermarket. Here's a roundup of annoying problems, and how to provide first-class first aid.

PROBLEM	SOLUTION
Burned grease in the bottoms of pots and pans	Fill each one with water, drop in 6 antacid tablets, and let them soak for an hour.
Clogged drain	Drop in 3 antacid tablets followed by a cup of white vinegar; give it a few minutes, and then run the hot water.
Dirty toilet bowl	Drop a couple of antacid tablets into it; wait 20 minutes, then brush and flush.
Mildewed caulking around tubs and showers	Wipe the area with rubbing alcohol, using a sponge or plastic scrubbing pad.
Mustard stains on clothes, table linens, or carpet	Scrub the spots with a solution of 2 parts water and 1 part rubbing alcohol, then wash the item as usual.
Scratches on wood furniture	Use a medicine dropper to drip iodine into the marks. Use new iodine for mahogany. For cherry-stained mahogany and cherry wood, use older iodine that's turned a dark brown. To mask scratches in maple, dilute brown iodine with a few drops of denatured alcohol.
Wax buildup on a wood or tile floor	Scrub it with a solution of 3 parts water to 1 part rubbing alcohol, then rinse thoroughly with clear water. (Make sure the room is well ventilated before you begin.)
Yellowed linens	Sponge the spots with hydrogen peroxide or, if the whole piece is yellowed, submerge it in peroxide. Leave it for an hour or so, rinse with cold water, and launder as usual.

Make vinyl glisten. This simple formula is just the ticket for cleaning outdoor-furniture cushions, your car's upholstery, or anything else that's made of vinyl. Here's all there is to it: Mix 1/4 cup of alcohol, 1/4 cup of baby shampoo, and 2 cups of water in a bowl or small bucket. Wipe it onto the surface with a soft, clean cloth (or maybe a sock whose mate has gone astray). Then buff with a second cloth. *Note:* This cleaner also works like a dream on leather.

Keep car windows frost-free. If you have to leave your vehicle outdoors on a cold winter night, wash the windows with a solution made from 1/2 cup of alcohol per quart of water. The glass will stay crystal clear. This trick also works to keep Jack Frost from leaving his calling card on the windows of your house or greenhouse.

Defrost your car's windshield. When it's too late for preventive measures, fill a handheld sprayer bottle with alcohol and spritz the windshield. Then simply wipe the frost and ice away with a clean, soft cloth—no need to scrape and scrape…and scrape.

 # Aspirin

Keep your houseplants healthy. My Grandma Putt had the happiest, healthiest houseplants I've ever seen. Her super-simple secret: She dosed each of them once a month with an aspirin dissolved in 1 cup of weak tea.

Make cut flowers last longer. Don't let your big, beautiful blooms go downhill faster than they need to. Instead, add two crushed aspirin tablets for each quart of water in the vase. Then sit back and enjoy the show!

Immunize your plants. Scientists have discovered that aspirin increases a plant's natural defenses against deadly bacteria, fungi, and viruses, *and* it repels insects. To put this miracle drug to work in your flower beds and vegetable garden, mix 1$\frac{1}{2}$ uncoated, finely ground aspirin tablets

Here's to
YOU!

When the bug bites or the bee stings, don't just sit there and remember your favorite things. Instead, remember this: A whole lot of products in the First Aid & Health Supplies aisle of your local supermarket will ease the pain and itch and reduce swelling of any insect attack—and fast, too! (In the case of a bee sting, get the stinger out before you proceed with the treatment.) Here are your some of your best supermarket super options:

* Dissolve two antacid tablets in a glass of water. Then moisten a soft cloth with the solution and hold it on the bite for 20 minutes.

* Wet your skin, and rub an aspirin tablet over the stricken site.

* Make a solution of Epsom salts and warm water. Soak a clean, soft cloth in the liquid, then apply it to the sting site for 15 to 20 minutes. If the sting was on your foot or your hand, soak your appendage in the solution instead.

* Rub a hemorrhoid remedy (like Preparation H®) over the afflicted area.

* Massage mentholated rub into your assaulted skin.

* Dab some milk of magnesia (magnesium hydroxide) onto the bite site.

* Slather Pepto-Bismol® onto the "crime scene."

and 2 tablespoons of baby shampoo in 2 gallons of water. Pour the solution into a handheld sprayer bottle, and spray your plants every three weeks throughout the growing season. Whatever you do, though, *don't* use a stronger solution—an overdose of aspirin will actually harm plants. *Note:* To grind the tablets, you can use a coffee grinder, a mortar and pestle, or (as a friend of mine does) the skinny end of a wooden spoon in a shot glass.

Improve seed germination. A mild aspirin solution (1½ finely ground, uncoated tablets per 2 gallons of water) also encourages seeds to sprout. In fact, tests have shown that it produces almost 100 percent germination in flowers and vegetables. In this case, apply it to the seedbed or flat with a watering can. Don't bother adding baby shampoo; its only purpose in the foliar spray (see "Immunize your plants," immediately above) is to help the mixture stick to the leaves.

Kill soilborne fungi. Many kinds of these foul felons can cause plants' crowns, roots, or stems to wilt or rot. Sometimes the damage is fatal; but if you reach the scene early, you can often save the day—with the help of good old-fashioned aspirin. Mix 1 crushed tablet per quart of water, and drench the soil thoroughly. Try to avoid getting any of the solution on the victim's leaves, though, because in this concentration, aspirin will most likely cause serious injury to foliage. (See "Immunize your plants," on page 172.)

Remove corns and calluses. Is one of these painful bumps putting a damper on your outdoor work (or play)? Then try this old-time formula: Mash 5 aspirin tablets, add equal parts of water and lemon juice (just enough to make a thick paste), and apply it to the annoying C-spot. Wrap the area in a warm towel, put a plastic bag over your foot, and leave it in place for 10 minutes. Take off the wrappings, and scrub the bump away with a pumice stone.

Aspirin

Castor Oil

Make moles move on. These tiny varmints don't eat grass or any other plants. Instead, they eat only insects—and plenty of them. But they can sure make a mess of your lawn as they tunnel through the soil in search of dinner. Here's a simple way to get rid of them: Just mix 1 cup of castor oil with 3 gallons of water, and drench the moles' mounds with it. The critters will head for the hills!

Tell voles to vamoose. Unlike moles, voles have a humongous appetite for any kind of plant material under the sun, but they're especially partial to the bark of trees and shrubs. Your woody plants are at greatest risk in the winter, when other food is scarce. So before the first snow flies, mix ½ cup of castor oil and ½ cup of dishwashing liquid in your 20 gallon hose-end sprayer, and saturate the area around all of your trees and shrubs. *Note:* Anytime a recipe calls for dishwashing liquid, do not use detergent or any product that contains antibacterial agents.

Keep the Christmas in Christmas cactus. Chances are that you bought your plant so you could enjoy its beautiful flowers during the holiday season. So to make sure it blooms *this* December, dribble 2 tablespoons of castor oil around the roots in October.

Perk up ailing ferns. In my Grandma Putt's day, folks swore by castor oil as an all-around pick-me-up tonic. And you know what? It works that same magic on ferns that are feeling (or at least looking) less than chipper. Just mix 1 tablespoon of castor oil and 1 tablespoon of baby shampoo in 1 quart of warm water. Then pour ¼ cup of the solution on the soil around each plant. They'll turn green and fresh almost overnight!

Lubricate pruning shears. When those cutting blades aren't moving as smoothly as they should, just put a drop or two of castor oil in the mechanism. They'll be right back in the swing of things. *Note:* This trick works just as well on scissors, tongs, and any other utensils that have moving parts.

Soften up stiff leather. You say you left your favorite leather gardening gloves out in the rain, and now they're stiff as boards? Don't fret: Just dip them in a sink full of warm water, squeeze them dry in a towel, and then rub a little castor oil into the leather. Those gloves will be as soft as the day you bought them!

MARVELOUS MiX

Gopher-Go Tonic

Like moles, gophers tunnel through your lawn, wreaking havoc in the process. But they're not really gunnin' for grass; they want more substantial vegetation in the form of flowers, vegetables, and the roots of fruit trees or grape vines. These gluttons don't discourage easily (to put it mildly), but this fabulous formula has worked well for me.

4 tbsp. of castor oil
4 tbsp. of dishwashing liquid*
4 tbsp. of urine
1/2 cup of warm water
2 gal. of warm water

Combine the oil, dishwashing liquid, and urine in 1/2 cup of warm water, then stir the solution into 2 gallons of warm water. Pour the mixture over any problem areas, and the gophers will gallop away!

*Do not use detergent or any product that contains antibacterial agents.

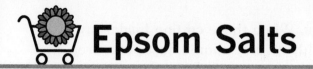

Epsom Salts

Start your herbs off right. Whether you're starting your herbs from transplants or direct-sown seed, spur them into action with this soil-building booster "shot": Mix together 5 pounds each of lime and gypsum, 1 pound of 5-10-5 dry, organic fertilizer, and $1/2$ cup of Epsom salts. Work the formula into each 50 square feet of herb garden area to a depth of 12 to 18 inches. Then let it sit for 7 to 10 days before planting. Those young'uns will get off to a rip-roarin' start!

Grow sweeter melons. No matter what kind of melons you grow, they'll be the tastiest treats in town if you use this simple trick at planting time: Mix 5 pounds of earthworm castings (available in catalogs), $1/2$ pound of Epsom salts, and $1/4$ cup of instant tea granules in a wheelbarrow or big tub. Then put 1 cup of the mixture into the bottom of each planting hole. Your melons will grow sweet and juicy beyond your wildest dreams!

Feed your lawn. Keep your grass in tip-top shape with my classic feeding plan: In the spring and fall, mix 3 pounds of Epsom salts per 50-pound bag of dry, natural/organic lawn food, and apply the mixture at half of the recommended rate with your broadcast or drop spreader. (If you use a slow-release synthetic/chemical fertilizer, spread the fertilizer first, clean your spreader to remove any residue, then follow up with the salts; otherwise, the salts will cause an additive in the lawn food to dissolve, and you'll end up with a gooey mess on your hands.)

Here's to **YOU!**

Sooner or later, nearly every gardener and outdoor-project builder winds up with a splinter that just doesn't want to budge. Here are two easy—and painless—ways to coax those annoying slivers to the surface:

Method 1. Pour about 2 tablespoons of Epsom salts into a cup of warm water, and soak the sore digit in the solution. It'll draw the invading fragment right out. (It should take only a few minutes, depending on the depth of the splinter.)

Method 2. No Epsom salts on hand? Then cover the splinter with adhesive tape or the sticky part of an adhesive bandage, and leave it on overnight. Come morning, peel off the tape, and the sliver should be poking out far enough so you can easily grab it with tweezers. If it's still under your skin, replace the sticky cover with a clean one, wait another few hours, and take another peek.

Super-charge grass seed. Getting ready to start a new lawn, or patch up an old one? Then here's a little secret you ought to know: Mix 1/4 cup of baby shampoo and 1 tablespoon of Epsom salts in 1 gallon of weak tea. Drop your grass seed into the container, and stash it in the refrigerator for at least 24 hours. Spread the seeds out on your driveway to dry, then sow them in the usual way. The result: almost 100% germination!

Give plugs a grand sendoff. Are you using plugs to start a new lawn, or patch up an old one? To get them up and growing great, mix 3 pounds of Epsom salts with 1 bag of dry, natural/organic lawn food (enough for 2,500 square feet). Using a handheld broadcast or drop spreader, apply the mixture at half the rate recommended on the fertilizer bag. (If you prefer to use a synthetic fertilizer, spread the Epsom salts and lawn food separately.)

Wake up your roses. My Grandma Putt's roses were always the toast of the town, and she said she owed it all to this simple formula. She served it up first thing each spring, when the soil temperature had reached 50°F or so. (The recipe makes enough for one plant.) To make it, mix 1 cup of Epsom salts, 2 cups of alfalfa meal, 1 cup of dolomitic lime, and 2 dried banana peels in 5 gallons of water. Pour the mixture around the base of the plant, and work the solids into the soil, along with any compost that you've used as mulch over the winter. Your roses will rush out of the starting gate like three-year-old colts on Derby Day!

MARVELOUS MiX

Container Garden Booster Mix

When you're planting vegetables in containers (as more and more folks are doing), add this miracle food to a half-and-half mixture of good commercial potting soil and compost. You'll get a harvest that will put many an inground plot to shame!

> 1/2 cup of Epsom salts
> 1/4 cup of coffee grounds (rinsed clean)
> 1 tbsp. of instant tea granules
> 4 eggshells (dried and crushed to powder)
>   per 2 gallons of soil

Combine the ingredients thoroughly with your potting mix. Then plant your seeds or set in your transplants, and get ready to enjoy a bountiful harvest.

Give extra "oomph" to flowering shrubs. Azaleas, forsythias, lilacs, and all your other colorful woodies will bloom their little hearts out if you perform this ultra-simple chore twice a year: In spring and fall, sprinkle Epsom salts around the root zone at a rate of $1/4$ cup of salts per 9 inches of circumference (measured at the farthest tips of the branches). Then sit back and enjoy the show!

Nourish your shade trees. After a long winter's nap, trees like maples, elms, and sycamores wake up mighty hungry in the spring. Here's how to serve them a hearty breakfast: Start by mixing 25 pounds of dry, organic fertilizer (5-10-5) with 1 pound of sugar and $1/2$ pound of Epsom salts. Then drill holes in the ground out at the weep line (a circumference at the tip of the farthest branch). Make the holes between 8 and 10 inches deep and 18 to 24 inches apart. Then pour 2 tablespoons of the breakfast mix into each hole, and sprinkle the remainder over the top of the soil.

Produce robust roses. In May and again in June, give each plant 1 tablespoon of Epsom salts with its regular feeding. This will encourage new growth from the bud union of the bushes—and, hence, stronger plants. (To get your roses off to a rousing start in the spring, see "Wake up your roses," on page 178.)

Make spring-blooming bulbs last longer. When your daffodils, tulips, and hyacinths burst into bloom each year, don't you just wish they'd keep going all summer long? I know I sure do! Unfortunately, I don't know of any way to pull off that trick, but I can tell you how to give those pretty flowers some extra staying power. When you see the first signs of growth in the spring, mix 2 pounds of bonemeal with 2 pounds of wood ashes and 1 pound of Epsom salts, and sprinkle this mixture on the soil around your plants. It'll fortify the bulbs and give them added strength for their blooming journey.

Make geraniums bloom in the winter. With their big, beautiful, boldly colored blooms, *Pelargoniums* are classic summertime favorites. And if you bring your potted geraniums indoors in the fall and put them in a sunny window, you can keep the show going all winter long. To jump-start the performance, sprinkle the soil with 1 tablespoon of Epsom salts for every 3 inches of pot size. Then mix 1 cup of beer, 4 tablespoons of instant tea granules, and 2 teaspoons of baby shampoo in 1 gallon of water, and use the solution to water the salts into the soil around your plants. If you follow this routine, you'll bid farewell to the weary-winter blues!

Increase your vegetable yields. This trick works for all kinds of veggies, but it's especially effective at producing bumper crops of tomatoes and peppers. Here's all you need to do: Dissolve 3 tablespoons of Epsom salts in 1 gallon of warm water, and give each plant 1 pint of this mixture just as it starts to bloom. Come harvest time, you'll be picking tons of tomatoes and pecks of peppers.

Fend off whiteflies—maybe. Why "maybe"? Because these tiny pests are most attracted to plants that aren't getting enough phosphorus or magnesium in their diet. If they're showing up in greater numbers than their natural predators can handle, send a soil sample off to a testing laboratory. Then, if the results show a deficiency of magnesium, add Epsom salts to your soil (the lab report will tell you how much). On the other hand, if phosphorus is lacking, your remedy is to add bonemeal, fish emulsion, poultry manure, or seaweed to the soil (all available at your local garden center). So now you can see why Epsom salts just *might* be the answer.

Hydrogen Peroxide

Transplant trees and shrubs. Whether you're setting a new tree or shrub into the ground, or moving an older one to a new location, it's a stressful experience for the plant. But you can ease that strain—by serving up a healthy dose of this soothing potion. Mix $1/3$ cup of hydrogen peroxide, $1/4$ cup of instant tea granules, $1/4$ cup of whiskey, $1/4$ cup of baby shampoo, and 2 tablespoons of fish emulsion in 1 gallon of warm water. Then after you've set your tree or shrub into its planting hole, pour about a quart of the solution onto and over the roots.

Give roses a healthy start. Getting ready to plant a new rose-bush, or transplant an older one? Then do a little home cookin' first. This is a super-powered breakfast for either bare-root or container-grown roses. In a watering can, mix 1 tablespoon of hydrogen peroxide, 1 tablespoon of dish-washing liquid, 1 teaspoon of whiskey, and 1 teaspoon of vitamin B_1 plant starter in $1/2$ gallon of warm water. Pour the solution all around the plant's root zone. Then step back and get ready to smell the roses! *Note:* Anytime a recipe calls for dishwashing liquid, do not use detergent or any product that contains antibacterial agents.

Bathe your bulbs. In the fall, when you dig up your dahlias, cannas, gladiolas, and other tender bulbs and tubers, don't even think of tucking them away with dirt on their "faces." Instead, before you store them away for the winter, wash them in a solution of 2 tablespoons of baby shampoo and 1 teaspoon of hydrogen peroxide mixed in a quart of warm water. This will get rid of any pests or disease germs that may be hiding in the soil. Just make sure you dry the bulbs thoroughly when you're finished—otherwise, rot will sneak in, and your hard work will have been in vain!

Keep your herb garden chipper. By and large, herbs are as easy to please as a plant can get. But they do enjoy a good cocktail every now and then, and their beverage of choice is 1 cup of tea and ½ tablespoon each of hydrogen peroxide, bourbon, and ammonia mixed in 1 gallon of warm water. Mix up a batch every six weeks throughout the growing

Down with Damping-Off

It happens to every new gardener (and even to not-so-new ones): Seedlings that looked fit as a fiddle when you went to bed are barely alive the next morning. The problem: damping-off. It's a fungus that whips like lightning through a seedling tray. The prime causes are nonsterilized soil, stagnant air, and dirt from hands, pots, or tools. Seedlings with wet foliage are the most common victims. The good news is that if the disease has felled only a few seedlings in a flat, there's a fair chance that you can save the rest of your babies. Just mix up a half-and-half solution of hydrogen peroxide and water, saturate the affected area, and hope for the best!

To head off future attacks, follow these guidelines:

* If your containers have been used before, soak them for 15 minutes in a solution made from 1 part household bleach to 8 parts hot water. Also use this mixture to clean any tools that will come into contact with your seeds or starter mix, like tweezers or soil scoops.

* Use only sterilized seed-starter mix in your starting pots.

* Make sure the tykes' nursery has good air circulation (use a fan turned on low if you need to).

* Water from the bottom up. Set your starter pots into a tray that has no holes, then pour the water into the tray. The roots will take up the moisture they need, and the baby foliage will stay nice and dry.

season, and pour it around the root zone of each of your herb plants. They'll lift their glasses and say "Here's to you!" (Well, they would if they could.)

Help your houseplants breathe better. An extra jolt of oxygen every now and then will make all kinds of indoor plants grow faster and produce more blooms. To deliver this breath of fresh air (so to speak), just mix 2 tablespoons of hydrogen peroxide with 1 quart of water in a handheld sprayer bottle. Every couple of weeks, mist-spray the leaves with the solution, and pour the remainder onto the soil at the base of the plant.

Fend off mildew. Both downy mildew and powdery mildew can plague roses and a great many annuals and perennials. Prime targets include asters, black-eyed Susans, mums, and (the champion mildew magnet of all) garden phlox (*Phlox paniculata*). To keep your plants free of both of these foul fungal diseases, spray them every week in the spring with a mixture of 1 tablespoon of hydrogen peroxide, 1 tablespoon of baby shampoo, 1 teaspoon of instant tea granules, and 2 cups of water in a handheld sprayer.

Cure mildew in your lawn. When your turfgrass starts sporting tiny patches of white to light gray fungus, it can mean only one thing: Powdery mildew has struck. So strike back fast! Mix 1 cup of hydrogen peroxide, 1 cup of baby shampoo, and 4 tablespoons of instant tea granules in a bucket, pour the mix into a 20 gallon hose-end sprayer, and fill the balance of the sprayer jar with water. Spray the affected area every week to 10 days, and your lawn will soon be spotless once more. *Note:* This foul fungus generally strikes only shady parts of a lawn during periods of high humidity and temperatures between 60° and 72°F. Bluegrass is most susceptible, but any grass that's growing in a shaded area (like the north or east side of your house or garage) is a candidate for powdery mildew.

MARVELOUS MiX

Summer Soother Tonic

Automatic sprinklers provide a simple, efficient way to water your lawn. But every now and then, on a warm summer morning, I like to take a garden hose in hand and do the job the old-fashioned way. When I do that, I soothe my whole yard with this nice, relaxing shower.

> 2 cups of weak tea water*
> 1 cup of hydrogen peroxide
> 1 cup of baby shampoo

Mix these ingredients in a 20 gallon hose-end sprayer, and give everything in sight a good soaking. It makes for a really delightful summer shower, and your yard will thank you for it!

*To make weak tea water, soak a used tea bag in a solution of 1 gal. of warm water and 1 tsp. of dishwashing liquid until the mix is light brown. Store any leftover liquid in a tightly capped jug or bottle for later use. *Note:* Anytime a recipe calls for dishwashing liquid, do not use detergent or any product that contains antibacterial agents.

Remove garden-variety stains. Think about it: How many times have you come in from working in your garden *without* wearing souvenirs in the form of either dirt, grass, or blood stains? If you're anything like me, the answer is probably, "Oh, maybe once or twice." Well, the next time you pick up any of those annoying marks, just reach for the hydrogen peroxide. Apply it to the soiled areas, rub it in until the spots disappear, and then launder as usual. Your duds will come out clean as a whistle. *Note:* If you're not sure about an item's colorfastness, first test-treat a hidden area, like a shirttail hem.

Get out mystery stains. For those times when you don't know what on earth caused the splotches on your (or your youngster's) clothes, try this old-time routine: Mix 1 teaspoon of hydrogen peroxide with a dab of non-gel toothpaste (if you only have the gel type on hand, use a pinch of cream of tartar instead). Rub the paste onto the spot with a clean, soft cloth, and rinse with clear water. The mystery will remain unsolved, but the stain will be history.

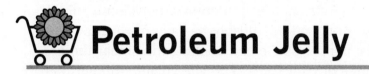

Petroleum Jelly

Keep rose borers at bay. Many kinds of borers—all the larvae of flying insects—target roses. You'll know that these pests have struck if you see spirals just under the bark of pruned canes and your plants' growth is less vigorous than normal. And, of course, if any canes break off, you'll see the invaders' tunnels. Now for the good news: Borers don't cause fatal damage. All you need to do is cut any afflicted canes back farther than the damaged section (tunnels usually extend only $3/4$ inch or so), and put a dab of petroleum jelly on the cut end to seal the opening. And from now on, use this same petroleum jelly treatment on all your pruning cuts. Your roses will be bored no more!

Trap bad bugs. Many flying insects find certain colors irresistible. And you can turn that craving into the cause of their downfall: Just coat a piece of appropriately colored wood, corrugated cardboard, or poster board with petroleum jelly, and hang it on or next to your plagued plant. Every few days, toss out the old trap and replace it with a new one. Or, if you've used a sturdy piece of wood, just use an old rag to wipe off the bug-studded jelly, and recoat the board. As for what color to use for your traps, see "Color Them Gone," on page 17. *Caution:* If your traps are catching beneficial insects like bees, butterflies, or ladybugs along with the bad guys, change your tactics. Throughout this book, you'll find plenty of ways to get rid of destructive pests without harming garden-variety heroes.

Stop slugs and snails. Here's a tip for all you Sunbelt dwellers. You know how much slugs and snails love sliming their way up into your citrus trees and nibbling the leaves to shreds? Well, you can put an end to those shenanigans with this simple trick: Mix $1^{1}/_{4}$ cups of petroleum jelly, 1 cup of castor oil, and 3 tablespoons each of cayenne pepper and hot pepper sauce in a bucket, and smear the goo on the trunks of your trees. The vile villains will get their kicks elsewhere.

Keep wasps out of birdhouses. Wasps are infamous for moving into empty birdhouses and nesting boxes—thereby depriving house-hunting birds of places to raise their families. But there's a simple way to keep the intruders out: Just smear a coat of petroleum jelly on the inside top of the house or box. The sticky stuff will prevent the buzzers from setting up housekeeping, but it won't bother your fine-feathered friends one bit.

Make extra-strong anti-cutworm collars. No matter what kind of barriers you use to protect your seedlings from these hungry larvae, go one step further to make sure the pests don't crawl over the top: Coat the top of each collar with petroleum jelly. Then sit back and rest easy!

Heal bruises. Ouch! You pulled your shovel up out of the soil a little too fast and banged it against your shin! Well, don't chew yourself out for your clumsiness (as my Grandma Putt used to say, what's done is done). Instead, just measure out 5 parts petroleum jelly to 1 part ground cayenne pepper, melt the jelly in a saucepan over low heat, and stir in the pepper. Let the gel cool, pour it into a clean glass jar, and apply it to the bruised area once a day. (Just be sure to wear rubber or plastic gloves when applying the gel, because this stuff is *hot*.)

Feed birds, not squirrels. If the greedy rascals are climbing up the pole to your feeder and helping themselves to your pals' dinner, here's an easy way to close the dining room door: Just grease the pole with petroleum jelly. When the rascals start to scamper up, they'll slide right back down again.

Foil nectar-craving ants. To keep the little sugar-holics out of your hummingbird feeder, rub petroleum jelly on the support wire. The tiny tightrope walkers will get a sticky surprise!

Winterize your garden tools. Before you put your shovels, hoes, and other gear away for the season, rub down the metal parts with a little petroleum jelly on a clean, soft cloth. It'll keep the tools free of rust and ready to go when duty calls in the spring.

Keep your mower moving. And your garden cart, wheelbarrow, and the kids' red wagon, too. How? Just lubricate the wheels by smearing petroleum jelly around the cylinders. The gear will keep rollin', rollin', rollin' along.

Here's to YOU!

The same mentholated rub that clears up your chest and nasal passages when you have a cold can do you another health-related favor: It fends off ticks, mosquitoes, and other biting (and disease-spreading) bugs. Just smooth the rub onto your arms, legs, and neck before you head out to your garden—or out to your deck for a relaxing evening. The flying fiends will keep their distance.

Remove bird offerings. No matter how much you may love watching your fine-feathered friends in action, it's no fun when one of them leaves a "present" on your leather bag, your jacket, or (yikes!) your convertible's leather upholstery. Well, when a splatter does fall from above, don't panic. Just rub the stain away with a little petroleum jelly on a clean, soft cloth.

Many first aid and health supplies come equipped with packaging that's every bit as useful as the product itself (though in different ways, of course). Here are some good examples of potential trash that you can turn into house and garden treasure:

Boxes from bandages and gauze. Save these boxes until Christmastime rolls around, then wrap them like tiny presents and hang them from the tree. You'll have one-of-a-kind ornaments for free!

Cardboard rolls from gauze. Dismantle the nests of rubber bands in your junk drawer, and snap them around the reel.

Plastic and metal boxes from throat lozenges. Use them to corral all kinds of tiny odds and ends, like buttons, nails, needles, paperclips, stamps...the list could go on—and on.

Reels from adhesive tape. Or any other kind of tape, for that matter. Wrap aluminum foil around them, attach a string, and hang them in your fruit trees and berry bushes to discourage fruit-eating birds.

Any of the above. Turn it into dollhouse furniture. Just cover the box, reel, or roll with fabric or decorative paper, and presto! Depending on the size and shape of the object, you've got a bed, coffee table, dining table—or whatever your future interior designer desires.

Vitamins

Jump-start bare-root roses. Garden catalogs may *promise* you a rose garden. But, of course, what they actually send you are dormant plants with their whole root system free of soil and gently swathed in sphagnum moss (or a similar wrapping). If you're new to rose growing, this may be a pretty scary sight, but don't worry: Bare-root roses actually seem to settle in more quickly than their potted counterparts. But they do need a bit of special handling. So before planting, soak the roots for 24 hours in a solution made from 1 crushed vitamin B_1 tablet, 1 tablespoon of Epsom salts, and 1 teaspoon of baby shampoo all mixed in 1 gallon of water. Before you know it, those bushes will be blooming to beat the band!

Perk up your houseplants. Are your houseplants looking less than their best? Then give them a nutritional boost with this old-time chow. In a bucket, mix 2 crushed multivitamin-plus-iron tablets; $^3/_4$ cup of ammonia; 1 tablespoon each of Epsom salts, saltpeter (available at drugstores), and baking powder; and $^1/_2$ teaspoon each of baby shampoo and unflavored gelatin. Add a few drops of food coloring if you'd like, so the clear solution stands out from other uncolored liquids. Pour the mixture into a container with a tight lid. (Use several jars if you don't have one that's big enough.) Then once a month, use 1 cup of this potion per gallon of water instead of your regular fertilizer. Your plants will all but jump for joy!

Help stem cuttings form roots faster. Getting ready to propagate shrubs or perennials? Then make sure you serve up healthy doses of vitamin B_1. For future plants started in water, add $^1/_2$ tablet per 8-ounce glass. If you're using a commercial starting mix, use 1 tablet per quart each time you water your cuttings. (Either way, dissolve the vitamin tablet in hot water first.)

Here's a trivia question for you: What does the discovery of vitamins have to do with rice? The answer: In 1905, an English doctor named William Fletcher found that eating unpolished rice (that is, rice with the husks intact) prevented the disease beriberi. But once the covering was removed from the kernels, the rice ceased to fend off the ailment. The reason, Dr. Fletcher figured, was that the hulls contained some kind of special, health-giving nutrients. A year later, another Englishman, bio-chemist Sir Frederick Gowland Hopkins, also discovered that certain food factors were important to health.

From there, the A to E train speeds forward to 1912, when Polish scientist Cashmir Funk (also investigating the importance of rice husks) coined the term "vitamine." Vita (of course) means life; "amine" was in honor of compounds Dr. Funk found in the thiamine he isolated from the rice husks. Later, the *e* was dropped, and Drs. Hopkins and Funk went on to formulate the hypothesis that a lack of vitamins could make you sick.

Feed flowering houseplants. Your cyclamen, gardenias, Amazon lilies, anthuriums, and other indoor bloomers will shower you with flowers if you water them with this elixir every two weeks or so. Mix 1 crushed multivitamin-plus-iron tablet, $\frac{1}{4}$ cup of instant tea granules, and $\frac{1}{2}$ tablespoon each of hydrogen peroxide, ammonia, and vodka in 1 gallon of warm water. Store the solution in a lidded container. To use it, add 1 cup of the potion per gallon of water.

Keep your Christmas tree fresh. Before you put the tree into its stand, cut 1 inch off the bottom of the trunk and soak the tree overnight in a bucket of very warm water with 4 crushed multivitamin-plus-iron tablets, 2 cups of clear corn syrup, and 2 tablespoons of bleach. After that, make sure you keep plenty of water in the stand at all times.

Soothe your sore face Spring has sprung, and you were so eager to start planting that you rushed out to the garden without applying any sunscreen—and you stayed outdoors way too long. Now your face is feeling the results. Instead of chewing yourself out, treat your face to this intensive treatment: Drain the contents of 5 vitamin E capsules into a bowl, and add 2 teaspoons of plain yogurt and 1/2 teaspoon each of honey and lemon juice. Mix well, and apply it to your face with a cotton ball. Wait about 10 minutes, and rinse with warm water. Your skin will feel like new!

MARVELOUS MIX

Groundcover Picnic Tonic

Groundcovers are miracle workers when it comes to covering shady spots where turfgrass refuses to thrive, or slopes that are too steep to mow safely. And they'll keep their good looks well into the fall if you give them a midsummer serving of this terrific tonic.

> 4 multivitamin-plus-iron tablets, dissolved in 1 cup of hot water
> 4 tbsp. of hydrogen peroxide
> 1 tbsp. of Epsom salts
> 1 tbsp. of baking powder
> 1 tbsp. of ammonia
> 1/2 tsp. of unflavored gelatin powder
> 1/2 tsp. of dishwashing liquid*
> 1 gal. of water

Mix the vitamin liquid, peroxide, Epsom salts, baking powder, ammonia, gelatin, and dishwashing liquid in a bucket. Then mix 1 cup of this liquid with the water in a watering can, and serve it up generously to your groundcover.

*Do not use detergent or any product that contains antibacterial agents.

Vitamins

191

Laundry & Cleaning Products

AMMONIA
BLEACH
BLUING
BORAX
CLEANERS & CLEANSERS
CLOTHESPINS
DISHWASHING LIQUID
DRYER SHEETS
FABRIC SOFTENER
LAUNDRY DETERGENT
PLASTIC LAUNDRY BASKETS

Ammonia

Prevent damping-off. Getting ready to start seeds indoors? Then keep in mind that one of the prime causes of this foul fungal disease is dirty containers. So if you're using pots or flats that have been used before, wash each one in a solution made from 8 parts water to 1 part ammonia, with a few drops of dishwashing liquid added to it. Then fill the container with sterilized seed-starting mix. You'll be well on your way to a healthy crop of young flower or vegetable seedlings. *Note:* In this case, feel free to use whatever kind of dishwashing liquid you have on hand—mildness doesn't matter here.

Hasten the harvest. When winter is heading in fast and your garden is still full of unripe vegetables, get the show on the road with this routine: Mix 1 cup of apple juice, $\frac{1}{2}$ cup of baby shampoo, and $\frac{1}{2}$ cup of ammonia in your 20 gallon hose-end sprayer, filling the balance of the sprayer jar with warm water. Apply the mixture to your plants to the point of runoff. Your tomatoes, squash, and other garden-variety goodies will be ready to pick before you know it.

Start your lawn off right. If you're gearing up to sow your field of dreams, then this tip is just for you. Two or three days before seeding, apply a good starter fertilizer according to the manufacturer's directions. (You'll find many different brands at your local garden center; just make sure the one you choose has roughly equal amounts of nitrogen, phosphorus, and potassium.) Then mix 1 cup of fish emulsion, $\frac{1}{2}$ cup of ammonia, and $\frac{1}{4}$ cup each of baby shampoo and corn syrup in a bucket, pour the mix into a 20 gallon hose-end sprayer, and saturate the soil. This will get your grass seed up and growing in no time flat!

Make flowering shrubs bloom indoors. The first hint of spring is in the air, and you just can't wait to see your flowering shrubs burst into bloom. So don't wait! When the plants first start to show buds, clip off as many branches as you like, and take them inside. Put them into buckets of warm water, and into each pail, drop a cotton ball saturated with ammonia. Put the branch-filled container into a giant trash

MARVELOUS MiX

Tire-Track Remover Tonic

When your lawn is damp, anything on wheels can leave its mark in the turf—delivery trucks, cars, bicycles, wheelbarrows, and even your lawn mower. The good news is that regardless of what caused them, getting rid of those ruts is simple. Just wait for the soil to dry out a little, and then stroll across the area with your aerating lawn sandals, or punch holes in the ground with a garden fork. Spread gypsum over the damaged area at the recommended rate, and overspray it with this fantastic formula.

> 1 cup of ammonia
> 1 cup of beer
> $1/2$ cup of baby shampoo
> $1/4$ cup of weak tea water*
> Warm water

Mix the ammonia, beer, shampoo, and weak tea water in a 20 gallon hose-end sprayer, filling the balance of the sprayer jar with warm water. Apply to the point of runoff. Repeat this treatment every three weeks to get your lawn on the road to recovery!

*To make weak tea water, soak a used tea bag in a solution of 1 gal. of warm water and 1 tsp. of baby shampoo until the mix is light brown. Store any leftover liquid in a tightly capped jug or bottle for later use.

bag, and tie it tightly shut with twine or a twist tie. Check your branches every day or two because almost before you know it, the ammonia fumes will make those baby buds burst into bloom. *Note:* This trick works like magic with lilacs, pussy willows, crab apples, and any other flowering trees or shrubs.

Keep raccoons out of your garbage cans. To you, the leftovers you tossed out after dinner may be mere trash—but to a raccoon, that chow is a five-star fine dining experience. There's a super-simple way to close the restaurant: Dip a large wad of paper towels in ammonia, douse it with hot sauce, and toss the wad into the can. The rascals will dine elsewhere.

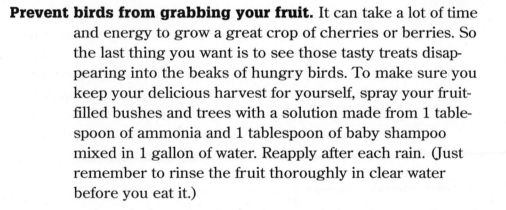

Prevent birds from grabbing your fruit. It can take a lot of time and energy to grow a great crop of cherries or berries. So the last thing you want is to see those tasty treats disappearing into the beaks of hungry birds. To make sure you keep your delicious harvest for yourself, spray your fruit-filled bushes and trees with a solution made from 1 tablespoon of ammonia and 1 tablespoon of baby shampoo mixed in 1 gallon of water. Reapply after each rain. (Just remember to rinse the fruit thoroughly in clear water before you eat it.)

Spray your bad-bug blues away. If you'd rather shoot than pick, send the culprits to you-know-where by spraying them with a half-and-half solution of ammonia and water. *Caution:* In order for this potion to be effective, it needs to make direct contact with the bugs; so whatever you do, don't spray an entire plant in the hopes of seeing residual action. (Aside from being counterproductive from a bug-elimination standpoint, it could do major damage to the plant.)

Ammonia

195

Deter four-legged garden pests. Most critters, including gophers, groundhogs, squirrels—and even skunks—will flee from the scent of ammonia. Just soak rags in the stuff, tuck them into old panty hose legs, and hang them in the areas you want to protect. If there's no hanging space, pour the ammonia into wide-necked bottles (like the kind that juice comes in), and bury them up to the rims in the soil.

Drown destructive insects. For my money, the most effective way to deal with beetles, caterpillars, and just about any other kind of large insect pests is to grab a pair of old tongs, pick the villains off your plants, and drop them in a bucket of water laced with a cup or so of a lethal ingredient—like good old-fashioned ammonia.

Get rid of mites. These tiny terrors can strike any kind of plant, and in big numbers, they can cause major damage. If they've moved into your garden in full force, act fast! Mix 3 teaspoons of ammonia and 1 teaspoon of dishwashing liquid in $2\frac{1}{2}$ gallons of water, and pour the solution into a handheld sprayer bottle. Spray the leaves and stems thoroughly every five days for three weeks, and the mites will be gone for good. *Note:* Anytime a recipe calls for dishwashing liquid, do not use detergent or any product that contains antibacterial agents.

Keep up your slug defenses. A mini fence made from copper strips works like magic to protect your plants from slugs (and snails, too). When the vile villains try to slither over the barrier, something in the metal reacts with the slime on the pests' bodies to produce a fatal jolt of electricity. There's just one catch: When the copper gets dirty, it loses its firepower. So every now and then, clean the copper by rubbing it with a soft cloth dipped in a half-and-half solution of ammonia and salt. Rinse with clear water. That'll keep the current coming!

Chase squirrels out of your chimney. You say the ornery rascals have set up housekeeping right in Santa's pathway? How rude! But don't fret—you can clear Santa's way by pouring about half an inch of ammonia into a pan and setting it on the hearth. (First, though, make sure that the flue is open and the fumes can travel up the chimney.) The critters will scurry in a hurry!

As unlikely as it might seem, a few potent laundry and cleaning products can help ease some of the most common—and uncomfortable—outdoor mishaps. Here's your Laundry & Cleaning Products aisle first-aid manual:

Here's to
YOU!

Bee stings. After scraping out the stinger, dab a few drops of bluing onto the spot, and—bingo—instant relief!

Fire-ant bites. Douse the flames by dabbing the area with a half-and-half solution of bleach and water. If it's applied within 15 minutes of the bite, it'll ease the pain and swelling. (But if the pain is severe, or spreads beyond the bitten spot, hightail it to the closest doctor.)

Mosquito bites. Nix the itch and swelling by dabbing the spot with a few drops of ammonia. Act fast, though, *before* you start scratching. If you apply ammonia to broken skin, the sting will feel a whole lot worse than the skeeter's bite!

Poison ivy. Relieve the pain and itch by patting the nasty red blotches with a solution consisting of a teaspoon or so of bleach per quart of water.

Rash. Grab a can of spray starch, and spritz that itch goodbye!

MARVELOUS M̲i̲x̲

All-Season Green-Up Tonic

I've been singing the praises of this remarkable recipe for well over half a century now—and for good reason: It's one of the best ways you'll ever find to give your plants all the nutrients they need for good health and great performance.

> **1 can of beer**
> **1/2 cup of ammonia**
> **1/2 cup of dishwashing liquid***
> **1/2 cup of liquid lawn food**
> **1/2 cup of molasses or clear corn syrup**

Mix these ingredients in a large bucket. Then pour the solution into your 20 gallon hose-end sprayer, and saturate your lawn, trees, flowers, and vegetables every three weeks throughout the growing season.

*Do not use detergent or any product that contains antibacterial agents.

Make your car's headlights sparkle. Those front-end lamps pick up more than their fair share of grime, especially in the winter. To cut right through that road dirt, use a solution made from 2 tablespoons of ammonia and 1 tablespoon of cornstarch mixed in 1 quart of water. (The cornstarch will act as a mild abrasive.) Wipe the mixture onto the lights with a clean, soft cloth, and then rinse with clear water.

Clear up oil spills on concrete. Oh, boy! You were changing the oil in your car, and somehow the stuff found its way onto your concrete driveway. Now what do you do? Exactly what I do when this mishap occurs: Mix 1 cup of ammonia in a bucket with a gallon of warm water, and brush that petro-puddle away. Follow up by rinsing the area with clear water. (And next time, be more careful!)

Remove milk stains from wood. Has someone spilled milk on your wooden patio furniture? Remove the spots by putting a few drops of ammonia on a soft, damp cloth and rubbing gently. The moo juice should come right out.

See the road clearly. Driving with a smeared windshield is more than just annoying—it can be downright dangerous. To make sure your view stays crystal-clear, perform this simple chore every week or so (or more often if you need to): Pull each wiper away from the windshield and rub down both sides with a rag soaked in ammonia.

 # Bleach

Keep plant diseases from spreading. Many ailments—especially those caused by foul fungi—can fly like lightning through your whole garden (or your lawn, in the case of a turfgrass disease). So do yourself and your whole green scene a favor: Whenever you're working with ailing plants of any kind, clean your tools before you move on to healthy plants. A simple rubdown with a solution of 1 part bleach to 3 parts water will do the trick.

Give your plants a healthy start. Are you starting seeds or cuttings in containers that have already been used? Then before you add any planting mix, soak the flats or trays for about 15 minutes in a solution of 1 part household bleach to 8 parts hot water. This will kill off any lingering fungi or other germs that could harm your infant plants. If you're fresh out of bleach, substitute the same amount of ammonia, and add a few squirts of dishwashing liquid to the water. *Note:* In this case, feel free to use whatever kind of dishwashing liquid you have on hand—mildness doesn't matter here.

According to the folks who keep such statistics, four out of five American households have at least one bottle of bleach lying around the laundry room. But here's something you may not know about this popular product: Even though household bleach is often called "chlorine bleach," there's no chlorine in it! That chemical (Cl, in scientific circles) is used in the manufacturing process, but none remains in the end product.

Protect plants of any age. Before you set any of your plants into a pot that's been used before, disinfect the container by soaking it for 15 minutes or so in a solution of 1 part bleach to 8 parts water.

Bash iris borers. When you see irregular tunnels or mines in iris leaves or flower stalks, it can mean only one thing: that iris borers are hard at work, and chargin' for the rhizomes—if they're not there already. To eliminate the pests in a leaf or flower stalk, just take each plant part between your fingers and squeeze hard, from the base up. When you hear a "pop," you'll know that a borer has bitten the dust. Or, if the thought of squashing makes you squeamish, cut off the whole fan of leaves and destroy it. You'll lose this year's big flower show, but you'll save the rhizome from invasion.

Then in midsummer—the time for dividing irises—dig up the rhizomes and look for tunnels. When you see one, poke a wire into it, and you'll hook the borer. (There's only one pest per rhizome, though droves of 'em might haunt the leaves.) Then dip the rhizome in a solution of 1 part household bleach to 3 parts water, let it dry, and replant. First, though, scrape out a few inches of the soil, add an equal amount of compost, and mix it in.

First Aid for Flopping Flowers

Just a few days ago, you cut a big basketful of flowers and arranged them in your best vase. Now they're lookin' as limp as overcooked spaghetti. Well, don't toss those bloomers onto the compost pile—at least not until you try this treatment. If they're not too far gone, you can give them a new lease on life, at least for a while. Here's the routine:

1. Fill a clean vase with a solution made from 1 cup of lemon-lime soda (not diet) and $1/4$ teaspoon of bleach per 3 cups of warm (110°F) water. Use only enough of this Flower Saver Solution so that all the stem tips are under water, and so that the vase is heavy enough not to topple over. Too much liquid will only make the stems rot faster.

2. Pull off any leaves that will be under water in the vase.

3. Hold each flower stem under running water. Using a sharp knife or scissors—and with the water still running—cut the stem at a 45-degree angle, about 1 inch from the bottom. Then set the flower into the vase.

4. When all the flowers are in the container, put it in the refrigerator for an hour or two. Just make sure the temperature is above 35°F. Also, keep the bouquet far away from unwrapped fruits and vegetables—they give off ethylene gas, which will make those posies go downhill *fast*. If there's no room in the fridge, just use the coolest spot in the house.

5. Move the flowers to a place that's out of direct sunlight, and away from both cold drafts and heat sources. Add fresh doses of Flower Saver Solution as the level goes down, and change it completely every two to three days until your posies have perked up.

Bleach

Treat bacterial soft rot. This dastardly disease turns iris rhizomes soft, mushy, and foul-smelling (to put it mildly). You may also see withered tips and water-soaked streaks on the leaves. The bacteria that cause the ailment sneak into the plant through wounds made by iris borers or (whoops!) by careless cultivation. Fortunately, if you reach the scene in time, there is hope. Simply dig up the infected rhizomes, then cut out and discard the rotten parts. Dunk the healthy portion in a solution of 1 part bleach to 3 parts water, and let it dry before replanting. (To keep the bacteria from spreading, don't forget to dip your tools in the solution, too.)

Kill moss on masonry surfaces. Is your patio or walkway starting to look almost as green as your lawn? If so, here's an easy way to change the picture: Just spray the mossy patches with a half-and-half mixture of bleach and water, and wipe them clean with a damp cloth. *Note:* This procedure works on anything that's made of brick, concrete, or stone.

MARVELOUS MIX

Down-Home Deck and Porch Cleaner

My Grandma Putt's house had big, wide, wraparound porches, and she kept them spotless with this simple formula. And it works just as well today on any wooden structure, including 21st-century decks.

> **1 qt. of bleach**
> **1/2 cup of powdered laundry detergent**
> **2 gal. of hot water**

Mix all of the ingredients in a bucket, and scrub the porch or deck using a stiff broom or brush. Then hose it down thoroughly.

Prevent moss attacks. To keep the fluffy green stuff from growing on your home's roof or siding shingles, try this: Make a solution of 2 capfuls of bleach per gallon of water. Sponge the solution onto the mossy areas, and don't rinse. How often you need to repeat this procedure depends on your climate and the location of your house. In a damp, shady spot, it's a good idea to use this treatment at least once every two years or so.

Remove skunk odor from surfaces. When a skunk or two come a-callin' and leave some fragrant evidence behind, this is the remedy to reach for: In a bucket, mix 1 cup of bleach, 1 tablespoon of dishwashing liquid, and $2^{1}/_2$ gallons of warm water. Use this solution to thoroughly saturate walls, stairs, or anything else your local skunk has left his mark on. *Note:* In this case, feel free to use any kind of dishwashing liquid that you have on hand, but use this potion only on nonliving things—not on humans, pets, or plants.

Get mildew off of plastic-mesh lawn furniture. If you leave your chairs outdoors all summer long, that's an open invitation to mildew spores. But it's a snap to send the spores packing. Just scrub the fabric with a solution of 1 cup of bleach per gallon of water. (But first, test for colorfastness by wiping it onto an inconspicuous spot.) Rinse well with clear water, and make sure the mesh is completely dry before you put the furniture away indoors for the winter.

Freshen up old sponges. If you like to use sponges for outdoor cleaning chores, you know how they can get *really* grungy *really* quickly. But that doesn't mean you have to throw them away. They'll come out clean as a whistle if you simply soak them for 5 to 10 minutes in a mixture of $^3/_4$ cup of bleach per gallon of water. Then rinse well, and put 'em right back to work!

 **Bluing**

Turn white flowers blue. How? Simply by adding ¼ cup or so of bluing to the water in the vase. The color will travel up through the stems and into the petals. (Of course, the more bluing you use, the darker the shade will be.)

Tint the water in your swimming pool. Would you like that H_2O to be an enticing shade of Pacific Ocean blue? Then take a tip from pool dealers and hotel poolkeepers from coast to coast: Add bluing to the water. To color a 20- by 40-foot pool, pour in one or two 8-ounce bottles at the point where the water flows in from the filter. Wait a couple of hours to let it circulate thoroughly, and dive right in. Over time, the sun will fade the color. When you notice that starting to happen, simply pour in another bottle of bluing. Just a few words of caution: Take care not to splash the bluing on your pool's walls or coping, and don't use it in aerated models like whirlpools or hot tubs. Although this stuff won't hurt a single living thing, in undiluted form, it may leave spots on some hard surfaces.

Give budding sailors a summertime treat. How? Just add a few tablespoons of bluing to the water in their wading pool. They can sail their toy boats across their own mini ocean!

Keep your birdbath algae-free. To feel comfortable in a bath, birds need to have good traction underfoot—and they won't get it if the surface is covered with slimy algae. (And you probably don't want to look at the ugly stuff, either.) You could keep it at bay by emptying your birdbath and cleaning it frequently, but here's a simpler solution: Add a few drops of bluing to the water. It'll reduce the growth of algae without harming so much as a feather on your fine flying friends.

Most laundry products, like soaps, detergents, and bleaches, actually remove dirt and stains. But bluing works its washday magic by optical illusion. Here's the scoop: Of the 300-odd shades of white that exist in the world, the brightest ones have a slight bluish tinge. But undyed cotton and wool are yellowish, linen has a distinct hint of brown, and most synthetic fibers rank somewhere on the gray scale. In order to get the snowy look that we think of as "pure" white, manufacturers bleach their material, then treat it with bluing, which is actually a very fine iron powder. It adds microscopic blue particles to the fabric, thereby making it look whiter. Over time, the bleach and bluing wash out, and the fabric regains its natural "dingy" appearance. When that happens at your house, just add about $^1/_4$ teaspoon of bluing to a gallon of cold water, pour it into your washing machine at the start of the wash cycle, and bingo—your whites will come out as snowy as Frosty's belly! But bluing can also come to your aid outside the laundry room. Here's a trio of examples:

* To check for a leak in your toilet's flush tank, pour a tablespoon or so of bluing into it. If the water in the bowl turns blue, you know you've got a leak to repair!

* Prevent algae from building up in a humidifier by adding a tablespoon of bluing to the water each time you fill the reservoir.

* When you wash the crystals in a chandelier, add a few drops of bluing to the rinse water. It'll repel dust particles and keep the glass clean for a longer time, which means less work for you.

Borax

Stop creeping Charley. Or at least keep it under control. This invasive perennial weed (also known as creeping Jenny, ground ivy, and gill-over-the-ground) is one tough customer. If it's running rampant in your lawn or garden, apply a mixture of 5 tablespoons of borax per gallon of water early in the spring, using a watering can.

Kill weeds while they sleep. I'm talking about the especially annoying kind that spring up and out of all the cracks and crevices in your driveway, sidewalk, and other paved surfaces. Here's the battle plan: In early spring, before you see any signs of life, sprinkle borax in all those tight spaces where you know the weeds will soon appear. The potent powder will kill them before they have a chance to take root.

Remove hard-water deposits. When those unsightly blotches build up on flowerpots, stone or concrete patios, water spigots, or any other hard surface, reach for a box of borax. Dissolve 1/2 cup of the powder in 1 cup of warm water, and stir in 1/2 cup of vinegar. Sponge the mixture onto the spots, and let it sit for 10 minutes or so (longer for really stubborn stains). Then wipe the surface clean with a damp sponge. The ugly spots will be history!

Preserve flowers and leaves. When you're setting out to dry plant parts to make wreaths, potpourri, and other craft projects, you could buy a commercial preservative. But don't waste your money! This simple supermarket alternative works every bit as well. Here's all there is to it: First, find a cardboard box that has a lid and is big enough to hold your flowers, leaves, and stems. Next, mix 1 part borax and 2 parts cornmeal, and pour a 1-inch layer of the mixture into the box. Lay your plant material on top, then very gently cover it with more of the mix, taking care to leave no air space around the flowers. (If you're working with many-petaled posies, such as roses or carnations, sprinkle some of the mixture directly into each bloom before you place it in the box). Tape the carton closed, and store it in a dry place at room temperature for 7 to 10 days. At the end of the waiting period, pour or brush away the covering, and carefully lift out your treasures. *Note:* Because the preservative doesn't absorb moisture from the flowers, you can use the same batch again and again—just store it in an airtight container.

Bring On the Boron

Boron is what gardeners call a micronutrient; but when some vegetables don't get enough boron, they suffer from macro-trouble. Fortunately, a deficiency is simple to fix: All you need to do is sprinkle about a tablespoon of borax around each plant. At the end of your growing season, have your soil tested, and add whatever amount of borax the results call for. But how do you know when your veggies are crying out for the big B? It's simple—just keep an eye out for these symptoms.

VEGETABLE	SIGNS OF BORON DEFICIENCY
Beets	The inside of the root turns brown and corky.
Cabbage	The whole head turns brown.
Celery	Margins of leaves show brownish mottling; later, horizontal cracks appear on the stems.
Corn	New leaves develop elongated, watery, or transparent stripes; ears (if they appear at all) have corky, brown bands at the base.
Rutabagas	The inside of the root turns brown and corky.
Swiss chard	Horizontal cracks appear on the stems.
Turnips	The inside of the root turns brown and corky.

Borax

Wipe out ants. When the little buggers are driving you to drink, mix equal parts of borax, alum, sugar, and flour with enough water to make a batter. Pour the mixture into shallow containers, and set them in the areas where ants congregate—but only in spots that children or pets can't get to.

Clean mud-splotched clothes. If you're anything like me, you rarely come in from your garden without a lot of brown mud on your clothes. Well, my Grandma Putt knew exactly how to get those stains out. I still use her method—and you can, too. After brushing off as much of the dirt as you can, rub the spots with a solution of 1 tablespoon of borax in 1 cup of water. Toss those duds in with the rest of the wash, and they'll come out clean as a whistle.

Cleaners & Cleansers

Kill slugs. Are the slimy thugs making a ragged mess of your flowers and vegetables? Then don't pull any punches. Pour $1/2$ cup of ammonia, 1 tablespoon of Murphy® Oil Soap, and $1^1/2$ cups of water into a handheld sprayer bottle. Shake it until the ingredients are well mixed. Then take aim and fire!

Clobber caterpillars. Are cabbage worms running roughshod through your cole crops? Hornworms terrorizing your tomatoes? Armyworms marching through your lawn? No matter what kind of crawling larvae are buggin' your plants, a jolt of this aromatic blend will do 'em in. To make it, gather up $1/2$ pound of wormwood leaves (*Artemesia absinthium*) and simmer them in 2 cups of water for 30 minutes. Strain out the leaves, then add 2 tablespoons of Murphy® Oil Soap and 2 more cups of water. Pour the solution into a 6 gallon hose-end sprayer, and apply it to your plants to the point of runoff.

Kill slugs, take 2. Another Laundry & Cleaning Products aisle weapon in the slug wars is pine-based cleaner. You have a choice between two methods of slugicide. Either pour a half-and-half batch of pine cleaner and water into a hand-held sprayer bottle, take aim, and let 'er rip, or pick up the slimy villains and drop them into bucket of water with a cup of the cleaner added to it. (The second tactic will also bid bye-bye to snails.)

Turn away tomcats. And a lot of male dogs, too! It's no fun when the four-legged boys are making their mark on fences, walls, or other surfaces in your yard. But there's an easy way to let 'em know it's your territory: Just fill a handheld sprayer bottle with a half-and-half solution of pine-based cleaner and water, and regularly spritz the visitors' targets. The scent will confuse the rascals, and they'll take their spray guns else-where. Just one word of caution: Pine-based cleaner can kill plants, so use it only on nonliving things—or weeds.

MARVELOUS MiX

Herb Booster Tonic

Even hardy herbs enjoy a nice, cool drink when the going gets hot. Quench their thirst with this summertime pick-me-up.

> **1 can of beer**
> **1/2 cup of Murphy® Oil Soap**
> **1 cup of ammonia**
> **1/2 cup of corn syrup**

Mix these ingredients in a small bucket, pour the mix into a 20 gallon hose-end sprayer, and apply to your herbs every six weeks during the growing season. They'll lift their glasses in a toast to you! (Well, they would if they could.)

Eliminate chinch bugs. If these suckers have invaded your lawn and the problem areas are too big for the flannel-sheet treatment (see "Drench chinch bugs," on page 216), use this broader-reaching remedy: Mix 1 cup of Murphy® Oil Soap and 3 cups of warm water in a bucket, pour the mix into a 20 gallon hose-end sprayer, and saturate your lawn. After it dries, apply gypsum to the bug-infested areas at the rate of 50 pounds per 2,500 square feet of lawn.

Here's to
YOU!

Study after study has shown that communing with nature improves folks' mental and physical health—and even increases their productivity at work. But you don't have to trek off on a photographic safari to enjoy these benefits. Something as simple as watching butterflies flit around your backyard works just as well. They'll show up in droves if you plant a wide assortment of nectar-rich flowers, but you'll entice them even more quickly (and get a close-up view, besides) if you install a nectar feeder or two near your house. You can buy special butterfly feeders, but my advice is, don't waste your money! The reason: Nearly all of these devices come equipped with a moat that you fill with water, which is supposed to keep crawling insects out of the sweet syrup. But a lot of small butterflies also get trapped in the water, often with fatal results. Fortunately, there's a simple—and safer— way to serve refreshments. Just get a thin, green, plastic-fiber scrubbing pad in the Laundry & Cleaning Products aisle, and saturate it with sugar water (1 part water to 4 parts white sugar is good). Set the pad on a plastic plate that you've screwed to a post or other flat surface. Then sit back and wait for the show to begin!

Make moles move on out These dastardly diggers spend most of their lives underground, so you rarely see them. But when they're in your lawn, it's easy to find their homes: At the entrances to their tunnels, they leave large, round piles of loose dirt. When you spot these doorways, you can say "Please go now" by squirting pine-based cleaner into the hole, straight from the plastic squeeze bottle. (If the cleaner you have is in a regular bottle, pour it into a squeezable container that formerly held dishwashing liquid, or a condiment like mustard or mayonnaise.)

Vote "No!" for voles. These little rodents generally do the most damage in the winter, when they scamper through mole runs and eat any roots they come across, or tunnel through the snow to chew on the bark of trees and shrubs. But I know a trick that will make the varmints pack up and spend the snowy season elsewhere: Just mix equal parts of diatomaceous earth and Bon Ami® cleansing powder, and sprinkle it around your trees, shrubs, and planting beds, too. For good measure, mix the same powdery duo in with your fall lawn food. You'll make the voles vamoose and pep up the grass at the same time!

Protect bulbs from voles. If you plant spring-flowering bulbs under your trees, make sure you give them extra protection, because bulbs are a vole's idea of gourmet treats. When you tuck the bulbs into the ground, sprinkle a teaspoon or so of Bon Ami® cleansing powder into each hole.

Say "Nuts!" to squirrels. To keep the pests from making off with your crop, spray your fruit and nut trees with this spicy potion: In a large bucket, mix 1 tablespoon of Murphy® Oil Soap and 3 tablespoons each of cayenne pepper and hot pepper sauce per quart of warm water. Pour the solution into a handheld or tank sprayer, and coat your trees from top to bottom. (Be sure to rinse the fruit well before you eat it!)

Clothespins

Simplify fall yard cleanup. When it's time to rake up all those autumn leaves, remember this helpful hint: Grab a giant trash bag, shake it vigorously to open it wide, and use two clip-type clothespins to fasten one side of the sack to a sturdy support. (A chain-link fence, a trellis, or two branches of a shrub would all do the trick.) With these handy helpers, you'll be able to toss in armfuls of leaves without struggling to keep the bag open.

MARVELOUS MiX

Clothespin Cleaner

Nowadays, just about every household in the country has a clothes dryer. But I know a lot of folks who still get a kick out of drying at least some of their laundry the old-fashioned way, by hanging it outdoors on a laundry line, using wooden clothespins. If you're one of those traditional folks, you probably want to keep your little clipping devices as clean as the clothes you clip them to. And with this simple recipe, you can do just that.

$1/2$ cup of bleach
1 tbsp. of laundry detergent (either dry or liquid)
2 gal. of warm water

Mix the ingredients in a bucket, and soak the clothespins for about 10 minutes. Then pin them on the clothesline to dry in the sun. Repeat the process every couple of weeks. *Note:* Even if you use your wooden clothespins for non-laundry jobs, this routine is still a great way to fend off both dirt and mildew.

Hang outdoor Christmas lights. When Santa's on his way and you're rushing to get everything done on time, every minute counts. And here's a terrific timesaving trick that comes straight from the Laundry & Cleaning Products aisle: Instead of twining light cords around tree branches or fastening elaborate hooks to your gutters, hold your light strings in place with clip-type clothespins. Clear plastic ones work best, because (of course) they just fade out of sight.

Avoid pricked fingers. Going out to your garden to cut some roses for bouquets? Then take along a clip-type clothespin, and use it to hold each thorny stem as you snip it off. That way, you'll get no unexpected jabs.

Plan to plant bulbs. Are there some noticeable patches of bare ground when your big spring bulb display bursts into bloom? If so, don't fret. Just stick clothespins into the places where there should be tulips, daffodils, or whatever. That way, you'll know exactly where to plant more bulbs in the fall.

Identify your seedlings. When you start flower or vegetable seeds indoors, use a clothespin to clip a label to the side of each container. It's a great way to keep track of your plantings. If you're growing the same kind of flower in a variety of shades—and you want to keep the colors separate in the bed—be sure to specify each one on its label. That way, come planting time, there'll be no chance of putting (for instance) your white cosmos where you wanted pink ones, or vice versa.

Clothespins

213

Dishwashing Liquid

I've Said This Before...

But it bears repeating: Whenever you're shopping for dish-washing liquid to use in your yard or garden, make sure you choose a brand that's made with pure, mild soap. Avoid any product that contains detergents or degreasing agents. They can harm your grass (or any other plants that they touch). And whatever you do, avoid all products that boast their anti-bacterial prowess. Not only will they damage your greenery, but they'll also kill off good bacteria along with the bad—and that can cause *big* trouble.

There is one exception to this rule, and that is when the soapy solution will not come in contact with valuable plants. If you're aiming to destroy weeds, clean inanimate objects, or kill pests that you've removed from your plants, feel free to use any kind of soap or detergent you have on hand—and make the "medicine" as strong as you like. (For more on soapy pest-control methods, see "Into the Drink," on page 217.)

Guard your grass from salt. If you live in the Snowbelt, you know all too well how much damage deicing salt does to your lawn. Unless you have a lot of clout at city hall, there's no way you can get the road crews to bypass your yard; but you can give your turf a protective suit of armor. Here's how to go about it: First, in late fall, liber-ally spread gypsum over the turf in a 5-foot band along roadsides, walkways, or any other surface that will be on the deicing list. Next, mix 1 cup of dishwashing liquid, $1/2$ cup of ammonia, and $1/2$ cup of beer in a 20 gallon hose-end sprayer, and apply it over the gypsum to the point of runoff. Your soil and grass should sail through the winter in fine shape.

Rev up your vegetable garden. Your tomatoes, squash, melons, and other crops will take off like racehorses out of the starting gate when you give your soil this pre-planting treatment: Two weeks before you sow your seeds or set in your transplants, mix 1 can of beer, $1/2$ teaspoon of instant tea granules, and $1/2$ cup each of dishwashing liquid, antiseptic mouthwash, and regular cola (not diet) in your 20 gallon hose-end sprayer. Saturate the soil with the mixture, and get ready for action! (This recipe makes enough to cover 100 square feet of garden area.)

Put your garden to bed. After you've harvested all your vegetables and it's time to close up shop (so to speak), spread a thick layer of organic mulch over the planting beds, then serve up this nightcap: Mix 1 can of regular cola (not diet), 1 cup of dishwashing liquid, and $1/4$ cup of ammonia in your 20 gallon hose-end sprayer, and fill the balance of the jar with warm water. Then spray until the mulch is saturated. During the cold, dark months, the soil will soak up the nutrients, and it'll wake up rarin' to go in the spring.

Bash beetles and weevils. These pests have hard, waxy bodies that are impossible for most sprays to penetrate. But this one has what it takes to go the distance. To make it, mix 2 tablespoons of dishwashing liquid and 2 teaspoons of peppermint oil in 1 gallon of warm water. Pour the solution into a handheld sprayer bottle, take aim, and fire!

Clobber cutworms in your lawn. These ugly larvae are best known for the damage they do in flower beds and vegetable gardens. But in the spring and summer, they can also make a mess of your grass plants by munching on the crowns, where the blades meet the roots. The easiest way to end their dining pleasure is to mix 3 tablespoons of dishwashing liquid with 1 gallon of water, and pour it on the trouble spots. The soap will bring the cutworms to the surface, where hungry birds will get 'em in no time flat.

Dishwashiing Liquid

Drench chinch bugs. These lawn pests suck sap from the grass blades and, at the same time, inject a poison that kills the plants. The outward symptoms are round, yellow patches that quickly turn brown and die. Fortunately, it's a cinch to send the menaces packin' from a small lawn, or just a few trouble spots. Here's how to do it: First, make a solution of 2 tablespoons of dishwashing liquid to 1 gallon of water, and pour it on the area. (I use a sprinkling can to ensure good, even coverage.) Then, put a white flannel sheet or other soft, white cloth on top of the grass. Wait 15 or 20 minutes, then peek under the fabric. It should be teeming with chinch bugs that've crawled toward the surface to escape the soap. Gather up the cloth, and dunk it into a bucket filled with soapy water. Finally, get out the hose, and spray your lawn thoroughly to remove the soap residue. (If a large area of your lawn is infested with these pests, see "Eliminate chinch bugs," on page 210.)

Kill *really* stubborn weeds. When you've tried everything, and the so-and-so's just won't knuckle under, pull out the big guns. Mix 2 tablespoons each of dishwashing liquid, gin, and white vinegar per quart of hot water. Pour the solution into a handheld sprayer bottle, and blast those weeds to you-know-where!

Rejuvenate clay pots. I know some folks who like their terra-cotta containers to look as though they've been sitting in the garden for years. But if you prefer your pots to look like you just brought them home from the garden center— even if they *have* been sitting in the garden for years— here's your cleanup plan: Wash them in a mixture of 1 tablespoon of dishwashing liquid, 1 teaspoon of bleach, 1 tablespoon of instant tea granules, 1 teaspoon of antiseptic mouthwash, and 1 teaspoon of hydrogen peroxide per quart of warm water. (Use a sponge, a soft cloth, or a brush.) Then rinse the pots with clear, cool water. They'll look almost like new.

Into the Drink

Believe it or not, a simple bottle of dishwashing liquid can help ensure that you never have a major pest problem. Of course, there is one catch: You need to inspect your plants (including flowers, vegetables, woody plants, and turfgrass) every day, or at least every couple of days. That way, you can deal with any little problems before they turn into big ones. Here are some simple ways to battle pests—using that potent weapon in the plastic squeeze bottle:

Handpick them. This is the most effective way to deal with larger insect pests, such as slugs, snails, beetles, weevils, and caterpillars. Just pluck them off the plants and drown them in a bucket of water laced with a cup or so of dishwashing liquid.

Dunk them. If you'd prefer a less hands-on approach, hold a bowl of soapy water under a bug-infested plant, and jostle the leaves; the pests will tumble into the drink and drown.

Vacuum them. Put about 2 inches of soapy water into the reservoir of a wet/dry vacuum cleaner (a.k.a., a Shop-Vac®), and suck up the culprits. Or use a regular, handheld model and empty the contents into a bucket of soapy water. Vacuuming works especially well for insects that tend to scamper rather than fly, like lace bugs, harlequin bugs, rose chafers, and carrot weevils.

Clip their damage off. When you find that a few leaves or stems are covered with bugs, just cut off the afflicted plant parts and stick them into a bucket of soapy water.

Pull up their plant homes. Sometimes, one plant will be seriously infested, while its neighbors are clean, or nearly so. In that case, simply throw an old sheet over the buggy plant, pull it up by the roots, and dump it into a tub of water laced with 2 cups or so of dishwashing liquid. Leave it for a minute or two, then drop it in the trash. If any stragglers have found their way to nearby plants, just handpick them off.

Reduce the mosquito population. My Grandma Putt used this super-simple technique to pick off these bloodthirsty menaces, and it's still one of the best skeeter-control methods that I know of. All you need to do is fill some old pans with water, add a few squirts of dishwashing liquid, and set them around your yard. When the skeeters set down to lay their eggs, they won't get up again!

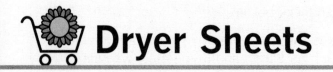 # Dryer Sheets

Deter mice. To you, a dryer sheet might smell like the freshest thing this side of a violet patch. But that strong, flowery scent sends mice scurrying. This go-away power lasts longer indoors (I use the sheets to safeguard the contents of my garden shed), but as a temporary measure, tie a few sheets to the lower trunks of your shrubs. They'll keep mice and other small critters at bay at least until rain washes the aroma away.

Send bigger critters packin', too. Cats, deer, gophers, moles, and skunks all flee from that distinctive dryer-sheet aroma. Just tie the sheets to trees, shrubs, or fence posts in the area you want to protect, or (in the case of moles and gophers), stuff a wad of sheets into each hole.

Cover drainage holes. If you're still using pot shards to cover the drainage holes in planting containers, here's something you should know: Although that technique *will* keep the potting mix from escaping each time you water your plants, it *won't* improve drainage—in fact, it can actually hinder it. So here's a better idea: Put a used dryer sheet over the hole in each pot. It'll keep the soil in, but let water drain out freely.

Prevent bites and stings. Our friends the bees and our enemies the mosquitoes have several things in common. Two of them are obvious: Both of them fly, and both can definitely put a damper on your outdoor fun if you happen to be in the wrong place at the wrong time. But here's something you may not know: Bees and skeeters both flee from the odor of scented dryer sheets. So before you head outside in the good old summertime (especially if you're allergic to bee stings!), tie one of these aromatic squares through one of your belt loops or buttonholes. Then rest (or work or play) easy!

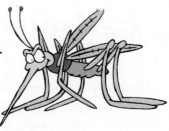

Repel packing "peanuts." A classic trick for taking up space in very large plant containers is to fill the bottom third or so with foam packing peanuts. It's a great idea, because you save money on potting mix and reduce the weight of your pots (that's especially important if they'll be sitting on a deck or balcony). There's just one minor drawback: When you're working with the static-producing nuggets, they act like magnets on your skin. The simple solution: Before you start to work, rub a dryer sheet over your hands (and arms, too, if you're wearing short sleeves). This way, the clingy devils will stay in the pot, where they belong—and not "crawl" all over your body.

Round & Round Round & Round

Even after you've reused a fabric softener sheet, you may be able to get one more garden-variety use out of it: Tear it into strips and use them to tie up your beans, peas, tomatoes, or other floppy plants.

Dryer Sheets

Fabric Softener

Remove hard-water marks from glass. It's frustrating, all right: You've just finished washing your car's windows, but the chemicals in your tap water have left them littered with spots. Fortunately, this problem has a simple solution. Just wipe fabric softener onto the marks, wait about 10 minutes, and wipe again with a damp cloth (no need to dry). Presto—spotless glass! Of course, this trick works on any type of glass, including the windows of your home or greenhouse, and the glass-topped tables on your patio.

Clean paint-covered brushes. Just painted your garden fence or deck? Speed up your cleanup by soaking the brushes for 10 seconds in a mixture of $\frac{1}{2}$ cup of fabric softener per gallon of water. They'll come out soft and spotless. *Note*: This only works on water-based paints, not oil-based products.

Here's to YOU!

Yikes! You've just discovered that a skunk has moved into your garden shed, and your mind is racing. How can you get rid of the critter without setting off his, um, aromatic alarm system? Just hightail it down to your local supermarket, head straight to the Laundry & Cleaning Products aisle, and find the strongest, most perfumed-smelling room deodorizers they've got. Take a few of them home and hang them in and around the invaded area (while your new tenant is out foraging for dinner, of course!). There's nothing most skunks hate more than the scent of perfume. So unless your little rascal varies from the norm, he'll clear out fast.

Preserve delicate flowers and foliage. Are you getting ready to dry some lacy or fine-textured plants like ferns, statice, and baby's breath? Then use this simple routine, which works better on those frothy types than any other technique I've tried: Fill a large plastic container with fabric softener (either a new food-storage container, or a tub that held ice cream, yogurt, or whipped topping will work). Then snap on the lid and cut a dozen or so quarter-inch Xs in it, using a box cutter or the tip of a sharp knife. Insert a stem into each X, making sure it reaches well into the softener. Let the arrangement sit for three or four weeks until the plant parts are thoroughly dried. Then pull them out and have fun creating long-lasting works of floral art.

Soften up your jeans. You got some new pants to wear when you work in your yard, but the dang things are so stiff, you can hardly bend your knees—much less get down on them to weed your garden. Well, here's a fast way to break in those dungarees (as Grandma Putt used to call them). Just fill your washing machine with water, add 1 capful of fabric softener, and soak those dungarees overnight. In the morning, run them through the rinse cycle, then pop them in the dryer. They'll come out feeling soft, comfortable, and ready for action.

 # Laundry Detergent

Fire fairy ring. This is a fungal disease that leaves your lawn littered with unsightly circles of mushrooms or puffballs. Fortunately, the cure is as close as the Laundry & Cleaning Products aisle at your local supermarket (or even your own laundry room). First, sprinkle dry, mild laundry soap on the affected area, and water it in well. Then mix 1 cup each of ammonia, baby shampoo, and antiseptic mouthwash in a 20 gallon hose-end sprayer, and apply it to the point of runoff. Those 'shrooms will be history! *Note:* Choose a mild laundry soap, such as Ivory Snow®, and use 1 cup for every 2,500 square feet of affected lawn area. Don't use more than the recipe calls for—it will be no more effective at solving the problem, and it could damage your grass. (That rule goes for all of the tips, tricks, and tonics in this book.)

Beef up your lawn fertilizer. When you feed your lawn, add 1 cup of dry, mild laundry soap and 3 pounds of Epsom salts per 50-pound bag of natural/organic lawn food. Apply the mix at half of the recommended rate with either a broadcast spreader or a drop spreader. *Note:* If you use a synthetic/chemical fertilizer, spread the soap and Epsom salts mixture first, then clean your spreader and apply the food. Otherwise, an additive in the fertilizer will react with the Epsom salts and make a gooey mess.

Wash your hands. When messy outdoor chores leave you with greasy, grimy hands, reach for the laundry detergent instead of hand soap. (Either dry or liquid detergent will do the trick.) Detergent will cut through that grease and grime better than hand soap will.

Make white wicker sparkle. If you're a fan of this classic, all-American furniture, do what my Grandma Putt did with the wicker treasures on her porch: Dust them on a regular basis, and each spring and fall, give each piece a deep-cleaning. Her formula still works as well as ever. Here's all you need to do: Put about 1 tablespoon of mild laundry soap in 4 cups of water, and mix until it's frothy. Apply the suds to the furniture with a soft cloth, working one area at a time. Wipe each piece with a clean, damp cloth, and your wicker will stay as dazzling white as new-fallen snow!

Round & Round Round & Round

When you buy a bottle of liquid laundry detergent, bleach, or fabric softener, you get a lot more than a useful washday product. You also get one of the handiest outdoor helpers you could ask for: a big, sturdy plastic bottle. Here are some of the ways I put them to work in my yard and garden—and you can, too:

Drip irrigation system. Poke small holes in the bottoms and sides of bottles, bury them in the soil at strategic spots in your garden, and fill them with water. The moisture will flow out at a slow, steady rate, directly to your plants' roots.

Garden-tool caddy. Make a big hole in a giant bottle on the side opposite the handle. Then insert your trowel, pruning shears, and other small hand tools through the hole.

Paint bucket. Just cut a big hole in the side opposite the handle. You'll have a pail that's easy—and comfortable—to hold with one hand as you paint with the other.

Plant labels. Cut the sides of white or yellow bottles into strips, write on them with an indelible marker, and shove the strips into the soil next to the appropriate plants.

Scoop. Cut diagonally across the bottom, screw the top back on, and use it to scoop up sand, fertilizer, compost, cat litter, or just about any other nonedible substance.

Soil sifter. Slice the bottom off diagonally, as you would to make a scoop (above), but don't replace the top. Then cut a piece of $1/4$-inch hardware cloth that's just big enough to fit inside the bottle, and insert it so that it rests just above the handle hole. When you scoop up soil, it'll sift out through the narrow opening, and the wire mesh will snag any debris.

Watering can. Drill a dozen or more holes in the cap of a giant bottle. Fill the bottle with water, and screw the top back on. To water your plants, flip the bottle upside down, and let the H_2O flow!

Maintain vinyl and aluminum siding. These low-maintenance materials may not need to be painted, as wood siding does, but they still need a little regular TLC to keep them sparkling clean. Here's my method: Once a year, give the walls of your house a good, strong spray from a garden hose. Attack any spots with a scrub brush and a solution of ¼ cup of laundry detergent (either dry or liquid) per 2 gallons of water. Rinse with clear water, and let the siding dry naturally.

Plastic Laundry Baskets

Keep your flower beds beautiful. There's nothing more cheerful than a bed full of spring bulbs—that is, until the flowers fade and the foliage starts withering. You can't whack those leaves off, or you'll deprive the bulbs of the food they need to fuel next year's big show. Instead, plant your bulbs in plastic laundry baskets sunk into your planting bed. Then when the blooms go bust, pull up the baskets, whisk them off to a spot where the foliage can die down in private (maybe behind the tool shed or garage), and fill the vacant space with annuals. Come fall, sink the bulb-filled baskets back into the garden.

As for the planting procedure, it's simple. After checking the proper planting depth for your bulbs (the plant label or catalog description will tell you this), fill the basket with enough garden soil to reach the target level. Then set in the bulbs as you would in open ground, and fill the basket to the top with more soil. (Tuck the plant label in the basket so you'll know where to replant it in the fall.) Dig a hole about an inch deeper than the basket, lower the container into the hole, fill in around the basket with more soil, and water the whole thing. You're good to go!

Save your greens. In the late spring and early summer, cool-weather crops like lettuce and spinach respond to the heat by bolting. That is, they grow tall and leggy, blossom, and go to seed. In the process, the leaves become bitter, tough, and less than tasty (to say the least). Unfortunately, there's nothing you can do to prevent bolting, but you can delay it for  a little while. When the temperatures start climbing into the 80s, just set plastic laundry baskets, bottom side up, over your greens, and set some stones on top of them to keep the baskets from blowing away. This "awning" will cool and shade the plants underneath, and add a week or so to your good-eatin' time.

Harvest your crops—neatly. Nothing tastes better than your own homegrown vegetables, but washing those tasty treasures in your kitchen sink can be a dirty business. So do what I do: Whenever you go out to the garden to harvest your edibles (especially root crops), take along a plastic laundry basket. When you've filled it up, rinse off your veggies outside with the garden hose. Then either let the water flow out through the vents, or speed up the process by shaking the basket gently to remove the water. The dirt (and maybe some bugs) will stay outside, where it belongs.

Stash your hose. A garden hose may look neat and tidy hanging on a wall-mounted rack. But lugging a wet, dirty rubber tube over to the wall and hanging it up can be a messy process. Here's a cleaner idea: Store your coiled hose in a round, plastic laundry basket. Whatever you're wearing will stand a better chance of staying mud-free if you can simply drop the hose into the basket rather than wrestling around trying to hang it up.

Personal Care & Oral Hygiene

ANTISEPTIC MOUTHWASH

BABY OIL & BABY POWDER

BABY SHAMPOO & BABY WIPES

COTTON BALLS

DENTAL FLOSS

DENTURE-CLEANING TABLETS

GROOMING AIDS

HAIR CONDITIONER & HAIR SPRAY

PANTY HOSE

SOAP

TOOTHBRUSHES & TOOTHPASTE

Antiseptic Mouthwash

Jump-start sod "bandages." Getting ready to patch bare spots in your lawn with chunks of sod? If so, then this prescription is just what the doctor ordered: In a large bucket, mix 1 can of beer, $1/2$ cup of Epsom salts, and 1 cup each of antiseptic mouthwash, dishwashing liquid, and ammonia. Pour the solution into a 20 gallon hose-end sprayer, and apply it to your lawn-repair site to the point of runoff. Wait two weeks, then administer another dose. Before you know it, your lawn will be a seamless field of green again. *Note:* Anytime a recipe calls for dishwashing liquid, do not use detergent or any product that contains antibacterial agents.

Serve your lawn a cocktail. Make that *two* cocktails. In late May and again in late June, thoroughly mix 1 cup of antiseptic mouthwash, 1 cup of Epsom salts, 1 cup of dishwashing liquid, and 1 cup of ammonia in a bucket and pour this into a 20 gallon hose-end sprayer. Overspray your grass to the point of runoff, and drink to the health of your turf! (This recipe makes enough for 2,500 square feet of lawn area.) *Note:* Anytime a recipe calls for dishwashing liquid, do not use detergent or any product that contains antibacterial agents.

Give your plants a bedtime bath. Lawns and gardens that go to bed clean in the fall are more likely to wake up healthy and rarin' to grow in the spring. So before the temperature goes below 50°F, lull your whole green scene to sleep with this gentle routine: In a bucket, mix 1 cup each of antiseptic mouthwash, baby shampoo, chamomile tea, and Tobacco Tea (see Lawn Stress-Reliever Tonic, on page 228). Pour 2 cups of the mixture into a 20 gallon hose-end sprayer, filling the balance of the sprayer jar with warm water. Overspray your lawn and all the plants in your yard to the point of runoff, and they'll be able to fend off any wintertime woes.

Send summer patch packin'. Summer patch is caused by a fungus that aggressively attacks grass during periods of hot, dry weather from late spring to late summer. The most common victims are bluegrass and fine fescues that are heat-stressed, mowed too short, or growing in compacted soil. In the early stages, you'll see scattered, elongated patches that start out light green, then quickly turn to a straw-brown color. That's the time to strike—fast and

MARVELOUS MIX

Lawn Stress-Reliever Tonic

For those of you who live in the Sunbelt states, winter is feeding time for your lawn. First, apply any premium dry lawn food at half of the recommended rate, adding 1 pound of Epsom salts to each 25 pounds of lawn food. (If you're using a synthetic fertilizer, rather than a natural/organic type, spread the lawn food and the salts separately.) Then follow up with this tonic to keep your lawn relaxed through the winter months.

> 1 cup of antiseptic mouthwash
> 1 cup of baby shampoo
> 1 cup of tobacco tea*
> 3/4 cup of weak tea water**
> 1/4 cup of ammonia

Mix these ingredients in a 20 gallon hose-end sprayer, and apply the solution to your lawn once a month to the point of runoff.

*To make tobacco tea, put half a handful of chewing tobacco in an old nylon stocking and soak it in a gallon of hot water until the mixture is dark brown.

**Soak a used tea bag and 1 teaspoon of dishwashing liquid in a gallon of water until the mix is light brown. *Note:* Anytime a recipe calls for dishwashing liquid, do not use detergent or any product that contains antibacterial agents.

hard. Here's your battle plan: In a large bucket, mix 3 tablespoons of saltpeter and 1 cup each of antiseptic mouthwash, ammonia, dishwashing liquid, and Tobacco Tea (see Lawn Stress-Reliever Tonic, on the opposite page). Pour the solution into a 20 gallon hose-end sprayer, and apply it to your lawn to the point of runoff every three weeks during the growing season. *Note:* Anytime a recipe calls for dishwashing liquid, do not use detergent or any product that contains antibacterial agents.

Fend off root rot. Many kinds of fungi can turn the roots of flower or vegetable plants into mushy messes. But you can protect your garden treasures with this simple routine: Keep the soil well stocked with organic matter to ensure good drainage, and douse your plants' root zones in the early spring with a solution of $1/2$ cup of antiseptic mouthwash and $1/2$ cup of baby shampoo per 2 gallons of warm water.

Keep plant diseases from spreading. Foul fungi and bad bacteria can move from sick plants to healthy ones by way of gardening tools. So when you're working with ailing flowers, vegetables, trees, or shrubs, play it safe: Disinfect your tools between cuts by wiping them down with a solution made from 1 part antiseptic mouthwash to 3 parts water.

If you're battling an especially rampant disease—or you simply don't want to take any chances—here's one more safety precaution: When your chores are done, mix 1 cup of antiseptic mouthwash per gallon of water in a bucket, and soak your tools (including shovels and trowels) in the solution for an hour. Then rinse the gear with clear water and dry it thoroughly.

Seal pruning cuts. Whenever you're pruning either sick *or* healthy trees and shrubs, paint all the large wounds with a mixture of $1/2$ cup each of antiseptic mouthwash and interior latex paint, and 1 teaspoon of cayenne pepper. This will work like a bandage to keep germs and pests from moving in.

Do Tell!

At the 1876 Philadelphia Medical Congress, Sir Joseph Lister presented his theory that airborne germs were responsible for the high postoperative death rate throughout the world (in many hospitals, it was as high as 90 percent!). His speech received a lukewarm reception, but at least one doctor in the audience, Joseph Lawrence of St. Louis, took the message to heart. Back home in his laboratory, he developed an antibacterial liquid, which was manufactured by the Lambert Pharmacal Company (later to become pharmaceutical superstar Warner-Lambert). In honor of Sir Joseph—and to give the product an appropriately antiseptic image—they named it (you guessed it) Listerine®.

Stop woody-plant ailments in their tracks. Whenever you're pruning tissue from a diseased tree or shrub, kill any lingering germs with this routine: In a bucket, mix 1/4 cup each of antiseptic mouthwash, ammonia, and dishwashing liquid with 1 gallon of warm water. Pour the solution into a handheld sprayer, and drench all the places where you've pruned your woody plants. And don't forget to wipe your pruning tools after each cut with the mouthwash solution described on page 229 (see "Keep plant diseases from spreading"). *Note:* Anytime a recipe calls for dishwashing liquid, do not use detergent or any product that contains antibacterial agents.

Get rid of moss in your lawn. For a while, anyway. Why do I say that? Because moss thrives in exactly the conditions turfgrass hates—namely, damp, shady spots with acidic soil. To eliminate the soft, cushiony stuff permanently, you'll need to raise the pH of your soil to neutral or slightly above, improve drainage to the level of excellence, and let in more sunshine. The good news is that you can bid moss a short-term farewell with this timely tonic. Mix 1 cup of antiseptic mouthwash, 1 cup of chamomile tea, and 1 cup of Murphy® Oil Soap in a bucket, pour the mix into a 20 gallon hose-end sprayer, and apply to your lawn to the point of runoff every two weeks until the moss is history.

Unclog your hose-end sprayer. Attention, garden-tonic users! If your water has a high concentration of chlorine, you should be aware that it can make baby shampoo (or any other kind of shampoo) foam up like a bubble bath—clogging the sprayer mechanism in the process. If this happens to you, just remove the tonic from the jar, mix a tablespoon or so of antiseptic mouthwash with enough water to fill the container, and run this solution through the sprayer to cut the foaming action. Then bingo—you're back in business!

Keep cut flowers looking lovely longer. There's nothing more frustrating than cutting armfuls of flowers from your garden, arranging them just so in your favorite vases—then watching them go limp and lifeless. Unfortunately, nothing can make them last forever; but you can prolong the show by adding 1/2 teaspoon of antiseptic mouthwash per quart of water in each container.

De-skunk your dog. When Fido tangles with the wrong end of Pepe le Pew, don't panic. Just saturate your pal with full-strength mouthwash, carefully avoiding his eyes and ears. Follow up by washing him with a good dog shampoo, and rinse thoroughly. (If he's less than a year old—or less than 18 months for a giant breed like a Great Dane or St. Bernard—use a shampoo that's specially made for puppies.)

If you or your youngsters get up close and personal with a skunk, use that same remedy; it works just as well on humans as it does on pets. As for your clothes, take them to the local Laundromat and toss them into the washer with an alkaline laundry detergent.

Treat cuts and scrapes. Every gardener picks up his or her fair share of "owies" during the growing season—and in the wintertime, too. When you wind up on the casualty list and you're fresh out of antiseptic cream, do what I do: Pour a little antiseptic mouthwash over your wounds. It kills germs on your skin just as well as it does in your mouth.

Relieve poison ivy woes. When that dreaded rash has you scratchin' up a storm, douse the affected areas with antiseptic mouthwash, and rub it in well with a washcloth or sponge. But be forewarned: This treatment *will* sting, but it should stop the itch immediately.

Here's to
YOU!

What would the good old summertime be without mosquitoes? A whole lot more comfortable—that's what! Unfortunately, I don't know any way to guarantee that you'll never be bitten by one of these vile vampires. But, as you've seen throughout this book, I know tons of terrific tricks for easing the pain and itch that follow. And here are three more, straight from the Personal Care & Oral Hygiene aisle:

✴ Moisten a tissue with antiseptic mouthwash, hold it on the bite for about 15 seconds, and you'll kiss that itch goodbye.

✴ Gently wipe a little toothpaste onto each bite. You'll feel relief in a hurry.

✴ Rub a wet bar of soap directly on the spot. The itch will vanish quickly, and the swelling will soon disappear, too.

Baby Oil

Repel corn earworms. If you've ever grown corn, you know the damage these ugly rascals can do to your crop. But there's a simple way to make sure you keep all that sweet, golden goodness for yourself—and the guests at your barbecues, of course! Simply apply a drop or two of baby oil to the tip of each ear when the silks begin to brown. (I use a medicine dropper, a.k.a. eyedropper, for this job.) Repeat the procedure every five or six days, for a total of three applications per season. Not only will this keep the worms away, but it will also lessen your workload at harvest time because when you shuck the corn, most of the silk will come off with the husk.

Say "Gno!" to gnats. Tired of waving off clouds of no-see-ums every time you head outdoors to work or play? Well, stop waving and wipe a coat of baby oil onto your exposed skin. It forms a protective barrier against the minute monsters. Oh, yes—there is one little catch to this terrific trick: You need to stay out of the sun, or the oil will cause your skin to burn.

Say a louder "No!" to mosquitoes. Does your yard or driveway have low spots where water collects after a rain? Stop those puddles from becoming mosquito maternity wards by pouring a little baby oil into each one. (A tablespoon to half a cup will do the trick, depending on the size of the pool.) The oil will spread across the surface and smother any eggs or larvae.

De-sap your tools. Baby oil is perfect for removing tree sap from pruning shears, saws, and loppers. Wipe a little oil onto the blades with a soft cloth. It'll dissolve the gunk, so you can wipe the metal clean with a second cloth.

MARVELOUS MiX

Sweet & Soothing Sunburn Bath

The next time a day of gardening (or a day at the beach) leaves you feeling like your skin's on fire, beat the heat with this gentle treat.

1 cup of baby oil
$1/2$ cup of liquid hand soap
$1/2$ cup of honey
1 tbsp. of pure vanilla extract (not artificial)

Mix the ingredients together in a bowl, and pour the mixture into a bottle with a tight stopper. At bath time, pour $1/4$ cup of the mixture under running water. Then ease into the tub and feel the pain fade away.

Lubricate pruning shears. Fresh out of your usual lubricating oil? Use a few drops of baby oil instead. Those pruners will be ready to cut up a storm again.

Clean your hands. Whether your paws are sporting a coat of sap from your evergreen branches or grease from your car, reach for the baby oil. Massage it into your skin, wash with soap and water, and you're back in business.

Baby your leather upholstery. Does your car have genuine leather seat covers? If so, you can keep them as soft as a baby's bottom by rubbing them down every month or so with—you guessed it—baby oil. Use a soft, all-cotton cloth to apply a very thin coat, then buff with a second cloth of the same kind. (Of course, this trick works just as well indoors on leather-covered furniture.) Whatever you do, don't go on the theory that more is better, because the excess will come off on your clothes later.

Remove latex paint from your skin. You've spent all day painting your garden fence, and it looks terrific. Unfortunately, there's almost as much paint on your hands and face as there is on the fence. Well, we can fix *that* in a hurry. First, rub a little baby oil into your newly decorated skin, and follow up by washing with soap and hot water. The oil will help that paint slide right off.

Hide scratches on plastic. Has the lens on your car's gas gauge picked up a few scrapes? Or maybe your cold frame's cover has gotten a few minor wounds. That plastic will look as clean and clear as new if you rub over the marks with a drop or two of baby oil on a soft cotton cloth.

Here's to
YOU!

Have you ever noticed that there always seem to be outdoor chores to do on days when you'd rather be huddled in front of either a fireplace or an air conditioner (or maybe floating on your back in a swimming pool)? Well, I don't know any way to change that—short of hiring someone to do all your yard and garden work. But I *do* know how a couple of common baby-care products can help make you more comfortable in the not-so-great outdoors. Here's the deal:

* When the temperature plummets, you have a job to do, and you can't do it with gloves on, massage your hands with baby oil. It'll close up the pores and help prevent damage from the frigid air.

* In steamy weather, before you head out to mow the lawn or dig in the garden, rub some baby powder on your hands. It'll absorb excess perspiration and prevent blisters.

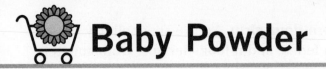

Baby Powder

Discourage ants. It's true that these hardworking insects perform a lot of good deeds around the yard and garden. But that doesn't mean you have to invite them to your barbecues and other outdoor events. To keep them from crashing the party, simply sprinkle a line of baby powder around the off-limits area. The tiny troublemakers won't cross the border.

Keep bulbs safe in their beds. When you spend hours preparing for your big flower extravaganza, the last thing you want is to have the stars of the show rot before the curtain goes up—or disappear into the mouths of a bunch of hungry critters. So don't take any chances: Before you tuck spring- or summer-flowering bulbs into the ground, dust them with medicated baby powder. It'll fend off foul fungi *and* four-footed felons.

Here's to YOU!

It's happened again. Modern medical science has confirmed one more of Grandma Putt's firmly held convictions: that the road to good health starts with a sound night's sleep. In fact, researchers at Cornell University have found that getting too little sleep may actually shorten your life span by as much as 8 to 10 years. But on hot, humid summer nights, if you don't have an air conditioner, drifting off to dreamland isn't all that easy. What to do? Just sprinkle a little baby powder between the sheets to absorb moisture and help you feel cooler. Before you know it, you'll be sleeping like, well, a baby.

Safeguard bulbs in winter storage. Your garden isn't the only place where bulbs are vulnerable. Tender bulbs and their close kin, corms and tubers, can easily fall victim to rot indoors, as well. So when you dig up dahlias, gladiolus, cannas, and other warmth-craving customers, be sure to give them a dose of medicated baby powder, too.

Close the deer diner. Has your yard become *the* bistro of choice for Bambi and his buddies? Well, there are a whole lot of deterrents you could try, but one that works for a lot of folks is this simple old-time trick: Sprinkle baby powder on rags, and hang them from your garden fence, or on the branches of trees and shrubs. And be sure to use the fragrance-protection plan described on page 260 (see "Save That Scent!").

Make rubber gloves glide on. These sturdy, waterproof wonders aren't just good for washing dishes—they come in mighty handy for outdoor chores, too. But sometimes, getting them onto your hands can take almost as much time as the job you need to do. That is, unless you sprinkle a bit of baby powder inside the gloves first. Then they'll slide right onto your paws with no muss and no fuss.

Remove grease stains from clothing. One minute you're turning a hamburger on the grill, and the next minute—splat! You've got a big, greasy blotch on the front of your shirt. Now what? First, don't panic. Second, reach for the baby powder (after you've changed your shirt, of course). Dab the powder onto the spot with a powder puff or cotton pad, rub it in well, and then brush off any excess. Repeat the procedure until the stain is history. Then go out and enjoy your barbecue!

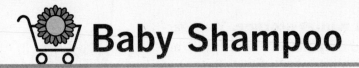

Baby Shampoo

Supercharge flower and vegetables seeds. When the calendar and the soil temperature both say "It's planting time!", it's all but impossible not to run out to the garden and start planting your seeds. But they'll germinate sooner and perform better if you can be patient long enough to give them a day's worth of TLC. Here's all you need to do: Mix 1 teaspoon of baby shampoo and 1 teaspoon of Epsom salts in 1 quart of weak tea water (see Lawn Stress-Reliever Tonic, on page 228). Bundle up your seeds in cheesecloth, or an old panty hose toe (one kind of seed per bundle, unless you're aimin' for a casual mix). Drop the bundles into the liquid, and put the container in the refrigerator to soak for 24 hours. Then spread the seeds on paper towels to dry, and plant them according to the directions on the packets they came in. Your flowers, herbs, and vegetables will all thank you by growing strong, beautiful, and (in some cases) tasty, too!

Supercharge grass seed. If your spring-planting project is a new (or renovated) lawn, this is the formula to use. In a large container, mix 1/4 cup of baby shampoo and 1 tablespoon of Epsom salts in 1 gallon of weak tea water (see Lawn Stress-Reliever Tonic, on page 228). Drop in your grass seed, put the mixture into the refrigerator, and leave it there for 24 hours. Strain out the seed, spread it out on your driveway to dry (on a non-windy day, of course!), and sow it in the usual way. The result: almost 100 percent germination every time—guaranteed.

Energize your new lawn. After you've sown grass seed and spread mulch over the top of the area, follow up with this super solution: Mix 1 cup of baby shampoo, 1 cup of beer, and 4 tablespoons of instant tea granules in a 20 gallon hose-end sprayer. Lightly apply the mixture to the mulch (do *not* apply it to the point of runoff). Then stand by with your mower, because your baby turf will be all grown up before you know it!

Cure mildew in your lawn. Flowering plants are not mildew's only victims. The powdery type can also strike shady parts of a lawn during periods of high humidity and temperatures between 60° and 72°F. Bluegrass is most susceptible, but any grass that's growing in a shaded area (like the north or east side of your house or garage) is a high-risk target. You'll know trouble has arrived if you see tiny patches of white to light gray fungus on the grass blades. It's easy to get rid of the stuff, but you need to act fast. Here's how: Mix 1 cup of baby shampoo, 1 cup of hydrogen peroxide, and 4 tablespoons of

MARVELOUS MIX

Bug-Off Bulb Bath

Before you plant either spring- or summer-blooming bulbs, treat them to this refreshing spa routine. It'll help fend off disease germs, as well as bulb mites and other pesky pests.

> 2 tsp. of baby shampoo
> 1 tsp. of antiseptic mouthwash
> 1/4 tsp. of instant tea granules
> 2 gallons of hot water (120°F)

Mix these ingredients in a bucket, drop in your bulbs, and let them soak for 2 to 3 hours (longer for larger bulbs). Don't peel off the papery skins, because the bulbs use them as a defense against pests. Plant the bulbs immediately after removing them from the bucket—otherwise, rot could set in.

instant tea granules in a 20 gallon hose-end sprayer, filling the balance of the sprayer jar with water. Spray the affected area every week to 10 days, and your lawn will soon be spotless once more!

Put your flower beds to bed. When it's time to close up shop for the season, cover the soil in each bed with finely mowed grass clippings. Then mix 1 cup of baby shampoo, 1 can of regular cola (not diet), $1/2$ cup of ammonia, and 2 tablespoons of instant tea granules in a 20 gallon hose-end sprayer, and saturate the grass-clipping blanket. All that's left is to wish your flowers sweet dreams as you head inside to relax by the fire!

Give tender bulbs a bedtime bath. Bulbs that don't get a thorough cleaning before they go into winter storage are sitting ducks for pests and disease germs. So each fall, when you dig up your dahlias, cannas, gladiolus, and other tender bulbs, corms, and tubers, wash them in a solution of 2 tablespoons of baby shampoo and 1 teaspoon of hydrogen peroxide mixed in a quart of warm water. Just make sure you dry the bulbs thoroughly when you're finished—otherwise, rot could sneak in over the winter, and all of your hard work will have been in vain!

Repel vegetable-garden villains. Garden webworms, tomato hornworms, asparagus beetles, and a whole lot of other bad bugs flee from this tangy tonic. To make it, gather 1 cup of pot marigold *(Calendula officinalis)* leaves and flowers (or buy them at your supermarket's florist section). Mash the plant parts in a bowl, mix them with 2 cups of water, and let the slurry marinate for 24 hours. Strain it through cheesecloth, stir in $1^{1}/2$ quarts of water, and add $1/4$ teaspoon of baby shampoo. Pour the solution into a handheld sprayer bottle, and spray your vulnerable plants from top to bottom. Reapply the tonic after every rain. Destructive insects will stay away in droves!

Out, Out, Dang Spot!

When nature calls, dogs answer (after all, a smooth, green lawn is *our* goal, not theirs). The spots that occur are simply the result of too much of a good thing—namely, nitrogen and salts. The same brown, burned-looking patches would occur if you spilled fertilizer on the grass. If the deed has just been done, it's a snap to head off damage: Just turn on the hose, and flush the site thoroughly. After more than a day or so, though, follow this routine:

1. Lightly sprinkle gypsum over and around each spot to dissolve the accumulated salts.

2. Pour 1 cup of baby shampoo into a 20 gallon hose-end sprayer, and overspray the lawn to the point of runoff.

3. One week later, overspray the turf with my Lawn Stress-Reliever Tonic (see page 228).

Prevent mildew on your flowers. Garden phlox *(Phlox paniculata)* is known far and wide as a world-class mildew magnet. But both downy and powdery mildew can also plague roses and a great many annuals and perennials, including asters, black-eyed Susans, and mums. To keep your plants free of both of these foul fungal diseases, spray them every week in the spring with a mixture of 1 tablespoon of hydrogen peroxide, 1 tablespoon of baby shampoo, 1 teaspoon of instant tea granules, and 2 cups of water in a handheld sprayer bottle.

Refresh a thirsty lawn. When your grass is dying for a drink, it'll speak up loud and clear! Well, not in English, of course. Like all plants, grass communicates in sign language. When you walk across your lawn and the grass doesn't spring right back up, it's time to turn on the sprinklers or haul out the hose. But before you do that, put on your

Baby Shampoo

spiked golf shoes or a pair of aerating lawn sandals, and take a stroll around your yard. Follow up by filling a 20 gallon hose-end sprayer with 1 can of beer, 1 cup of baby shampoo, and $\frac{1}{2}$ cup each of ammonia and weak tea water (see Lawn Stress-Reliever Tonic, on page 228). Spray your grass to the point of runoff—and *then* give it a long, slow drink of H_2O.

Deliver post-mowing TLC. No matter what kind of mower you use, or how carefully you mow, having that little bit taken off the top is a shock to your grass. To help it recover, apply this gentle, effective elixir once a month: Mix 1 cup each of baby shampoo, ammonia, and weak tea in a 20 gallon hose-end sprayer, filling the balance of the sprayer jar with warm water. Then just after you mow your lawn, apply the solution to the point of runoff.

 # Baby Wipes

Make scale scram. And mealybugs, too! Almost no plant is off-limits to these sap-sucking pests, but you don't have to put up with their shenanigans. You can bid them goodbye with a baby wipe. Simply rub it over the stems and both sides of each leaf, and presto—happy ending to the story!

Pretreat minor wounds. If you're anything like me—and like every other gardener I know—you're forever picking up scrapes and scratches as you work among your plants. So do what I do: Stash a box of baby wipes in your garden tool bag. Then when you run into a prickly thorn or a wayward twig, clean the scene of the "crime" with a wipe. When you get indoors, follow up with a more thorough cleaning, and apply your favorite antiseptic product.

Make mildew take a powder. Have your flowering plants just come down with a case of powdery mildew? Well, I have good news for you: In the early stages, those fuzzy, gray spots are a snap to remove. Just wipe them away with a homemade baby wipe (see page 351 for directions).

Clean your lawn mower. When that old workhorse (or brand new supertool) winds up wearing grease, oil, or some kind of mystery gunk, reach for the baby wipes. They'll clear the mess away without harming the paint job. Wipes can work this same magic on cars, bikes, boats, and any other vehicles in your life.

Degrease your hands. You say your machinery is as clean as a whistle, but your hands are coated in oily crud? No problem! A few swipes with a baby wipe will have your skin spotless again. In fact, in my humble opinion, no garage, workshop, garden shed, or automobile glove compartment should be without a box of these moist marvels.

Say "No" to rust. To keep the nasty stuff at bay, periodically rub a wipe over the metal parts of your shovels, trowels, rakes, and metal tools. Besides fending off rust, this will also keep them clean and in better working order.

Keep dirt in its place. Namely, in your yard—not in your house. There's a super-simple way to pull off this feat. Just keep a box of baby wipes by the back door and ask everybody to clean up before stepping inside.

Soothe sunburn. When you linger too long in the yard—or anyplace else where Ol' Sol's rays are beating down—a baby wipe is a short-term soother. Simply slide it gently over your stricken skin. It'll bring blessed short-term relief until you can use one of the longer-lasting remedies you'll find throughout this book.

Round & Round
Round & Round

The sturdy plastic boxes that hold baby wipes can perform almost as many jobs as the wipes themselves—indoors or out. Just take a gander at these possibilities:

Building blocks. Just collect 'em and let the kids build towers, bridges, castles, and even whole towns. They're sturdy and waterproof, and with their rounded corners, they're safe for even tiny tykes to play with.

Clutter busters. Use them as mini storage chests for all kinds of tiny odds and ends, such as hobby, craft, and sewing supplies; spare electrical parts; and small office gear.

First-aid kits. Fill 'em up with essentials like bandages and antiseptic ointment, and keep them in your car, workshop, garden shed, or kitchen—anyplace accidents tend to happen.

Pitching-practice targets. Stack 'em up outdoors, wind up, and let 'er rip. Three strikes and you win!

Seed-starting trays. Sow your seeds in individual containers with drainage holes, and set two planting pots into each box.

Seed-storage containers. When you don't use up all the seeds in a packet, or if you save seeds from your flowers or plants, stash them in baby wipe boxes. In each box, mix 1 part seed to 1 part powdered milk, snap the lid closed tightly, and stash them in the refrigerator (not the freezer). The milk—and the airtight container—will keep the seeds dry and fresh all winter long.

Snail and slug traps. Sink the boxes in the soil (minus the lids, of course), leaving about $1/8$ inch sticking up above the surface. Then pour in your bait of choice (you'll find some dandy ones throughout this book). The slimers will belly up to the bar, fall in, and die happy.

Traveling trash can. Tuck a wipes box under the seat of your car, or in your bicycle saddlebags. It's sturdier than a bag, and when you have anything, um, fragrant to dispose of, you can snap the lid closed to contain the odor.

Cotton Balls

Keep houseplants feline-free. When your cats nibble on the leaves of your indoor greenery, it can be a lot more than a nuisance—it can be catastrophic for the kitties. That's because many kinds of plants are highly toxic to pets. So play it safe. Saturate some cotton balls with lemon-oil furniture polish, and set them on top of the soil in the pots. Use one ball for a small to medium-sized plant, and two or three for big ones. Fluffy and Puffy will do their nibbling elsewhere.

Discourage deer. As you've noticed, I've included a whole lot of deer-deterring tips in this book, and there's a good reason: Deer quickly get used to anything in their day-to-day environment that doesn't eat them up. So when you're trying to discourage them from devouring your lovely landscape, you need to vary your tactics frequently. Here's another trick to tuck into your arsenal: Saturate cotton balls with peppermint oil, stuff them into old panty hose feet, and hang them from your garden fence, or the branches of trees and shrubs. Half a dozen balls per foot should do the trick. Just be sure to give each pouch a "garage" like the one described on page 260 (see "Save That Scent!").

Kill deer ticks. If Lyme disease is a problem in your area (its range is expanding daily), you no doubt know that deer mice carry the small ticks that spread the ailment. What you may not know is that those little rodents can help you wipe out the minute menaces—or at least reduce the population. All you need to do is soak cotton balls in a pet shampoo that contains permethrin, a potent flea- and tick-killer, and push them into an empty toilet-paper tube. When you've filled a half dozen tubes or so, set them out in brushy areas or other sheltered spots where deer mice are likely to find them. The mice will take the fluffy cotton home to line their nests, and the disease-spreading ticks will be history. *Note:* Unfortunately, this trick will not end your dog-tick problems—it works on deer ticks alone, because they're the only kind carried by deer mice.

Repel raccoons and squirrels. Are you going nuts trying to keep these furry felons from robbing your bird feeders? Well, here's some good news: Just like deer, 'coons and squirrels flee from minty aromas (at least most of the time). Prepare your cotton-ball-and-peppermint-oil deterrents as described on page 245 (see "Discourage deer") and hang them from your bird feeder, or anyplace else you don't want the rascals roaming.

Annihilate ants. You say you've tried every repellent in the book, and the little pests still refuse to take their appetites elsewhere? Then bite the bullet and send 'em to the big anthill in the sky. Mix 1 cup of borax, $2/3$ cup of sugar, and 1 cup of water in a bowl. Dip cotton balls into the solution, and set them at points along the ants' travel routes (but *only* in places where children or pets can't reach them). The tiny terrors will eat the poison, and that'll be all she wrote.

Do Tell!

Coming up in Chapter 9, we'll talk about a whole passel of supermarket products that grow on plants (namely fruits, nuts, and vegetables). But if you don't hail from Dixie, you may not remember that one product in the Personal Care & Oral Hygiene aisle also grows on plants. Cotton balls start life as beautiful white flowers on a cotton plant. Each flower blooms for just a day. Then as it withers, a cotton boll appears, chockfull of the fluffy white fibers.

Make hollow-stemmed cut flowers last longer. Tulips, daffodils, delphiniums, lupines, and all other flowers with hollow stems have one common (and annoying) trait: When you cut them and put them in a vase, they seem to go downhill at the speed of light. That's because air enters each stem as soon as it's cut, forming an air lock that prevents life-sustaining water from getting in. Fortunately, a simple conditioning routine can pick that lock. First, cut each stem at a roughly 45-degree angle, and remove any leaves that would be underwater in the vase (they attract bacteria). Turn the stem upside down, fill it with tepid water, and plug it with pieces of cotton ball to keep the liquid from flowing out. Then set the stem into a vase that's filled with fresh water and the floral preservative of your choice (you'll find many good ones throughout this book). Just one word of caution: The stems of daffodils exude a sap that's poisonous to other flowers, so always give your daffs their own private living quarters.

Save your rubber gloves. If you like to wear these sturdy hand covers when you work outdoors—and you have long, sharp fingernails—you've probably put holes in a *lot* of rubber fingers. And, unless I miss my guess, you're tired of constantly running out to buy new gloves. So try this trick: Before you put on your next pair, push a cotton ball (or a piece of one) onto each finger.

Dental Floss

Floss your sweet peas. Talk about bad timing! Your sweet pea seedlings are ready for a lightweight trellis, you're fresh out of string, and you don't have time to go out and get some. The simple solution: Use (unflavored) dental floss. It's not the cheapest way to support vines, but in a pinch, it'll do the job just fine. FYI: The waxed kind stands up best to the weather.

You can also tie a vine to a trellis with dental floss. The green, mint-flavored kind works especially well for this job because it blends right in with the foliage. Just be sure to leave plenty of slack in your knot, or the floss will slice right through your plant's tender stems.

Keep flowers upright in a vase. Here's the problem: The neck of your vase is just a tad too wide for the bouquet of flowers you have, so the stems flop toward the sides, leaving a gap in the middle of the arrangement. The simple solution: Use green, mint-flavored dental floss to tie the stems loosely together just under the flower heads. The stems will stay upright, but the display will still look full and lush.

How Dry They Are

Unwaxed, unflavored floss is perfect to use for an old-time drying technique called "leather britches," which is one of the easiest ways to preserve your homegrown produce. It works for just about any kind of vegetable or tree fruit, but I especially like to use it for green beans. Here's the simple four-step process:

Step 1. Pick a bucketful of young, tender snap beans (or buy them at the supermarket).

Step 2. Thread some dental floss through a darning or embroidery needle, and string the beans on it, in the same way you'd string cranberries and popcorn for a Christmas tree.

Step 3. Hang them in a shady spot to dry (a screened-in porch is perfect).

Step 4. In a day or so, or when the beans are about the consistency of a leather belt, cut them down and store them in a brown paper bag.

Create a *ristra*. Want to add a touch of Southwestern flair to your kitchen? All you need are dental floss and some red chili peppers with their stems intact. (If you don't grow your own peppers, you can probably find them in the produce section of your local supermarket.) Start by tying the stems of three peppers together with floss. Repeat until you've got as many trios as you'd like. Tie all the strings together to form a long line of peppers that you can twist or braid around each other. Then hang your masterpiece from a ceiling rafter or door frame. *Note:* Unless you live in a very dry climate, don't hang your ristra outdoors—the peppers will turn moldy in a flash.

Make an instant bird feeder. Just tie dental floss around a bagel or a donut, and hang it from a tree limb, deck railing, or trellis. You'll attract Carolina wrens, chickadees, titmice, and scads of other pretty (and melodious) songbirds.

Repair leather work gloves. I don't know about you, but once I've found a good pair of gardening gloves and broken 'em in thoroughly, they become almost like a member of the family—and there's no way I'm going to toss 'em out just because a seam comes loose. Instead, I just stitch up the damage with dental floss. It's much stronger than cotton thread and a whole lot easier to work with than leather lacing or nylon cord.

Denture-Cleaning Tablets

Clean a hummingbird feeder. For my money, there's almost nothing more fun than watching those tiny birds flit around a nectar feeder. And there's almost nothing *less* fun than cleaning the sticky thing. That is, unless you know this simple trick: Fill the tube with hot water, and drop in half of a denture-cleaning tablet. Wait 5 minutes or so, and rinse it out with clear water. Then fill 'er up with sugar water, and you're back in business!

Get gunk out of glass vases. We all know how crud collects in the bottoms of flower vases. Instead of trying to scrub it out with a brush, take a tip from the folks who make Waterford® crystal: Fill the vessel about halfway with water, and pop in two denture-cleaning tablets. Let it stand for an hour or two, and rinse. Presto—crystal-clear crystal! (Of course, this trick works just as well with cruets, decanters, and any other glass vessels where residue builds up.)

De-cloud glass. You say you found a vintage glass vase at a flea market, but it's cloudy inside *and* out? No problem! Just set it in a bucket of water, pop in two or three denture-cleaning tablets, and let it soak until the clouds drift by. (About 2 to 3 hours should do it.)

Wash super-grimy windows. Whether the offending surfaces are on your car or your house, denture-cleaning tablets can save the day. Just dissolve several tablets in a bucket of water, dip a soft cloth in the solution, and wipe the glass clean. Then rinse with clear water, and dry with a second cloth.

Make your hubcaps sparkle. Time to spiff up your lawn furniture for a backyard barbecue? Or maybe you're getting ready to drive your '57 Chevy in the Fourth of July parade. No matter what surface is adorned by chrome at your place, it's a snap to make it shine like a full moon. Just plop a denture-cleaning tablet into a glass of water, and use a soft cloth to wipe the fizzing solution onto the chrome. Rinse with clear water, buff to a shine, and you're good to go!

Here's to YOU!

Effervescent denture-cleaning tablets first hit the supermarket shelves in 1967, and it didn't take long for folks to discover that these fizzing marvels could do a whole lot more than just clean false teeth. Here are just some of the chores these bubbling powerhouses can perform at your place:

Clean a toilet bowl. Drop three tablets into the bowl, wait a minute or two, scrub, and flush your troubles away.

Clear a clogged sink. Plop several tablets into the drain, and let it sit overnight. In the morning, rinse with cold water.

Freshen up electric coffee and tea makers. Put a tablet in the filter basket (without the filter), add some hot water, and then run it through a cycle as you would a normal pot of coffee or tea. Follow up by "brewing" one or two pots of clear water before you make the real deal.

Remove stains from clothes and linens. Put the fabric in a container that's large enough to hold the soiled portion, fill it with warm water, and drop in two tablets. Leave the material in the solution for the time suggested on the package, then launder it as usual. *Caution:* Use this trick only on colorfast fabrics. To play it safe, test a hidden spot, like an inside seam, before you plunge full-speed ahead.

Polish diamonds. Soak them for 2 minutes or so in a glass of water with one tablet added to it. *Caution:* Don't even think of using this trick with pearls or opals—the cleanser will actually dissolve them.

Grooming Aids

Support your local vines. Clematis, morning glories, and other
flowering vines do a fine job of clinging to or twining
around their supports—once they get established, that is.
But in the beginning they need a little help holding on.
And you can give it to them with plastic hair clips. Just
point a stem in the direction you want it to go, and clip it
to the trellis. Check it out every day or two, and remove
the holder when the plant's got a grip of its own.

De-thorn your roses. June is bustin' out all over, and so are your
roses. You've cut oodles of them to fill vases all over your
house. There's just one problem: As you try to arrange your
flowers, the dang thorns keep gouging your skin. The simple solution: Trim the thorns off with nail clippers. (These
dandy grooming gadgets are also great for snipping off the
ultra-sharp tips of yucca leaves—thereby preventing cuts
and gashes when you're working in their planting beds.)

Deadhead in close quarters. If you've ever had to clip one over-
the-hill rose out of a cluster, or snip off dead fuchsia
blooms in a crowded pot, you'll love this idea: Do the job
with manicure scissors instead of full-sized models. They'll
give you pinpoint precision every time.

Find your tools. Lots of folks paint their tool handles bright orange
or neon yellow so the tools won't vanish among the grass.
But I know an easier—and fun—way to make your garden
gear stand out: Buy a bunch of colorful hair scrunchies at
the supermarket. (In case you don't have a teenage girl in
the house, these are the ruffly elastic fasteners used to hold
ponytails.) Slip them onto the handles of your trowels, hand
rakes, and anything else that tends to disappear just when
you need it most. As a bonus, when you're working in the

garden and decide that you want to get your hair out of your eyes *right now,* you can simply slide an "ID bracelet" off its handle and slip it onto your hair!

Thin seedlings in a flat. When it's time to weed out some of your baby plants, never pull them up—that's likely to damage the roots of the seedlings that you want to keep. Instead, clip the stems off at soil level, using manicure scissors. They'll fit into the tightest spots without disturbing any of the little green residents.

Identify pests. It's frustrating, all right: You know that some tiny terrors are lurking on the undersides of your plants' leaves, but you're not sure what kind. Well, here's an easy way to make a positive ID: Just glue or tape a small mirror on the end of a yardstick, and shove it under the foliage for a look-see.

Round & Round
Round & Round

When tent caterpillars set up camp in your trees, there's no chance of mistaken identity—their housing accommodations give them away every time. The dwelling is a gauzy tent where a whole crowd of the pests live together in early spring. They hunker down inside at night and during stormy weather; on balmy days, they venture out to devour huge numbers of leaves. Thanks to their group living quarters—and with the help of a retired round hairbrush—you can wipe out a whole colony of the vile villains in one fell swoop. You want to perform this maneuver in the early evening or on a cloudy day, when you know the creeps are at home. First, fasten the brush to a long pole. Twirl the brush around inside the tent until the gauzy stuff completely clings to your brush. Then scrape it off into a fire or a bucket of soapy water. Any worms that escape will be fair game for birds and other predators, of which they have many.

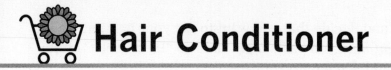

Hair Conditioner

Clean your houseplants. Is your dracaena looking a little drab? Your ficus fairly filthy? Just squeeze a small dab of hair conditioner onto a soft cotton cloth and wipe it gently onto the leaves. They'll shine like the morning sun!

Unstick your windows. Do you have to struggle every time you open your windows—or maybe the sliding doors to your deck? Lubricate their tracks with hair conditioner, and you'll struggle no more.

Silence a screeching faucet. Even outdoors, you don't want to have your ears assaulted every time you turn on the water. But it doesn't take a plumber to bring blessed relief. Just remove the handle and stem, coat both sets of metal threads with hair conditioner, and put the pieces back in place. Ahhh...quiet again!

Put the hush on hinges. You say your water faucets are just fine, but the door to your toolshed is squeaking like a penful of piglets? And what's more, you're fresh out of lubricating oil? Don't fret—and don't rush down to the hardware store. Instead, squirt a few drops of hair conditioner onto the moving parts. They'll open and close like a dream.

Rustproof your tools. Every gardener—and every do-it-yourselfer—knows that any job goes more smoothly when your tools are in tip-top shape. One way to keep them that way is to wipe them with hair conditioner every now and then. It'll keep the working parts clean, free of rust, and rarin' to go whenever you are.

Here's to YOU!

In the winter, before you take your dog for a walk on de-iced sidewalks, rub his paws with hair conditioner. It will help keep salt and other chemicals from irritating his foot-pads. When you get back inside, wash Fido's feet (including the hair between his toes) with dog shampoo and rinse thoroughly—before he has a chance to lick off any of the toxic chemicals.

Lubricate wheels. Whether the sticking or whining roll-arounds are on your wheelbarrow, your golf cart, or Junior's roller skates, simply rub a little hair conditioner on the axles. You'll be movin' right along again.

Winterize leather footgear. The same de-icing salts that wreak havoc on turfgrass can make a mess of leather, too. So before you head outdoors to work (or play) in messy winter weather, give your shoes or boots a good rubdown with hair conditioner. It'll protect them from the nasty chemicals and condition the leather at the same time.

Hair Spray

De-bug container plants. When aphids, mealy bugs, whiteflies, or spider mites are ganging up on your potted plants—indoors or out—get rid of the pesky pests with this simple trick: Grab a trash bag that's big enough to hold the plant and its pot. Then spray the inside of the bag (not the plant!) with aerosol hair spray. Put the victimized plant inside, fasten the bag tightly with a twist tie, and set it in a spot away from direct sun (otherwise, the heat will build up and kill the plant). Wait 24 hours, and remove the bag. Those little villains will be dead as doornails!

Get bugs on the fly. No matter what kinds of flying insects are buggin' you or your plants, a direct hit with aerosol hair spray will being 'em down fast. Just one word of caution: If you try this trick indoors, make sure you use water-soluble hair spray. That way, if any spray hits the wall, you can easily wipe it clean.

Make cut flowers last longer. Of course you know that hair spray makes your "do" last longer. But did you know it can do the same thing for the big, beautiful bouquet on your coffee table? It's true! Just stand about a foot away from the vase, and give the petals and leaves a quick spritz—on the undersides only.

Extend the life of your Christmas greenery. As soon as you bring your trees and wreaths home, spritz them from top to bottom with hair spray. It'll trap moisture in the needles and help your Yuletide treasures keep their festive looks longer. *Note:* A coat of super-hold hair spray will also pro-

Here's to **YOU!**

If you use a hair spray that comes in a pump bottle, rather than an aerosol can, good for you—you're not only doing your part to save the environment by forgoing chemical-spewing aerosols, but you're also giving yourself reusable bottles. Washed and rinsed, they're perfect for holding and dispensing garden tonics, homemade spray cleaners, or even vegetable-based wood stains (see "Color It Fresh," on page 297).

long the good looks of ribbons and bows on outdoor wreaths. Just don't hang them where they'll get rained or snowed on, or the hair spray will wash off.

Keep wooden tool handles shipshape. To my way of thinking, well-kept tools can spell the difference between a gardening job that's a joy to do—and one that's a royal pain in the grass. One of the simplest ways to make your work a pleasure is to give the handles of your shovels, rakes, and other tools a thin coat of hair spray every now and then. (Either pump or aerosol will do the job.) It'll give the wood a smooth, splinter-free surface that always feels good in your hands.

Put rubber handle grips on a bicycle. As you know if you've ever tried it, this can be a real dickens of a job. But it'll be a snap if you lightly coat the inside of each grip with hair spray before you slide it onto the handlebars. The spray works as a lubricant when it's wet, but it'll dry like glue to keep the grips firmly in place.

Protect garden-variety paperwork. Outdoors or in a workshop, planting plans, project diagrams, and how-to instructions can get grimy fast. Keep the paperwork clean and readable by coating it with hair spray before you use it.

 # Panty Hose

Fend off squash borers. You *could* head off borer problems by covering your melon, squash, and cucumber plants in the early spring so the adult moths can't get in to lay their eggs. That can be tricky, though, because if you don't get the covers off in time, bees and other insects can't pollinate the flowers—and you won't get any crop at all. So here's a better idea: Just wrap panty hose around the base of each plant. That's where these villains generally strike, and if they find the door closed, they'll probably go elsewhere. (Don't take chances, though: Keep a lookout for clusters of bright red eggs, and wipe them away pronto.)

Protect your corn from critters. Raccoons, skunks, and squirrels share one trait with most of us humans: a great love of sweet corn. Depending on the size of your crop, this trick may take some patience—but it *will* ensure that you get to keep your whole harvest. Just put an old panty hose toe over the top of each ear after the pollen drops. Then touch

MARVELOUS MiX

Compost Tea

Compost tea is the healthiest drink a flower or vegetable plant could ever ask for. It delivers a well-balanced supply of all the essential nutrients—major and minor—and fends off diseases at the same time. Here's how to make it.

> **1 gal. of fresh compost**
> **4 gal. of warm water**

Pour the water into a large bucket. Scoop the compost into a panty hose sack, tie the sack closed, and put it in the water. Cover the bucket and let the mix steep for three to seven days. Pour the solution into a watering can or handheld sprayer bottle, and give your plants a good spritzing with it every two to three weeks throughout the growing season. *Note:* You can make manure tea (another wonder drink for your plants) using this same recipe. Just substitute 1 gallon of well-cured manure for the compost, and use the finished product the same way.

the top of the stocking with just a dab of perfume (the cheap stuff, of course). The furry little fiends will take their appetites elsewhere!

Store onions and garlic. If you want to keep these pungent bulbs fresh and close at hand, give them a leg—of panty hose, that is (or use nylon stockings or knee-high hose). Drop in a bulb, tie a knot, drop another one in, and so on. When you want to use one of the bulbs, cut just below the knot above the bulb.

Save your melons. When you thin out your cantaloupes, casabas, or honeydews (or whatever kind of sweet treats you're growing), slip a panty hose foot over each fruit that's staying on the vine, and tie the end closed. That way, you'll fend off more pesky pests and dastardly diseases than you can shake a spray bottle at. And here's a grape idea: This terrific trick works just as well with clusters of grapes.

Keep raccoons out of trash cans. Clank! There it goes again. Rocky Raccoon and his pals are staging another midnight raid. Well, if your cans have open handles on the sides and lid, you may still be able to get some shut-eye. Just rummage through your drawers for an old pair of panty hose, and use them like a bungee cord to tie the lid down tight.

Give tender bulbs a winter home. When you dig up gladiolus and other tender bulbs in the fall, make sure they'll be healthy, pest-free, and rarin' to grow come spring. How? Simply dust them with medicated baby powder, drop them into an old panty hose leg, and hang it in a cool, dry place.

Tie up your plants. There are plenty of good ways to fasten vines and floppy plants to their support structures. But when you do the job with strips of panty hose, you get a special bonus: The nylon will attract static electricity, which will give your plants an added boost of grow-power.

Make a fish net. Attention, water gardeners! Does your net always seem to vanish just when you need to scoop a fish out of your pond? Well, here's a simple way to make an extra one to keep close at hand. All you need are a wire coat hanger, a rubber band, and an old panty hose leg. First, stretch out the triangular part of the hanger so that it forms a diamond shape. Pull the panty hose leg over the diamond, leaving a little slack to achieve a cuplike effect. Use the rubber band to fasten the open end to the hook of the hanger. There you have it: a first-class fish net for free!

Strain Marvelous Mixes. Anytime you whip up a recipe that contains solid ingredients (like chopped garlic, dried peppers, or even instant tea granules), it's important to strain the tonic before you pour it into a hose-end or handheld sprayer bottle. Otherwise, tiny bits of stuff could get caught in the sprayer mechanism and spoil your chances for a successful delivery. So what's the strainer that I recommend? You guessed it—a piece of old panty hose. It'll head off (and strain out) trouble every time.

Save That Scent!

One tried-and-true deer-chasing trick is to tuck deodorant soap, smelly old socks, pouches of baby powder, or other strong-smelling stuff among their target plants. It works, too, unless the deer are on the brink of starvation. There's just one drawback: Rain or snow will wash away the scent (and in the case of soap, the whole shebang). So, before you hang up your deterrent of choice, put it into an old panty hose foot, and tie the pouch closed with a string. Tuck the bag into a plastic flowerpot, pull the string through the drainage hole, and tie it into a loop. Then fasten the loop to the branch of a tree or any other sturdy plant. Your repellent should keep its odor for about a year, no matter how much rain falls from the sky.

Soap

Say "So long" to spiders. Don't let Miss Muffet mislead you—many kinds of spiders are true garden-variety heroes, gobbling up scads of destructive insects. Still, that *doesn't* mean you want the web spinners setting up housekeeping in your house. To discourage them, simply tuck perfumed soap chips into old panty hose toes, and hang the pouches in the would-be construction sites. Or, if you'd prefer, scatter the chips around the area.

Bid anthills *adieu*. Are ants making a major mess of your lovely lawn? If you've tried all of the gentle "please-go-away" methods in the book, and the unwelcome guests still haven't gotten the message, haul out the big guns. Mix ¼ cup of liquid hand soap and 1 gallon of water in a bucket, and pour the solution onto the ant mound. Repeat the procedure about an hour later to make sure the liquid penetrates to the queen's inner chamber. She and her court will wish they'd set up shop in your neighbor's yard instead!

Make many Marvelous Mixes. Does the dishwashing liquid that you normally use contain antibacterial or grease-cutting agents? Then here's some good news: There's no need to buy a mild, soap-based product just to use in my garden tonics. Instead, in any recipe that calls for dishwashing liquid, simply substitute liquid Castile hand soap—it performs exactly the same function.

Cook at your fire pit—neatly. Do you love to cook over an open fire, but hate the chore of getting the soot off of the pans afterwards? Try this trick: Before you start cooking, rub a bar of soap over the bottom of each pan. When dinner's over, cleanup will be a breeze!

Do Tell!

Trivia time again! Did you know that a popular product in the Personal Care aisle owes its name to a biblical Psalm? It's true! Here's the story: One morning in 1878, Harley Proctor had a brainstorm: He decided that the soap and candle company founded by his father should produce a soap to compete with the creamy white, delicately scented Castile soaps then being imported from Europe. He discussed his idea with his cousin, a chemist named James Gamble, who quickly developed a smooth, white soap that produced a lavish lather, even in cold water. Proctor and Gamble dubbed the stuff simply "White Soap." Full-scale production began, and the product sold well.

Then one day, the factory worker in charge of the soap vats left for lunch, forgetting to turn off the master mixing machine. He returned to find that too much air had been whipped into the soap solution. Rather than toss the batch out, he poured it into the hardening and cutting frames, and the resulting bars were delivered to local stores in Cincinnati.

Almost immediately, letters began pouring in from consumers requesting more of this amazing soap that floated on the surface, rather than sinking into their bath water. Recognizing a good thing when they saw it, Proctor and Gamble ordered that all White Soap be given an extra-long whipping time. But one thing nagged at them: Such a novel product deserved a more clever name than "White Soap." Harley Proctor was mulling over some possible choices one Sunday in church as the pastor read the 45th Psalm: "All thy garments smell of myrrh, and aloes, and cassia, out of the ivory palaces, whereby they have made thee glad."

In October 1879, the first bars of Ivory Soap® hit the grocery store shelves (supermarkets as we know them would not come along for another 37 years)—and as they say, the rest is history.

Clean up a gas spill on your lawn. We've all been there before: You're filling up the old mower, someone calls to you from the house, and you turn around to answer. The next thing you know, there's gasoline running onto your grass. The good news is that if you act fast and the spill is small, you can probably head off any damage to the turf. Here's your action plan: Saturate the soil with a solution of $1/2$ cup of liquid Castile soap per gallon of water. Wait 3 or 4 minutes, then grab the hose and give the accident scene a thorough dousing. Let the water run for a good 10 to 15 minutes on the area and it'll be good as new.

Deodorize your car. Of course, you can buy disposable air fresheners that hang from your car's rear-view mirror. But why bother, when you can make a permanent version for next to nothing? Just punch or drill a dozen or so holes in the lid of a throat-lozenge tin or a plastic soap container (the kind meant for traveling). Tuck a small bar of sweet-smelling soap into the box, and slide it under the front seat of your car. Your vehicle will smell clean and fresh—and in a pinch, you can pull out the soap and use it to wash your hands!

Fog-proof your car's windows. There's nothing more annoying—or more dangerous—than driving without crystal-clear vision. So if fog is a fact of life where you live, don't take chances. Rub a bar of soap over your auto's glass, and polish it with a clean, soft cloth. *Note*: This trick works just as well on diving masks and ski goggles—just be sure to rub the soap only on the *outside* of the lens.

Remove a bee's stinger. If you spend any amount of time working around flowers, sooner or later, you're bound to find yourself on the wrong end of a bee. When that happens, your first job is to get the danged stinger out. And it couldn't be simpler: Just rub a bar of soap over the sting site. The buzzer's weapon should slide right out.

Soap

Old-Time Board Cleaner

You've found some beautiful old boards that you want to recycle into a garden fence, or maybe furniture for your deck. There's just one problem: The things are filthy! Well, don't fret about it. Just mix up a batch of this power-packed cleaner. It—plus just a little elbow grease—will make that vintage lumber sparkle like new.

> **3 parts sand**
> **2 parts liquid hand soap**
> **1 part garden lime**

Mix all of the ingredients together in a bucket, and scour the boards using a stiff scrub brush. Rinse with clear water, and rub dry with a clean towel. Then pat yourself on the back for your lucky find, because new wood could never look this good!

Zip your jacket. Rats! It's a cool, breezy day, you're headed out to work in your garden, and your zipper's stuck halfway up. Don't fret—and don't freeze, either. Instead, grab a bar of soap and rub it over the upper teeth. The zipper should slide right up to the top.

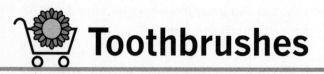

Toothbrushes

Dust your African violets. As you know if you grow these classic houseplants, the fine hairs on their leaves collect a lot of dust, which can block both air and sunlight. Trying to wipe the covering away with a damp cloth just makes matters worse—you end up with a sticky mess on the foliage. The simple solution: Gently whisk the dust away with a soft toothbrush. Your plants will look better and breathe a whole lot easier!

Harvest sunflower seeds. When the back of a sunflower head turns brown, that's the signal that it's time to gather the seeds. Whether you intend to toast and eat the seeds, feed 'em to the birds, or save 'em to plant next year, here's the easiest way I know to get at 'em: Rub a stiff-bristled toothbrush across the flower head. The seeds will loosen up and pop right out.

Plant tiny seeds. Many flowers and vegetables, like lobelias, impatiens, lettuce, and carrots, have seeds that are so small they're hard to *see,* much less plant evenly. But a toothbrush can help. Dampen the brush slightly and dip it into your seed packet. Then hold the brush over your indoor flat or prepared garden soil, and wipe the seeds off with your finger. And what about the seeds that stick to your finger? Scrape 'em off with the handle!

Make planting holes and trenches. The ideal planting depth varies from one type of flower or vegetable seed to another. But the general rule of green thumb is to set a seed into the ground (or a seed-starting flat) at a depth that's equal to twice its diameter. In most cases, you certainly don't need a shovel or even a trowel for that job. Instead, use a toothbrush handle to make a hole or a trench in the soil. Once the seeds are in place, gently sweep the soil over them with the brush.

De-silk your corn. For a lot of folks (including yours truly), shucking sweet corn brings back floods of happy, summertime memories. That is, until it's time to get all those final, clingy strands of silk off of the ears. I don't know any way to make that job a happy one. But I do know a way to make it a lot faster: After you've removed the husks, run a toothbrush vertically down each ear. Any reluctant silks will come right off.

Clean nooks and crannies. The compact, bristly head of a toothbrush is the best tool I've found for getting dirt out of hard-to-reach places like the crevices in garden tools, fancy terra-cotta pots, your lawn mower's engine—and even the treads in work shoes and sneakers. For extra-thorough and extra-easy cleaning, pick up an electric toothbrush in the Oral Hygiene aisle, and make it part of your outdoor tool kit. Don't get me wrong: I'm not suggesting that you splurge on one of those sophisticated sonic models that kills bacteria in your mouth! For home and garden hygiene, any inexpensive battery-powered brush will work just fine.

Here's to
YOU!

As any dentist will tell you, giving your toothbrush early retirement leads to healthier teeth and gums (besides providing you with a steady supply of gardening and cleaning aids). But did you know it can also help you lick a cold or the flu? That's because germs linger on a wet brush, and when you use the same one over and over, you keep reinfecting yourself. So the next time you come down with a sore throat, runny nose, fever...the whole nine yards...play it smart: Get yourself a fresh toothbrush and put the old one to work outdoors, doing the chores that you'll find in this section. (Just dip the brush in boiling water first, or run it through the dishwasher on the top rack.)

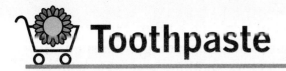# Toothpaste

Remove light scratches from auto glass. Even the best-kept cars pick up minor scrapes on their windows and mirrors every now and then. When that happens to the vehicle in your life, reach for a tube of mildly abrasive toothpaste (not the gel kind). Squeeze a little of it onto a soft, cotton flannel cloth, and rub the scratches very lightly until they're gone. (Of course, this trick works just as well on mirrors, windows, tabletops, or any other glass surface, indoors or out.)

Renew scratched plastic. Got some scuffs and shallow dings on your plastic deck furniture? Or maybe the cover of your cold frame is beginning to show its age. Here's a simple trick that will make just about any, um, "experienced" plastic surface look new again: Using a clean, soft cloth, cover the plastic with toothpaste. Wait a minute or two, and buff the surface with a second cloth.

Make grass stains vanish. If there's any way to work in your yard without picking up green streaks and splotches on your clothes, I don't know what it is. But I do know a lot of ways to get the marks out, and one of the simplest is this: Squeeze non-gel toothpaste onto the spots, and scrub it in with an old (but clean!) toothbrush. Rinse with clear water, and launder the garment as usual.

Get mystery stains out of your clothes. For those times when you come in from the garden wearing a substance that you can't identify, try this old-time routine: Mix a dab of non-gel toothpaste with 1 teaspoon of hydrogen peroxide. Rub the paste onto the spot with a clean, soft cloth, and rinse with clear water. The mystery will remain unsolved, but the stain should be history.

Treat minor burns. To my way of thinking, a tube of toothpaste belongs in every garage, workshop, and garden shed. How come? Because it's perfect for soothing your skin with you accidentally touch a hot car engine or power tool.

A Brush with History

If it seems as though the toothbrush has been around forever, there's a good reason: It has—although not always in the form that we know it today. Here's a brief look at the evolution of this indispensable personal-care product.

ON THIS DATE IN HISTORY	THIS IS WHAT HAPPENED
3000 B.C.	The Egyptians invent the toothbrush (actually, a pencil-sized twig with one end frayed to produce soft fibers).
1498 A.D.	The Chinese produce the first modern toothbrush, featuring bristles hand-plucked from the necks of hogs and fastened into handles made of bone or bamboo.
1938	DuPont markets the first nylon-bristle toothbrush under the name Dr. West's Miracle Tuft Toothbrush. A softer, more gum-friendly version, called the Park Avenue brush, came along in the early 1950s.
1961	The Squibb Company introduces the first electric toothbrush, called Broxodent. General Electric followed a year later with a cordless model that was both battery-powered and rechargeable.
1992	David Giuliani develops the Sonicare® tooth brush, featuring sonic technology that destroys bacteria at the gumline. It takes its first (highly successful) bow at a periodontal convention in Florida.

Produce

APPLES

AVOCADOS

BANANAS

CABBAGE

CITRUS FRUITS

CUCUMBERS

FRESH HERBS

GARLIC

ONIONS

PEPPERS

POTATOES

# Apples

Trap visiting voles. Mousetraps work just as well on these tiny plant-munching pests as they do on mice. Bait the traps with apple slices (voles *love* them!), and set them out among your trees. Just be sure to put the devices inside milk cartons or coffee cans, or cover them with "bridges" made of bricks or boards. Otherwise, you could catch birds, pets, or small human fingers instead of voles. Keep checking, emptying, and refilling your traps until your bait no longer has any takers.

Grow a grand and glorious groundcover. Here's a simple trick that will make your hardworking, living blanket thick enough to stop a jackrabbit: Top-dress the plants with a mixture of 10 cups of worm castings, 5 cups of ground apple, and ½ bushel of compost. Then overspray everything with my All-Season Green-Up Tonic (see page 198).

Feed your flowering shrubs. Want to hear one of the least-known growing secrets in all of gardendom? Here it is: Blooming bushes of all kinds go gaga over apples. Bury all of your peels and over-the-hill fruit an inch or two under the soil surface, and your hydrangeas, forsythias, and other flowering gems will bloom to beat the band!

Say "Phooey!" to fruit flies. You may think of these villains as apple maggot flies because it's the younger generation that causes so much trouble in apples and crabapples. But close relatives of the apple crowd attack cherries, pears, plums, peaches, blueberries, currants, and citrus fruits. Regardless of what kinds of fruit the flies are after at your place, your most effective weapon is waiting for you in the supermarket Produce aisle. Here's all you need to do: Before the blossoms on your trees turn to fruit, hurry on down to your local supermarket, and buy some red apples with the stems still attached. (All of these flies are drawn to the color red, even if the fruit they favor is some other color—go figure!) You'll need six to eight traps for a full-sized tree; for a bush or a dwarf tree (less than 9 feet tall), two traps should do the trick. Coat the apples with corn syrup, or spray them with a commercial adhesive, and hang them in your trees. The adult flies will zero in on the apples to lay their eggs, and get stuck in the stick-um. As the traps fill up, cut them down and replace them with new ones. By the time the real fruit appears, your fruit fly—and maggot—woes will be history, and you can take down your traps for good.

MARVELOUS MIX

Heirloom Flu-Stopper

In our grandparents' day, when antibiotics were few and far between—and a vaccine lay decades ahead—the flu was serious business. That's why, when anyone in our family showed signs of coming down with the Big F, my Grandma Putt pulled out the big guns in the form of this powerful potion. And you know what? It works just as well today.

- 1 large, tart, juicy apple
- 1 qt. of water
- 2 shots of whiskey (about 3 oz.)
- 1/2 tsp. of lemon juice
- Honey (optional)

Boil the apple in the water until the apple falls apart in pieces. Strain out the solids, and add the whiskey and lemon juice. Sweeten to taste with honey, if you like. Then get in bed and drink the toddy. If you do this in time, by morning, you'll be feeling fit as a fiddle!

Lure starlings away from your feeders. It's a wicked winter, and the greedy gluttons are hogging all the seed. But even starlings have to eat, and in this blustery weather, there's not much natural food to be had. So what do you do? Trot down to your local supermarket, and buy as many apples as your bird-watching budget will allow. (In most Produce aisles, you'll find a section of fruit that's slightly past its prime (but not rotten!) that costs next to nothing. If it's not on display, chances are the produce department manager can find some for you.) Take the fruits home, cut them in half, and set them on the ground, far away from your feeders. The starlings will happily devour the apples and leave the seed for the birds that you'd rather look at.

Support your local deer. They may be your summertime adversaries, but deer can suffer tragically during harsh winters. You can help them out by serving up a steady supply of apples (and pears, too). It's fine if the fruits are a little bruised or slightly past the supermarket's official sell-by date. Set the goodies out in places where you know the brown-eyed beauties roam. Just make sure that once you start this routine, you keep it up, because the deer will come to depend on your offerings. In return, you'll have the fun of watching the diners as they arrive at your "bistro" every evening. *Note:* If you *really* want to do your four-footed friends a lifesaving favor (especially if the ground is covered with ice, which deer can't dig through), offer some commercial deer food along with the fruit. You can buy sacks of it for practically peanuts at most feed stores.

Ripen green tomatoes. A heavy frost was headed your way, so you picked all the tomatoes that were left on your plants. Unfortunately, most of them were still green, and you're itchin' to turn them into your extra-special marinara sauce. No problem! Just pop those underripe fruits into a paper bag, along with some already-ripe apples. They'll give off ethylene gas, which will redden up your tomatoes in a flash. The tomatoes should be ready for eating (or sauce making) in a couple of days. For best results, use one apple for every five or six tomatoes.

Here's to YOU!

As you're beginning to see in this chapter, you can find some of your best garden helpers in the Produce aisle. But you know what? Those fruits and vegetables can do yeoman's work *inside* your house, too. Here are just some of the ways you can put them to good use:

Clean a stained aluminum pan. Fill it as full as you can with water, then add a handful of apple peels or chopped rhubarb, and gently boil it until the stains disappear.

Deodorize your refrigerator. Cut a raw potato in two, and set both halves inside, cut side up. When the surfaces turn black (as they will in a week or so), just shave off the discolored layer and put the clean sections back on the job.

Freshen the air in your kitchen. And fast, too! Heat the oven to 300°F, and set a whole, unpeeled orange inside. Bake it for about 15 minutes with the oven door slightly ajar, then turn off the oven. Let the fruit cool before you take it out.

Eliminate eau de paint. Before you start a painting project, drop some big chunks of onion into a pan of cold water, and set it in the middle of the room.

Polish pewter. Simply rub your treasures every now and then with cabbage leaves.

Protect your belongings from a teething puppy. Just give young Rover a steady supply of cold carrots to chew on. The cool temperature will soothe his sore gums, and he'll love the satisfying crunch.

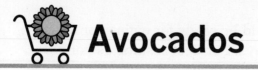

Avocados

Feed your plants. Avocados are a potent source of potassium and magnesium. Just bury their peels near your flowers, vegetables, or flowering shrubs, then stand back and watch the show. If you have any over-the-hill fruits, or leftovers that haven't been doused with salad dressing, that's even better for the soil.

Trap slugs and snails. Are these slimy mollusks wreaking havoc on your hostas, bashing your begonias, or making mince-meat out of your mint? If so, then assassinate the creeps with avocados—or rather, avocado peels. Just set them in your garden at night. Come morning, collect the slug-filled rinds, and drop them into a bucket of soapy water. Then dump it all on the compost pile, or bury it in the garden. *Note:* You need intact half-rinds for this job, so when you peel your avocados, cut them in half first, then

Do Tell!

Hey there, trivia fans! Ready for a few fun facts about fruit? Ready or not, here they come:

* Botanically speaking, some lovely, luscious fruits are members of the rose family, including cherries, pears, peaches, plums, and (of course) raspberries and blackberries.

* Also botanically speaking, grapefruits, lemons, limes, oranges, and pineapples are all classified as berries.

* Only a handful of major fruits are native to North America, including blueberries, strawberries, raspberries, cranberries, cherries, squash, and tomatoes.

pull the sections apart, remove the pit, and squeeze the skin gently to loosen the tender fruit inside. It should come right out.

Start seeds. In a pinch, carefully "unwrapping" your avocados can also give you a good supply of "travelin' pots." Using a large nail or awl, poke a few holes in the bottoms of the peels, and put them in a tray or shallow pan. Fill each little container with a commercial starter mix, and plant your seeds. When it's time to move the seedlings to the garden, plant 'em, pots and all.

Bananas & Banana Peels

Grow radiant roses. I have a good friend who grows absolutely show-stopping roses that (she swears) have never been troubled by pests or diseases. And do you know what her secret is? She feeds them banana peels, plus an overripe fruit every now and then. That's it—no fertilizers, no sprays, no dusts. The reason it works is simple: Both the skins and the innards of bananas are chock-full of nutrients that roses need for good health, including potassium, phosphorus, magnesium, calcium, sulfur, sodium, and silica. (Talk about power lunches!) To put this miracle food to work in your yard, add chopped peels to the hole when you plant any kind of rose. And give the plants a snack anytime you think of it. Just bury the peels, or whole fruits, anywhere in the root zone, about 1 inch deep. Although roses go absolutely bananas over bananas, all flowering and fruiting plants benefit from the health-giving properties of these mellow yellow fruits.

Make fabulous fertilizer. I know what you're thinking: "What can I do with my banana peels in the winter, when the ground is frozen and I can't feed them to my plants?" The answer: Spread the peels out on paper towels and let them air-dry until they're crisp (the timing depends on the humidity level in your house, but two or three days should do the trick). Crunch them up with your hands, and store the pieces at room temperature in a sealed container. Then during the growing season, when any plant needs a jolt of phosphorus or potassium, work a handful of crumbles into the soil and water them in well.

Serve breakfast to your roses. In the spring, when your roses show their first sign of life, pull back their winter mulch, whip up this wake-up tonic, and sprinkle it on. (This recipe makes enough for one plant.) Here's all there is to it: Pour about 3 gallons of water into a bucket and add 2 banana peels, 1 cup of Epsom salts, 2 cups of alfalfa meal or alfalfa pellets, and $1/2$ cup of dolomitic lime. Don't bother to let it steep. Just stir it up and pour it around the base of the plant (after pulling back any compost or other organic mulch that you've used over the winter). Then work the solids into the soil along with the mulch. Just like that, your roses will be off and running! Your clematis will respond in exactly the same way; give each of them a bucketful, too.

Prevent leaning lilies. Here's a rather perplexing problem: You ordered your short-stemmed, hybrid lilies because the catalog said they wouldn't need staking, as taller varieties do. But they're fallin' over anyway! Well, don't fret: You didn't get defective goods. Unless you planted those lilies where gusty winds can get 'em, the problem is a shortage of potassium in the soil. This deficiency leads to weak stems that'll topple over even on calm days. Just give your lilies a big helping of banana peels (two or three per bulb should do the trick) by working them into the soil *very* gently, so you don't damage the bulbs.

Banana power doesn't stop at the garden gate. These fabulous fruits can also work wonders for your health and well-being—in some ways you might not expect. Take these, for instance:

Here's to **YOU!**

Clear up annoying blemishes. Just before bedtime, mash an overripe banana, and smooth it thickly over the affected skin. Cover the mush with gauze, and tape it in place. Then toddle off to dreamland. While you're snoozing, the sugar and enzymes in the fruit will draw out the impurities.

Get some shut-eye. Having trouble sleeping through the night? Eat a few bananas during the day. The secret lies in the potassium, which encourages deep, restful sleep.

Lose weight. One study found that dieters who sniffed a banana scent whenever they felt like munching lost an average of 30 pounds in 6 months.

Lower your blood pressure. The high potassium content in bananas can prevent the thickening of artery walls and also help regulate your body's fluid levels—both crucial to regulating blood pressure.

Remove a plantar wart. Tape a piece of banana peel, inner side down, over the painful bump. Cover the peel with a bandage or tight sock, and leave it on overnight. Repeat each night—after three or four nights, the wart should start to disappear.

Soften cracked, dry, sore feet. Combine 1 ripe, smashed banana with 1 tablespoon of lemon juice, 2 tablespoons of honey, and 2 tablespoons of margarine. Stir the ingredients until creamy, then massage the mix onto clean, dry feet. Pull on a pair of cotton socks, and go to bed. By morning, you'll feel like dancing all day long!

Jump-start container plants. When you pot up flowers, vegetables, or fruits—indoors or out—plop an overripe banana into the bottom of the container (add about an inch or so of potting mix first). The fruit will break down quickly, providing valuable organic matter and nutrients to get your plants growing on the right root—and fast, too!

Repel aphids. These tiny sap-sucking pests can't stand the aroma of bananas. So if you love those tasty fruits as much as I do, you've got a never-ending anti-aphid arsenal. Just lay the peels on the ground under your plants, and aphids will keep their distance. As an added attraction, when those skins

MARVELOUS MIX

Tanager Temptations

These scarlet songbirds are so spectacular that they look like they should live in a jungle—which they do in the winter. But in the warmer seasons, they move back north. Here's the best part: If you can lure one to your feeder, the same bird is likely to return at the same time year after year. To issue your invitation, set out these treats from early to late spring, when the northward migration is at its peak. Trot them out again in early fall, when these lovely birds fly off for the Sunny Southland.

> 1/2 of a ripe banana, mashed
> 1 cup of cornmeal, regular grind
> 1/2 cup of peanut butter
> 1/2 cup of suet or fat scraps, chopped

Mix the banana and cornmeal in a bowl. Add the peanut butter and suet or fat scraps, and mix thoroughly. Put the mixture in a wire suet cage with a stick poked into it for a perch. Then stand by with your binoculars and camera at the ready. Chances are that orioles and bluebirds will stop by for a nibble, too!

break down (which they do with amazing speed), they'll infuse the soil with valuable potassium and phosphorus.

Trap a trio of terrible pests. Wasps, mosquitoes, and codling moths will all swarm to this simple snare: Put 1 banana peel into a clean, 1-gallon milk jug with 1 cup of vinegar and 1 cup of sugar. Pour in enough water to almost fill the bottle, put the cap on, and shake well to mix the ingredients. Tie a cord or piece of wire around the handle, remove the lid, and hang the bottle from a tree limb. The pests will fly in for a sip and drown. *Note:* If your target is codling moths, hang your trap in your apple tree before the blossoms open.

Shine your shoes. It never fails: Your dinner guests were due at any minute, you were scurrying to put the salad together, and discovered that you were one tomato short. So you charged out to the garden to pluck a nice, big, ripe one—and you charged back indoors with a few not-so-nice scuff marks on your favorite dress shoes. Well, we can fix that problem in a hurry: Just pull a banana out of the fruit bowl, remove the peel, and rub the inside surface over the leather. Buff with a soft cotton cloth. Then say "Goodbye" to the scuff marks and "Hello" to your guests!

 # Cabbage

Snag snails and slugs. Cabbage or lettuce leaves make great traps for these slimers. Really early in the morning, set the leaves on the ground near your infested plants. The villains will crawl under them during the heat of the day, and you can scoop them up and drop them into a bucket of water laced with a cup or so of salt, soap, vinegar, or ammonia.

Relocate pillbugs and sowbugs. Contrary to their name, these little round creatures are not insects; they're tiny crustaceans—kissin' cousins of crayfish and lobsters. Most of the time they feed on dead plant material, and in the process, break it down into rich, fertile soil. (You could think of them as earthworms with legs.) Once in a while, though, the population explodes, and there's not enough dead stuff to go around. Then the hungry hoards sink their chops into tender, young flower and vegetable seedlings. When that  happens, simply tuck cabbage leaves under upturned flowerpots. Every few days, check your traps, and relocate the prisoners to the compost pile. If you don't have a compost pile, just dig a hole in the ground, and bury the occupied leaves in a place that's well removed from your garden or flower beds. *Note:* If you don't have any cabbage on hand, substitute lettuce leaves, potato peelings, corncobs, or halved cantaloupe rinds.

Trap cutworms. Because new batches of cutworms come along every few weeks, your garden is never really out of the woods during the growing season. Once plants are past the seedling stage, the culprits aren't likely to cause fatal damage, but they'll still make a nuisance of themselves. They'll also turn into moths and lay next year's supply of cutworm eggs. The key to outwitting the rascals is persistence. Every evening throughout the growing season, set out cabbage leaves in your flower beds or vegetable garden. The next morning, the traps will be full of cutworms. What you do with them is your call: You can squash them, burn them, or dump them into a bucket of hot, soapy water. If you don't have any cabbage on hand, lettuce leaves will also do the trick.

Take another approach to molusk-icide. If you'd rather not deal with leaves that are filled with squirming slugs and snails, use this more hands-off technique: Slice some cabbage or lettuce leaves into thin strips and put them into shallow cat food or tuna cans that you've filled with salt water. The slugs will home in on the cabbage, fall into the drink, and drown.

Kill annual weeds. Cabbage and its cruciferous cousins, broccoli, kale, and Brussels sprouts, all contain *thiocyanate,* a chemical that's toxic to newly germinated seeds. Apply this potent herbicide in early spring: Blend the vegetables with just enough water to make a thick mush, and add about $1/2$ teaspoon of dishwashing liquid (any kind). Pour the mixture into cracks in your sidewalk or driveway, or anyplace you want to stop weeds before they germinate. Just one word of warning: Be careful where you use this stuff. Although thiocyanate won't hurt estab-

Don't Join the Club

Although cabbage can solve a lot of garden-variety problems, it and its close relatives (including broccoli, Brussels sprouts, and cauliflower) are prone to one big problem of their own: clubroot. This fungal disease arrives by way of infected transplants and causes your plants' roots to become gnarled, misshapen, and unable to take up enough water. Above ground, afflicted plants look stunted and yellowish, and they wilt easily. There is no cure for clubroot, but you will find some good preventive medicine in your supermarket's Produce aisle—namely, rhubarb. Bury stalks of the sweetly tangy fruit in the planting beds, and your cole crops should stay free of the foul fungus. (But to be on the safe side, grow your brassica crops in a different spot every year, and if clubroot is common in your area, don't buy any seeds or transplants that were locally grown.)

lished plants, it can't tell the difference between the seeds you've sown—or the volunteers you're hoping for—and the weeds you want to get rid of!

Stay cool. It's hot enough to fry an egg on the sidewalk, but you've got some outdoor chores that can't wait. How can you get your work done without risking heat stroke? Do what Babe Ruth used to do on steamy days in the Yankees' dugout: Wear a cabbage leaf under your hat. It'll keep you as cool as a cucumber—well, almost.

Jazz up a Christmas wreath. Looking for out-of-the-ordinary trimmings for that circle of evergreens on your door? Try Brussels sprouts. Fluff up the leaves a little, then poke a hole through the stem using a nail or a nutpick. Thread floral wire through the hole and attach it to the wreath. Group the mini cabbages in clusters as you would decorative fruits or dried flowers. (Design pros favor odd-numbered groupings of three or five for these purposes.)

 # Citrus Fruits & Rinds

Keep kitty out of your houseplants. Whether your resident feline is nibbling on the leaves or using the soil as a litter box, try this effective, purr-fectly safe trick: Saturate a few cotton balls with lemon juice, and set them in the off-limits areas. The scent will send a message that says, loud and clear, "Not here, my dear!"

And keep ants out of anyplace. Whether they're making mischief indoors or out, put fresh lemon slices in places where you don't want the tiny pests roaming. They dislike the tangy scent just as much as cats do.

Deter dogs and cats. Are neighborhood pets making a mess of your flower beds or your vegetable garden? Or maybe there are spots in your yard where you'd rather your own four-footed friends didn't roam. Here's a fast, easy—and entirely harmless—way to keep them out. Just sprinkle slivers of orange, lemon, lime, or grapefruit peel among your plants. Most canines and felines hate the scent of citrus, so they'll go elsewhere for their fun and games.

Put Out the Fire Ants

To wipe out a nest of fire ants, you need to kill the queen. That's all but impossible to do with poison bait, because the worker ants test all food before it reaches the boss's lips. Instead, your best option is to stage an ambush. For the surest—and safest—results, enlist a partner-in-crime for this escapade. Plan to attack early in the morning, or on a cool, sunny day (that's when the queen is usually holding court near the top of the mound). Then proceed as follows:

1. Toss 4 cups of citrus peels into a big pot with 3 gallons of water. Bring it to a boil, and let it simmer for about 10 minutes.

2. While the potion is simmering on the stove, put on the uniform of the day, and have your sidekick do the same: You'll need gloves, a long-sleeved shirt, and long pants that are tucked into high boots. To be extra-safe, wear rubber boots that you've smeared with a sticky substance like petroleum jelly. Arm your partner with a long, sharp stick or metal rod.

3. Together, tiptoe as softly as you can up to the mound—fire ants are super-sensitive to ground vibrations.

4. Have your cohort poke the entrance with the stick.

5. *Immediately* pour the boiling solution into the hole. Then run like the dickens! The boiling water will polish off any ants it reaches, and the citrus-oil fumes will send more to the gas chamber. Repeat every other day, until there's no sign of life in the mound.

Of course citrus fruits don't come packed in plastic baskets like strawberries come in—even though, as I mentioned earlier in this chapter (see "Do Tell!" on page 274), citrus fruits are technically classified as berries. But plenty of other berries do come in these sturdy, reusable containers. Here are nine nifty jobs they can do for you, indoors or out:

Bulb protector. Fend off hungry rodents by planting your bulbs inside berry baskets that you've set into the ground.

Cucurbit crop guard. Keep pesky pests and dastardly diseases away from your cucumbers, melons, and squashes by propping up each fruit on a basket, turned upside down.

De-clutterer. Turn a basket upside down, and fill the grid with skinny stuff that tends to get scattered all over the place, like pencils and pens, screwdrivers, and small paintbrushes.

Dishwasher basket. Put one on the top rack (never the bottom!), and use it for things that tend to slide around, such as small lids, baby-bottle nipples, and tiny spoons.

Easter basket. Deck it out with ribbons, fill it with cellophane "grass," and add a handle if you like.

Flower arranger. Put it upside down in the bottom of a vase, and tuck the stems into the holes.

Garden shed organizer. Berry baskets are perfect for holding things like seed packets, twine, twist ties, and plant labels.

Gift-wrap guardian. Before you pack up a present for mailing, set a basket, upside down, over the bow. That way, you'll know that it'll arrive in all its fluffed-out glory.

Seedling savior. Set the baskets upside down over seedlings to keep them safe from rabbits, squirrels, and other unwelcome diners. (Set stones on top of the "cages" to keep them from blowing away in the wind.)

Repel caterpillars. Plant-munching larvae loathe citrusy aromas just as much as dogs and cats do. In this case, though, your modus operandi is a little bit different. Put 1 cup of chopped citrus peels (orange, lemon, lime, grapefruit, or a combination thereof will work) in a blender or food processor. Pour $1/4$ cup of boiling water over the peels, liquefy, and let the mixture sit overnight at room temperature. Strain through cheesecloth or old panty hose, and pour the liquid into a handheld sprayer. Fill the balance of the jar with water, and spray your flower or vegetable plants from top to bottom. The crawling menaces will stay away in droves!

Get rid of aphids. When these sap-sucking so-and-so's stage a full-scale attack on your flowers, vegetables, or shrubs, don't just sit there and take it! Fight back with this super-simple—and super-potent—weapon. To make it, put 1 coarsely chopped orange or lemon peel, 1 tablespoon of baby shampoo, and 2 cups of water in a blender. Blend on high for 10 to 15 seconds. Strain out the pulp, and pour the liquid into a handheld sprayer. Before applying the tonic, get out your hose, attach a high-pressure spray nozzle, and blast your plants with water. This will dislodge many of the aphids. About 10 minutes later, thoroughly spray all leaves, buds, and stems with the citrusy potion. Repeat the procedure after four days, and your aphids should be history. This routine will also polish off destructive caterpillars and any other soft-bodied insects, including whiteflies, lace bugs, and leafhoppers.

Slaughter slugs and snails. When pests rank as high on the Most Unwanted List as this duo does, you know that determined gardeners have devised a zillion ways to polish 'em off. Here's one of the most effective: Shortly before dark, set hollowed-out orange or grapefruit rinds among your plants. By morning, the skins will be filled with the slimy troublemakers. Pick up the traps and dump them—and the pesky pests—into a bucket of water with about a half cup of liquid soap added to it. Then toss it on the compost pile. (If you don't have a compost pile, just bury it in your garden; the peels, soft bodies, and snail shells will all decompose and enrich the soil.)

Make container-plant sticky traps. When insect pests are bugging your potted plants—indoors or out—coat a lemon with corn syrup or petroleum jelly, and set it in the pot. The two-part secret to the success of this trick: Most bad bugs are drawn to the color yellow, and a lemon is just the right size to protect a small to medium container. (If you need to de-bug a tree-sized tub, use two or three of the tangy fruits.) When your traps are covered, throw them into the compost pile and start over with fresh recruits.

Polish your houseplants. When your indoor plants start lookin' a little drab, shine 'em up the old-fashioned way, with citrus juice (any kind will do). Just wipe the juice onto the leaves with a clean, soft cotton cloth. The dingy residue left by hard tap water or sprayed-on fertilizer will come right off, leaving the foliage bright, sparkling—and better able to absorb essential carbon dioxide from the air.

Power up your potted plants. Before you water your container plants—indoors or out—add a few drops of lemon juice to the watering can. It'll lower the water's pH, thereby allowing the plants to take up more nutrients from the soil.

Make seed-starter pots. Many vegetables and flowers, including beans, corn, and morning glories, don't like to have their roots disturbed. So when you start these plants indoors, you need to use containers that can go right into the garden at planting time. Some of the best travelin' pots I've found are hollowed-out half rinds of lemons, limes, oranges, or grapefruits. Just punch holes in the bottom of the rinds using an awl or large nail, and fill the rinds with starter mix. Then add your seeds, and set them in a tray. When your baby plants are ready for life in the great outdoors, they can stay right in their homes, and you won't have the bother of unpotting them.

Invite the orioles. No, I'm not suggesting that you invite the Baltimore baseball team over for a barbecue! I'm talking about luring those beautiful birds to your feeder. You can do that by mixing up this colorful treat in mid-spring, when orioles start returning from their winter homes in the South. Here's all there is to it: Split a peeled orange apart with your fingers, and finely chop the pulp, discarding the membrane and any seeds. In a bowl, combine the orange pulp with 1 cup of chopped suet or fat scraps, and mix them together thoroughly, using your hands. Stir $1/4$ cup of frozen blueberries (not thawed) into the mix. Form the fruity fat into a block to fit a wire-cage suet feeder, and add a perch by poking a stick into the fat. Keep refilling the feeder until the birds lose interest as natural foods become more abundant.

Don't let the name fool you: Rose chafer beetles do attack their namesake plants, all right; but they also target many other shrubs, perennial flowers, and both ornamental and fruit trees. The chafers appear suddenly in late spring or early summer, and that's the time to lure them to their death with an aroma they can't resist: the ultra-sweet smell of decaying fruit. Just fill some jars about halfway with water, drop in some chunks of over-the-hill fruit (any kind will do), and set the jars on the ground among your plants. The hungry hordes will hurry on over for a snack, fall right in, and drown.

Beef up your compost. Citrus fruits and rinds are rich in phosphorus and potassium, and they'll enrich your black gold if you toss a handful of rinds into the bin every now and then. And do the same with any leftover, past-its-prime fruit. When your plants "taste" the results, they'll show their pleasure by growing bigger, stronger, and healthier.

Make a mini bird feeder. When Old Man Winter arrives, birds need more calories than ever—but their natural foods are in short supply during the cold, snowy months. You can help your feathered friends by serving up extra-hearty grub. But you don't need to go buy more feeders; just mix 1 part black oil sunflower seed to 2 parts peanut butter, and pack the mixture into the rind of a grapefruit or large orange half. Make a sling using twine or wire, and hang the feeder from a tree limb or from a hook attached to an arbor or trellis.

Do Tell!

Have you ever ordered grapefruit in a restaurant, then glanced down at it and said, "Waiter, there's a hair in my fruit"? You haven't? I didn't think so. But you could—and you'd be right, too. That's because the sweet, juicy flesh of a grapefruit—and every other kind of citrus, too—is made up of fluid-filled sacs called vesicles, which are actually specialized hair cells. Here are a few more trivial tidbits about citrus fruits:

* Lemons originated in China more than 4,000 years ago, and lemonade was a favorite drink of the ancient Chinese emperors.

* The color orange was named for the fruit—not the other way around. The word "orange" comes from the Sanskrit *naranga*, which means "fragrant."

* Grapefruit got its name because it grows in grape-like clusters on the tree.

De-skunk a tiny dog. Is there a toy or miniature pooch in your
household? If so, then a bowl of lemons belongs in your
kitchen. How come? Because lemon juice will eliminate eau
de skunk, lickety-split. If your pal gets sprayed, just wash
him from head to toe with the juice, being careful to keep it
away from his eyes—it won't cause any permanent harm,
but it *will* sting like the dickens. Then rinse thoroughly
with clear water. (Of course, in theory, this trick works on a
dog of any size, but to deodorize a pup who's any bigger
than a Scottie, you'd need a whole *lot* of lemons!)

Remove moss from wood. I happen to be a big fan of moss—in its
proper place, that is—for instance, on a stone wall, or on
patches of ground under a big old shade tree. When the soft,
cushiony stuff starts growing on a deck, an arbor, or the
wood siding of your house, that's another kettle of fish alto-
gether. It'll hold in moisture and make the lumber rot before
you know it. Here's a simple and safe way to get rid of the
moss and discourage it from coming back: In a bucket, mix
1 part freshly squeezed lemon juice, 1 part water, and 2 parts
white vinegar. Apply the solution to the affected area with a
handheld sprayer. (If you're tackling a big space, use a tank
sprayer instead.) Let it sit for 45 minutes, and then hose it
off with clear water. This will loosen the moss so that you
can easily scrape it off. Just be sure you use a plastic scraper,
rather than a metal one, to avoid gouging the wood.

Remove rust from tools. Dang! Your favorite shovel picked up a
little rust over the winter. Or maybe you found a steal of a
deal on some vintage tools at an auction, but they're sporting a few rusty patches. No problem! You can rub those
spots away with a soft, dry cloth dipped in a mixture of
1 tablespoon of lemon juice per 2 tablespoons of salt.
Then rinse with clear water and dry thoroughly. To guard
against future trouble, spritz the metal surface lightly with
an oil spray—either the lubricating type or the cooking
type will do the trick.

Do your outdoor painting in peace. That is, without "help" from flying insects. To say "I can do this myself, thanks," simply add a few drops of lemon juice to the paint in your bucket.

Get berry stains off of your skin. You were jumping for joy when your new raspberry patch produced its first crop of plump, juicy berries. But after you plucked your harvest, you weren't so thrilled to see the colorful splotches all over your hands. Lucky for you, berry juice is no match for lemon juice. Just wash your paws with the full-strength stuff, and rinse with clear water.

Cool off—instantly. On steamy summer days, working (or playing) outdoors can make you feel like your whole body is on fire. That's why, as soon as the mercury starts creeping upward, I make a batch of this sensational soother and stash it in the refrigerator. It is simply marvelous for those hot summer days, especially when used ice cold from the refrigerator. Here's the routine: Cut about a cup of citrus peels into thin strips, put them into a heatproof bowl, and set them aside. Bring 1 cup of water to a boil, and add a

Here's to
YOU!

If you enjoy watching butterflies flit around your yard in the summertime (and who doesn't?), here's an idea that'll increase your viewing pleasure: Set out a feeder just for them, and stock it with fresh fruit. A platform-type bird feeder will do the trick, or if you like, fasten a plastic plate to your deck railing. Add slices of oranges, bananas, apples, melon, or whatever other sweet treats you find in the Produce aisle. The flying jewels will beat a path to your yard and linger long enough for you to enjoy a spectacular show.

vitamin C tablet (crush it first). Pour the boiling water over the citrus peels. Let the mixture cool, then strain out the solids and pour the liquid into a clean container with a tight lid. Keep it in the refrigerator, and whenever the need arises, pour the libation onto a cotton pad or washcloth and dab it onto your steaming skin. *Hot tip:* When you need to cool down *fast,* apply this (or any other cold fluid) to your left wrist. This way, you'll chill the blood that's headed for your heart, and your whole body will feel cooler instantly.

Soften calluses. You've just moved into a new house (new to you, anyway), and you've been working like crazy to get the yard in shape. In the process, you've developed a crop of annoying calluses on your hands. Don't worry—there's a dandy remedy waiting for you in the Produce aisle (or maybe right in your refrigerator). Just rub half a lemon on the rough spots once or twice a day, and they'll be gone in no time at all.

Cucumbers

Trap cucumber beetles. Don't let the name fool you: In addition to dining on their namesake crop and its relatives, these menaces chew ragged holes in the foliage, flowers, stems, and fruits of many vegetables and ornamental plants. What's more, as they feed, cuke beetles also spread three of the worst diseases that can strike any garden: bacterial wilt, fusarium wilt, and cucumber mosaic virus. Here's a super-simple way to get rid of the beastly pests: Set out shallow bowls of water with strips of cucumber peel added to them. The beetles will make a beeline for the tasty treats, fall into the drink, and drown.

Wired for Action

When wireworms are on the scene, your plants lose their get-up-and-grow power, and eventually, they wilt and may die. If you dig up the victims, you'll see obvious signs of an eating binge, and most likely, foul fungi will be finishing the destruction that the wireworms started. The munching marauders attack the roots and seeds of just about every kind of vegetable and fruit under the sun. But their favorite targets are root vegetables—and that gives you two foolproof ways to lure the villains to their death:

1. Punch medium-sized nail holes in the sides of some large cans (3-pound coffee cans are perfect). Fill them about halfway with cut-up carrots, and bury them so that the tops are just above ground level. Cover the openings with small boards, and put a little mulch on top. Once or twice a week, pull up the cans, empty the contents into a bucket of soapy water, and toss it on the compost pile. Then re-bait and re-bury your traps.

2. Spear chunks of potato on sticks that are about 8 inches long (bamboo skewers are perfect), and bury them so that about 3 inches of the stick shows above ground. Then every day or two, pull up the tater bits, toss 'em in a pail of soapy water to kill the worms, and toss the whole shebang on your compost pile.

Catch mice, too. Folks have been trying for years to build a better mousetrap, but you still can't beat the old-fashioned snap trap, indoors or out. Whether the munchkins are nibbling on your plants or they've invaded your garden shed, stage a full-scale blitz. Invest in as many traps as your budget will allow, set them out all at once, and repeat the process until your bait has no takers. As for what bait to use, my hands-down favorite is cucumber pieces with the rind left on. The tiny terrors just *love* it!

Declare a no-ant zone. Got ants wandering where you don't want them to be? Cut a cucumber into 1/4-inch slices, and scatter them on the ground in the problem area. (This trick works indoors, too. Just put the cuke slices at the ants' entry points, or wherever you want to discourage their presence.) Ants won't cross the cuke barrier.

Soothe your sunburn. Time sure flies when you're havin' fun in the sun! When you've lingered too long in the garden—or out on the golf course—do what Grandma Putt always had me do when I'd spent too much time at the old swimming hole: Soak in a tepid bath with a few tablespoons of cucumber juice added to it. Or, if you need relief in a hurry, apply the juice directly to your skin. Your steamy skin will cool down fast! (To make cucumber juice, just puree a cuke, strain out the seeds and pulp, and pour the juice into a bowl.) *Note:* Cucumber juice also helps relieve the pain and itch of eczema. Just dab it onto your skin once a day with a cotton pad.

Make a sunburn cooler. Here's a variation on the cucumber cure: It's a fresh, cooling lotion that eases the pain of sunburn or any other minor burn. It's worked so well for me and my family that we keep a bottle of it on hand all year 'round. To make it, mix 1 cup of witch hazel, 3 tablespoons of coarsely chopped cucumber, and the juice of 1 lemon in a clean, glass jar with a lid. Let it sit for two days, strain out the cucumber, and pour the liquid into a bottle. Keep it in the refrigerator, and dab it on with a cotton ball whenever the need arises.

Refresh your achin' feet. You've been on your feet doing yard work all day long, and now those dogs feel so tired and achy that you don't think you can stand up for another minute. Well, we can take care of that little problem in a hurry! Just reach for three or four cucumbers and chop them up (propping yourself against the kitchen counter, if you need to). Toss the pieces into your blender or food processor, and whirl them into a thick pulp. Put an equal amount into each of two pans that are big enough to hold your tootsies. Then sit back in your easy chair, put one foot into each pan, and think lovely thoughts. The next thing you know, you'll be ready to go out and dance the night away—or at least take Rover for a stroll around the block.

 # Fresh Herbs

Stop brown rot on fruit trees. This fungal disease strikes at peaches, plums, cherries, nectarines, and apricots. It starts out as a small, round, brown spot; in the blink of an eye, that little freckle grows to cover the whole fruit. It gets a toehold when the flowers first start to bloom, but you may not notice symptoms until picking time—and then it's too late. The key to protecting your bounty is to keep your eyes open. If the weather is warm and wet in the spring when the blossoms are developing, wait until three weeks before harvest time, and then spray your trees weekly with my Chive Tea. To make it, put 1 part chopped, fresh chive leaves and 4 parts water in a pan, bring the water to a boil, and remove the pan from the heat. Let the tea cool, strain out the leaves, and pour the liquid into a handheld sprayer. Spray your fruit trees every seven days, and say "Farewell, fungus!" *Caution:* Don't use any kind of spray when blossoms are forming, or you won't get any crop at all!

Make a hot and tangy insecticide. This fabulous formula is instant death to any kind of destructive insect—even hard-shelled beetles and weevils. To make it, boil 3 quarts of

MARVELOUS MIX

Garden-Fresh Stain

When you're fixin' to "color up" unfinished wood, don't head down to the paint store. Instead, hightail it to your supermarket's Produce aisle, pick up some colorful produce, and use this simple recipe to make your own stain. As for what kind of produce to use, you'll find a whole range of eye-pleasing shades on page 297 (see "Color It Fresh").

1–2 cups of fruits, nuts, or vegetables
4 cups of water
1/2 tsp. of alum*

Put the produce in a pan with the water. Simmer for an hour, adding more water as it evaporates. Let it cool to room temperature. Stir in the alum as a fixative, brush the stain onto your wooden object, and let it dry overnight. Recoat, if you'd like, until the wood reaches your desired color density.

*Available in the Condiments & Flavorings aisle of your supermarket.

water, and toss in a 1-inch piece of fresh horseradish, finely chopped, and 2 cups of fresh cayenne peppers, also finely chopped. Turn off the heat, and let the mixture steep for an hour or so. Wait until it's cooled to room temperature, strain out the solids, pour the liquid into a hand-held sprayer, and blast those bugs to you-know-where! (As with most insecticides, this one needs to make direct contact with its victim, so take careful aim before you fire.)

Keep your pet tick-free. And flea-free, too! One of the most effective repellents I know of is waiting for you right in your supermarket's Produce aisle. What is it? Rosemary. Just buy a bunch of sprigs, take them home, and dry them in your microwave (see *Note* below). Strip off the leaves and

Fresh Herbs

grind them up in a blender. Then rub the powder into your dog's or cat's fur, and sprinkle it around in their (and your) outdoor play areas. The blood-sucking, disease-spreading villains will look for a drink elsewhere. *Note:* To dry rosemary (or any other herb) in a microwave, put a single layer of sprigs between two paper towels, and nuke 'em for 2 to 3 minutes. Give them additional 30-second jolts as necessary until they're dry.

Repel ticks and fleas: the alternative. If you prefer your deterrents in liquid form, here's your mission: Boil 1 quart of spring water in a pan, and toss in 1 cup of rosemary needles, either dried or fresh. Cover the pan, remove it from the heat, and let it cool. Strain it into another pan or jar, and let it sit while you give Rover a bath with a high-quality dog shampoo—*not* the flea and tick kind. (Use puppy shampoo if he's less than a year old—or younger than 18 months for a giant breed like a Great Dane or St. Bernard.) Rinse well to remove all traces of the shampoo, then pour the rosemary tea onto his coat, work it in well, and let it dry. Blood-sucking bugs will dine elsewhere.

Keep mosquitoes away. Nothing spoils a barbecue faster than a bunch of hungry mosquitoes. But a couple of fresh herbs from the Produce aisle can help you and your guests dine in peace. What are these skeeter chasers? Sage and rosemary. Just toss a handful of either one of 'em onto the coals. (Use whichever one goes better with the food you're cooking.) You'll keep the biters at bay and spice up your chow at the same time!

Protect yourself from mosquitoes. A number of fresh herbs repel these little vampires, and there's a good chance you can find several of them in your supermarket's Produce aisle. Look for lemon balm, lemon basil, or lemon thyme. When you get the herbs home, crush the leaves to release their volatile oils, and rub them on your skin. When you do that, you can expect to stay bite-free for a couple of hours. The secret to their success lies in a strong, citrusy scent that's very pleasant to humans, but repugnant to mosquitoes and many other insects, too.

Turn away ants and mice. As unlikely as it may seem, these two little rascals have one thing in common: a strong aversion to mint. But you don't have to plant this cool-scented herb to take advantage of its power. Just pick up some sprigs of fresh mint at the supermarket, and lay them around wherever you don't want mice or ants roaming.

Color It Fresh

When you want to add real oomph to a wooden window box, planter, or unfinished outdoor furniture, color it up the natural way: with a stain made from fruits and vegetables straight from the Produce aisle (or, in some cases, the frozen-food section). You'll find the simple recipe for "Garden-Fresh Stain" on page 295, and here's your color palette.

TO GET THIS COLOR	USE THESE MATERIALS
Blue	Blackberries, blueberries, chestnuts, and red cabbage leaves
Brown	Walnuts
Green	Spinach
Green-gold	Golden delicious apple peels
Orange	Yellow onion skins
Purple	Blackberries or purple grapes
Red	Beets, cranberries, red raspberries, and red onion skins
Yellow	Shredded carrots, carrot tops (the green part), and lemon or orange peels

Fresh Herbs

Heal a bruise. Every gardener and do-it-yourselfer picks up his or her fair share of bruises. The next time an unexpected encounter with a stepladder or a boulder leaves you with a sore and unsightly souvenir, try this old-time remedy: Chill a handful of fresh parsley sprigs, crush them, apply them to the wound, and cover it with a bandage. Within 24 hours, those blues and purples will start to lighten up.

Put bruise relief on ice. Here's another way to enjoy the healing benefits of parsley—even when you don't have any sprigs on hand: Toss a handful of fresh leaves into a blender or food processor, and puree them with $\frac{1}{2}$ cup of water. Pour the mix into an ice-cube tray and stick it in the freezer. Then when some hard object jumps out and bonks your body, pull out a parsleysicle, wrap it in a thin cloth, and put it right on the sore spot. Hold it there for 15 to 20 minutes. Do this three or four times a day. The ice helps reduce the swelling, while the parsley goes to work on the discoloration, repairing the tiny capillaries that were burst in the crash.

Say farewell to frostbite. If you live in cold-winter territory and spend a lot of time outdoors, make up a batch of this old-time frostbite remedy, and keep it close at hand. Here's all there is to it: Pour $1\frac{1}{4}$ cups of white wine into a clean glass jar that has a tight lid. Add 1 tablespoon of fresh, coarsely grated horseradish, 1 tablespoon of fresh, coarsely grated gingerroot, and 2 tablespoons of whole black peppercorns. Let the mix sit for one week. Strain out the solids, using very fine cheesecloth or a coffee filter. Keep the liquid in a tightly closed bottle in a cool, dark place. Then anytime Jack Frost bites your fingers, nose, or other tender body parts, apply a generous coat of the solution to your affected skin, using a cotton ball or a very soft, clean paintbrush. You'll feel instant relief from the burning pain.

Garlic

Destroy soilborne fungi. When root and stem rots or other fungal diseases attack your flowers, vegetables, or turfgrass, this potent potion can come to the rescue. To make it, pour 1 gallon of water into a pot, and stir in 4 crushed garlic bulbs and ½ cup of baking soda. Bring the water to a boil, then turn off the heat and let the mixture cool to room temperature. Strain the liquid into a watering can, and soak the ground in the problem areas (removing any dead grass first). Go *very* slowly so the elixir penetrates deep into the soil. Then dump the strained-out garlic bits onto the soil, and work them in gently.

Prevent mildew. If you grow "mildew magnets" like garden phlox, asters, and mums, protect them with this ultra-easy spray that fends off both downy and powdery mildew. Just boil 10 cloves of garlic in 1 quart of water for half an hour. Strain, let the liquid cool to room temperature, and pour it into a handheld sprayer bottle. Then when you get a spell of warm days and cool, humid nights—which is prime mildew weather—spray your trouble-prone plants from stem to stern every four or five days.

Stamp out damping-off. The same garlic-tea recipe (see "Destroy soilborne fungi," above) will protect seedlings from the dreaded damping-off fungus. Start mist-spraying your baby plants with the brew as soon as their little heads appear above the starter mix.

Kill insect pests. Mince 1 whole bulb of garlic, mix it with 1 cup of vegetable oil, and put it in a glass jar with a tight lid. Set it in the refrigerator, and let it steep for a day or two. To test it for "doneness," remove the lid and take a whiff. If the aroma is so strong that you want to drop the jar and run, it's ready. If the scent isn't so strong, add half a garlic bulb, and wait another day. Then strain out the solids, pour the oil into a fresh jar, and store it in the refrigerator.

You can turn your "condiment" into a potent pesticide by whirling 1 tablespoon of the oil in a blender with 1 quart of water and 3 drops of dishwashing liquid added. Pour the mixture into a handheld mist sprayer, and let 'er rip. The potion will deal a death blow to any soft-bodied insects, including aphids, whiteflies, and destructive caterpillars. (Bear in mind that to be effective, this spray needs to make direct contact with its victim, so take careful aim before you pull the "trigger.") *Note:* Anytime a recipe calls for dishwashing liquid, do not use detergent or any product that contains antibacterial agents.

Make an extra-potent insect spray. When your whole garden seems to be disappearing into the mouths of leaf-eating bugs, strike back hard with this heavy artillery: Combine 4 to 6 garlic cloves, 1 small onion, and 2 hot peppers (or 1 teaspoon of ground cayenne) in a blender with 1 quart of water, and liquefy the mix. Let it sit overnight, then strain out the solids, and add 3 drops of baby shampoo. Pour the solution into a handheld sprayer, and fire when ready.

Mix up an extra-gentle repellent. Use this aromatic concoction to make your plants a no-munching zone for beetles, weevils, and all kinds of hard- and soft-bodied bugs. Because this formula contains no soap—which can damage tender, young plant parts—it's safe to use even on brand-new buds. Here's all you need to do: Mix 1/2 cup of finely chopped garlic and 2 cups of water in a bowl, let it sit for an hour or so, and strain out the solids. Pour the liquid into a handheld sprayer, and spray your plants once a week, paying special attention to new leaf and flower buds. Repeat after every rain, and after any overhead irrigation. If you don't have any garlic on hand, you can substitute onions or chives in the mix.

Protect your roses. From what? From the dreaded black spot fungus *and* from some of the most notorious rose-destroying pests of all, including cane borers, rose chafers, and Japanese beetles—that's what! The process couldn't be simpler: Just pick up a few garlic bulbs from the Produce aisle, and plant the cloves in your rose beds (or anyplace else in your yard where bad bugs and black spot are causing trouble). When the garlic plants come up, they'll work like knights in shining armor to keep your green friends happy, healthy, and pest-free.

Protect your other plants, too. In addition to fending off rose problems, garlic says a loud and clear "Keep out!" to deer, rabbits, and all kinds of other destructive insects, including aphids, cabbage loopers, plum curculios, and borers of all types.

MARVELOUS MiX

Flowery Farewell Formula

This potent repellent is tailor-made for container gardens, or any garden that's small enough to water by hand. It keeps destructive insects away from your plantings, without harming a single living thing.

- 1/4 cup of garlic cloves
- 1/4 cup of marigold flower tops
- 1/4 cup of geranium (*Pelargonium*) flower tops

Chop all of the ingredients (I use an old food processor), and mix them in a bucket with 5 gallons of warm water. Let it sit overnight, and strain it into your watering can. Sprinkle your garden with this elixir, then scatter the solids on the ground to deliver even more bug-chasing power.

Garlic

Make moles mosey on out. When these terrible tiny tunnelers are trouncing your turf, there's no mistaking the evidence: You'll see round piles of loose dirt around each tunnel entrance. A classic good-riddance maneuver is to pop an aromatic substance into the hole. It works, too—at least most of the time. One of your best smelly choices is a partially crushed garlic clove and a stick of Juicy Fruit® chewing gum. You might have to repeat the procedure a few times (with this or any other odiferous stuff), but eventually, the moles will give up and move away.

Keep your dried beans bug-free. If you grow beans to store for the winter (or "put by," as my Grandma Putt called it), here's an old-time trick you should know: Tuck a few

Here's to
YOU!

When you're looking for relief from sunburn pain, garlic probably isn't the first remedy that springs to mind—but it sure is one of the most effective. Don't just take my word for it, though. The next time you need to cool down an overheated hide (your own or someone else's), make up a batch of this super-soothing tea. Here's the easier-than-pie recipe: Simmer 2 chopped garlic cloves in 2 cups of water for 5 minutes. Turn off the heat, cover the pan, and let it steep for 45 minutes. When it's cooled to room temperature, strain out the solids, pour the tea into a covered container, and stash it in the refrigerator until it's chilled. Then soak a washcloth or hand towel in the chilly brew, wring out the excess liquid, and put the damp cloth on the painful area. Leave it in place for about 20 minutes or so. Replace it with a freshly moistened cloth until you feel relief from the discomfort.

cloves of garlic into each storage container. The aroma will deter bean weevils and other pests that might otherwise invade your supply.

Protect your pet from fleas and ticks. Here's one of the simplest—and most effective—ways to keep your dog or cat from picking up these nasty parasites: Just put a few garlic cloves into his bed, and mix a crushed garlic clove into his food once a day.

 # Onions

Repel pillbugs and sowbugs. Under normal circumstances, these little crustaceans do good work in the garden by recycling dead plant material into valuable humus. But once in a while, the population skyrockets, and your helpers are forced to nibble on living flowers and vegetables (most often, young seedlings). When that happens at your place, don't panic—and don't destroy your allies! Instead, just issue a gentle go-away-for-now message with this simple concoction. Puree 3 medium-sized onions with 1 quart of water in a blender or food processor, and strain out the solids. Pour the liquid into a handheld sprayer, and spritz the soil around any plants that need protection. Repeat after every rain until the crustacean population returns to a tolerable level.

Keep whiteflies away from your houseplants. No windowsill, sunroom, or greenhouse plant is off-limits to these sap-sucking pests. So guard your green friends by spraying them with onion skin tea. To make it, chop the skin of 1 medium onion, and let it steep overnight in 2 cups of water. Strain out the solids, add 1 quart of warm water,

If you're like most fruit and vegetable lovers, you tend to collect a lot of mesh bags. Here are some ways to put those handy things to work, indoors and out:

Arrange flowers. Wad up a mesh bag, put it in the bottom of a vase, and stick the stems through the holes. They'll stay exactly where you want them.

Clean dead bugs off of your windshield. Slosh soapy water onto the glass, scrub with a mesh bag, and wipe dry with a clean, soft cloth.

Dry out bathtub, wading pool, or beach toys. Load the dripping stuff into a mesh bag, and hang it from your shower nozzle, or a handy tree limb.

Dye Easter eggs to die for. Wrap a hard-boiled egg in a mesh bag, and dip the package into the dye. The egg will come out with a beautiful lattice pattern.

Feed the birds—fast. To make an instant feeder, slide a block of suet inside a mesh bag, and hang it from a sturdy tree branch.

Increase your tree-fruit harvest. Fill mesh bags with stones, and attach them to the tree's branches so they bend downward to a roughly 60-degree angle. This will shift the plant's energy away from foliage growth and into producing fruit buds. (Just be sure you don't make the weights so heavy that the limbs break!) This trick works with any kind of tree fruit.

Wash and dry your lettuce. Put the freshly picked (or just-bought) greens into a mesh bag and repeatedly dunk it into a sinkful of water. Then hang the bag from an upper-cabinet knob and let it drip onto a towel, or blot the leaves dry. Or do what I do: Take the bag outside and give it a few twirls.

Wash up outdoors. Tuck a bar of soap into a mesh bag, hang it on the outside faucet, and wash your grimy hands with it—there's no need to remove the soap.

and pour the liquid into a handheld sprayer. Apply the brew to your plants once a month, and you can wave your whitefly worries goodbye!

Get moles out of your yard. Here's one of the easiest mole-control methods that I know of: Simply tuck onion wedges every 4 to 5 feet in each run. The dreadful diggers will dash outta Dodge in a mighty big hurry.

Cure black spot. If you grow roses, you know what a pain in the grass this fungal disease can be. Well, here's good news: If you reach the scene at the first sign of a breakout, you can turn the tide. To start, gather up two small onions and 15 tomato leaves (if you don't grow tomatoes, borrow these from someone who does). Chop the bulbs and leaves into fine pieces, and steep them overnight in rubbing alcohol. Strain out the solids, then use a small, sponge-type paint-brush to apply the liquid to both the tops and bottoms of any infected rose leaves. The ugly spots will be gone before you know it.

Turn off mosquitoes. And other biting bugs, too. Just rub a slice of raw onion over your exposed skin, and the would-be diners will give you the cold shoulder. (But then again, so will your friends and family.)

Soothe a bee sting. One minute, you're having a great time at your barbecue, and the next minute, zap—a bee plants her stinger in your unsuspecting skin. Don't rush away from the fun. Instead, pull the stinger out, then grab an onion slice from the table and lay it on the sting site. It'll ease the swelling and soreness fast.

Shine up a rusty knife. Whether you use that blade indoors or out, you can get it shipshape the same way: Use it to slice up an onion or two. It'll soon be as clean as a whistle!

Dr. Onion Is In

Believe it or not, the humble onion is one of the best bronchial medicines you could ever ask for. The pungent bulbs are a rich source of quercetin, a chemical that helps relieve chest colds, bronchitis, and even asthma attacks. What's more, it works whether you eat your onions raw in a salad, stir-fry them with other vegetables, or make yourself a big bowl of onion soup. Take a gander at some of the other health problems that this medical miracle worker can solve.

HEALTH PROBLEM	TANGY SOLUTION
Athlete's foot	Massage onion juice into your tootsies twice a day to relieve the itching and burning sensation.
Banged shin	Immediately after the unfortunate encounter, cut a slice of raw onion (the stronger, the better), put it over the bump site, and leave it on for 15 minutes. If you've acted fast enough, no bruise should develop. That's because the same chemicals that make your eyes water also flush out excess blood from the area.
Chest congestion	Cut a large onion into thin slices, and cook it in a little water until it's very soft. Wrap the cooked onion in a clean towel, lay it over your chest for 20 minutes, and you'll start breathing easier.
Clogged sinuses	Cut one end off of an onion, hold it (cut side up) under your nose, and take a big whiff. Those nasal passages will be free and clear in no time flat!
Earache	Heat half an onion in the oven until it's warm (not hot). Wrap it in cheesecloth, and hold it against your sore ear. The chemicals in the onion will help increase your blood circulation, and draw out the infection.
Minor burn	First run cold water over the burned area, then apply a slice of raw onion. The same chemicals that make you cry also block the substances that make you feel pain. And here's a bonus: Onion juice has antibacterial properties that may help prevent infection. (Of course, if the burn is severe, hightail it to the emergency room!)

HEALTH PROBLEM	TANGY SOLUTION
Nagging cough	Put 1 finely sliced onion in a pot, and add enough honey to cover the slices completely. Simmer, with the lid on, over low heat for 40 minutes. Let it cool, and strain the syrup into a bottle with a tight stopper. Take a teaspoonful every hour or so until your cough has gone away.
Warts	Rub them with half an onion that's been dipped in salt. Use this treatment twice a day until the unsightly things disappear.
Wooziness	Hold a cut onion under your nose and try to breathe normally until the sensation passes.

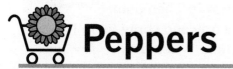 # Peppers

Keep roving pets out of your yard. We all know that the surest way to do this job is with a nice, solid wall or tall fence. But if you can't or simply don't want to enclose your property, this liquid barrier makes a fine stand-in. To make it, puree 3 or 4 hot peppers (the hotter the better) and 2 to 3 cloves of garlic, and mix them in a bucket with 2 gallons of water and a few drops of dishwashing liquid. Dribble the elixir around the edges of your lawn and sidewalk. Repeat frequently, especially after each rain and after you've watered your lawn. *Note:* Anytime a recipe calls for dishwashing liquid, do not use detergent or any product that contains antibacterial agents.

Make Japanese beetles go away. When you want to issue a get-lost notice to these vile, voracious villains, hot peppers are your best friends. That's because Japanese beetles hate hot, spicy flavors as much as a lot of people love them.

Here's your modus operandi: Put $^1/_2$ cup of fresh jalapeño peppers and $^1/_2$ cup of dried cayenne peppers in a pot with 1 gallon of water. Bring it to a boil, and let it simmer for half an hour. (Keep the pot covered, or the peppery steam will make you cry a river of tears!) Let the mixture cool, strain out the solids, and pour the liquid into a handheld sprayer bottle. Apply the potion to your plants from top to bottom to the point of runoff. To ensure continued protection, reapply after every rain.

Stop squirrels from robbing your bird feeder. The same hot trick that chases Japanese beetles away from your plants will keep squirrels from robbing your bird feeders blind. First, mix up the potion as described above (see "Make Japanese beetles go away"). Then pour a shallow layer of seeds into a tray and spray them lightly, but thoroughly, with the solution. When they're dry, put them into your feeder. The pests will take one nibble— and rush for cooler dining options. But the birds won't be bothered one bit—they have no receptors in their brains for spicy flavors, so they can't even taste the pepper!

Add punch to commercial repellents. Whether the product you bought is designed to fend off insects or four-legged critters, this simple trick will help it do a better job—and make your supply last longer, too. Here's all you need to do: Fill a bucket with water, and toss in a couple handfuls of chopped hot peppers (the hottest ones your supermarket has). Put the bucket in a sunny spot, and let the mixture steep for a week or so, until it's so spicy that it brings tears to your eyes. Then mix 4 parts of the pepper solution to 1 part of your commercial deterrent in a handheld sprayer. Apply the mixture to the pests' target plants, and sit back and watch the lack of action! One word of caution: If you use this spray on fruits or vegetables, be sure to wash them thoroughly before you eat them!

Vitalize your veggies. Here's an out-of-the-ordinary tonic that packs a double punch: It'll get your plants producing to beat the band *and* help repel pesky pests, too! To make it, first mince 1 green pepper, 1 onion, and 2 teaspoons of mint leaves, and whirl them in a blender with 1 quart of hot water. Strain out the solids, and mix 1/4 cup of the liquid with 1/2 can of beer, 3 tablespoons of fish emulsion, and 2 tablespoons of dishwashing liquid. Pour the mix into a 20 gallon hose-end sprayer, and apply the solution to your vegetable garden every three weeks throughout the growing season. You won't believe the results! *Note:* Anytime a recipe calls for dishwashing liquid, do not use detergent or any product that contains antibacterial agents.

Turn Up the Heat!

When you're setting out to repel pests by using hot peppers, you want the hottest ones your supermarket has to offer. What provides the steamy quality in these fruits is certain heat-producing chemicals, the prime one being capsaicin. How much capsaicin a pepper has—and therefore, how much firepower it delivers—is measured in Scoville Heat Units. (They're named for scientist William Scoville, who came up with the system back in 1912.) Here's Dr. Scoville's scorecard. You might want to keep these numbers in mind when you're shopping for peppers to use in my Marvelous Mix recipes.

PEPPER TYPE	SCOVILLE HEAT UNITS
Anaheim chili	250–1,400
Jalapeño	4,000–6,000
Serrano chili	7,000–25,000
Cayenne	30,000–35,000
Chili Pequin	35,000–40,000
Tabasco	30,000–50,000
Habañero	200,000–350,000

Deal a death blow to bad bugs. Almost no destructive insect can stand up to this fiery eliminator. To make it, puree 3 hot green peppers, 3 medium cloves of garlic, and 1 small onion in a blender. Pour the mixture into a large jar, and add 1 tablespoon of dishwashing liquid and 3 cups of water. Let it stand for 24 hours. Strain out the solids, pour the liquid into a handheld sprayer bottle, and blast the plant-trashing trespassers to kingdom come. If you don't get them all on the first try, repeat the process a few times. *Note:* Anytime a recipe calls for dishwashing liquid, do not use detergent or any product that contains antibacterial agents.

 # Potatoes

Test for worms in potted plants. If your formerly healthy container plants suddenly wilt (and you know it's not from dehydration), the cause may be root-damaging worms or maggots. To find out for sure, set a slice of raw potato on the soil. The worms will mosey on up to the surface to get at the taste-tempting treat—and you can catch them in the act.

Deter dogs (maybe). Grandma Putt told me that when she was a girl, folks swore that rotten potatoes were a first-class dog repellent. They scattered them in new planting beds, around garbage cans, and anyplace else where they didn't want Rover to roam. I've never used this trick myself, but if you find yourself with a few over-the-hill spuds and a trespassing pooch on your hands, it's worth a try!

Start roses from cuttings. Do you have a treasured old rose that you'd love to share with family and friends? If so, then grow more plants from cuttings. It's easier than you might think— especially with this old-time trick: After all of the flowers have fallen off in late summer, snip off 6- to 8-inch-long stem tips, and remove all of the leaves except for one or two at the top. Stick the cut end into a potato, then plant the cutting (potato and all) in your rose bed, with half of the stem's length below the ground. Water thoroughly, then invert a glass jar over the cutting. (Shove the jar a little way into the soil so it won't blow over in the winter wind.) Come spring, remove the jar, and you'll have a brand-new little rosebush.

Super-charge geraniums. The next time you're getting ready to pot up some *Pelargoniums,* pop over to the Produce aisle, and pick up some potatoes—one for each young transplant. Carve out a hole in the spud that's just big enough to hold the little rootball, insert it into the opening, and set the whole thing into your container. The potato will give the baby plant all the nutrients it needs to grow big, strong, and bursting with blooms.

Do Tell!

Calling all tomato lovers! As your garden-variety travel advisor, I'm here to tell you about a place you might want to go on your next vacation. It's a little town called Buñol, in the Valencia region of Spain. And why, you might ask, would you want to go there? Because Buñol is the site of La Tomatina, a weeklong festival held each August that's centered around the world's largest (maybe the world's *only*) tomato fight. Some 30,000 tourists and 9,000 or so townspeople join the fray, pelting one another with more than 100 metric tons of overripe tomatoes. Of course, although the messy fracas is the main event, it's not the only game in town. There's also music, dancing, parades, fireworks and, on the evening before the big fight, a *paella*-cooking contest. So what are you waiting for? Order your plane tickets now!

Arrange cut flowers. You've picked flowers from your garden, you're all set to make a fancy arrangement for your dinner party tonight—and you discover that you're fresh out of florist's foam! Don't fret—you don't need that stuff. Just grab a large potato, cut it in half, and put it flat-side down on a plate or cutting board. In the spud's rounded side, poke holes that are large enough to hold your flowers' stems. Set the holey potato into your vase, and insert the stems in the holes. If the vase is transparent or shallow, disguise the brown tuber with a bit of moss or fabric.

Coax a stubborn splinter out. Ouch! You were building a raised bed out of rustic lumber, and now a little sliver of that wood is stuck under your skin where you can't get at it. Well, you'll be able to reach it soon if you try this simple trick: Tape a slice of potato onto the affected site, or if the sliver is in your finger or toe, hollow out a space that's just the right size, and slip the digit into the spud. (Hold it in place with a sock if you need to.) Leave the tater in place overnight, and you'll be able to easily pluck the splinter out in the morning.

Cap your mower's gas tank. How on earth did you manage to misplace that gas-tank cap? All you did was unscrew it and set it aside so you could fill up your mower, and now poof—it's gone! No problem. Just fill the opening with a small potato or half of a larger one (whittle it down as much as you need to, so that it fits snugly). It'll keep fuel and fumes from escaping until you can buy a new cap, or the old one reappears. Don't use the spud for more than a day or two, though; after that, it'll start to decompose.

Clean scuffed leather. Your shoes and boots can sure take a beating in the great outdoors, but once more, America's most-eaten vegetable can rise to the challenge. Just rub your footgear with a raw potato, and follow up with your usual polish. Bingo—end of stubborn scuff marks!

We all know that potatoes make for some mighty fine eating. But the common spud can also do terrific things for the *outside* of your body. Here are a handful of ways you can put spud power to work for you:

Here's to YOU!

Ease the pain and itch of eczema. Just grate a raw potato, dip a cotton pad in the shreds to absorb some of the juice, and gently dab the trouble spots.

Cure hemorrhoids. Grate a tablespoon or two of raw potato, wrap it in cheesecloth, and put it in the refrigerator until it's good and chilled. Then pull out the pouch, go to your room, pull down your drawers, and—no kidding—sit on the spuds.

Reduce bags and dark circles under your eyes. Grate a raw potato and wrap the shavings in two pieces of cheesecloth. Lie down, put one sack over each eye, and relax for 15 minutes. Repeat daily, until the circles fade. (If you don't mind the messiness, you can dispense with the cheesecloth and apply the potatoes directly to your skin as a poultice.)

Soothe a minor burn. Slice the end off of a raw potato, and rub the affected skin gently with the cut surface. You'll feel almost instant relief!

Treat muscle aches and pains. Spuds retain both heat and cold well—which is just what the doctor ordered for making a good compress. If your injury calls for hot treatment, boil a potato, wrap it in a towel, and apply it to the ailing area. When it's time for the big chill, pop the tasty tuber into the refrigerator until it's nice and cold. If you're in a hurry, put it into the freezer instead, or use a second potato for chillin'.

Change a broken lightbulb. Your back-porch
lightbulb fell victim to a wayward
Frisbee, and you have to get the danged
thing out without cutting yourself. How
can you do it? It's easy: First, make sure
the power to the fixture is turned off! Next,
push half of a raw potato, cut-side first,
against the broken bulb. Turn the spud just
as you would to unscrew an unbroken light
bulb. It'll come right out. Then toss the whole thing in the
trash (don't try to separate the bulb from the tater).

Remove mud spots. When you spend any amount of time in your
yard or garden, you're bound to wind up with a lot of mud
on your clothes. I know I do! And I still get rid of the spots
the way my Grandma Putt did: by rubbing them with a
slice of raw potato, and tossing the duds into the washing
machine. They emerged spotless way back then, and the
same trick still works today!

Start a tree off right. When you're planting or transplanting a
tree, line the hole with baking potatoes. Initially, they'll
help hold moisture that the young tree needs to get started. Then once they decay, they'll provide much-needed
nutrients for the tree to grow on.

Distract slugs. If these vile villains are attacking your container
plantings, slice up a raw potato and place the slices around
your pots. The slugs will home in on the potatoes, and in
the morning, you can pick 'em up and plop 'em in a bucket
of soapy or salty water.

Sugar & Sweeteners

CORN SYRUP
HONEY
MOLASSES
PEANUT BUTTER
SUGAR

Corn Syrup

Start bare-root roses out right. A dormant rose with its roots stripped of soil *looks* pretty pathetic, all right. But for reasons that (I confess) I've never discovered, bare-root roses seem to settle in more quickly than their potted counterparts. You do need to give them a little special TLC at planting time, though. Specifically, you should soak the roots overnight in 1 gallon of warm water mixed with 1 tablespoon each of corn syrup, baby shampoo, and 5-8-5 or 5-10-5 organic fertilizer. After you've planted your bare-root babies, sprinkle the mixture around your established rosebushes—they'll love you for it!

Give bare-root roses speedier TLC. When you can't wait a whole day to get your plants into the ground, use this instant formula: In a bucket, mix 2 tablespoons of corn syrup, 2 teaspoons of dishwashing liquid, and 1 teaspoon of ammonia in 1 gallon of warm water. Dunk the roots into the drink, let them soak for about half an hour, and then put 'em in the ground. They'll be growin' great in no time flat. *Note:* Anytime a recipe calls for dishwashing liquid, do not use detergent or any product that contains antibacterial agents.

Prep your soil for a new lawn. Turfgrass is no different than any other kind of plant: To perform its best, it needs to sink its first, new roots into good, healthy soil. You can provide those root-pleasing conditions by digging plenty of organic matter into the ground, along with a good starter fertilizer and whatever amendments your soil test called for. (You *did* have your soil tested, didn't you?) Then about three days before you sow your seed or lay your sod, overspray the prepared ground with this fabulous foliar formula: In a bucket, mix 1/4 cup of clear corn syrup, 1 cup of fish emulsion, and 1/2 cup each of ammonia and baby shampoo.

Give 'Em a Warm Welcome

Whenever you're using corn syrup, honey, or molasses in a Marvelous Mix, make sure that you bring it to room temperature before you add it to the other recipe ingredients. If the sticky stuff is cold, it'll clog the tube in your hose-end sprayer. The same thing will happen if these or any other thick substances are not combined thoroughly. So for best results, always mix up your tonic in a bucket before pouring the solution into the sprayer jar.

Pour the solution into a 20 gallon hose-end sprayer, and saturate the soil. After planting, spray the area lightly with water three or four times a day. Before you know it, you'll be rollin' in the green—grass, that is!

Green up your yard. To keep your lawn, trees, shrubs, flowers, and vegetables in the pink of health all summer long, do what I've been recommending for more than half a century now: Serve frequent doses of my All-Season Green-Up Tonic. To make it, pour 1 cup of beer, 1 cup of ammonia, and $1/2$ cup each of corn syrup or molasses, dishwashing liquid, and liquid lawn food into a bucket. Mix the ingredients thoroughly, and pour the solution into a 20 gallon hose-end sprayer. Apply the mix to every plant in your yard to the point of runoff every three weeks throughout the growing season. You'll have the greatest-looking green scene in town! *Note:* Anytime a recipe calls for dishwashing liquid, do not use detergent or any product that contains antibacterial agents.

Grow moss on hard surfaces. Do you have a new stone wall that looks a little, well, raw around the edges? Or maybe some just-bought terra-cotta planters that look too pristine to suit you? If the answer is yes—and you can lay your hands on a little moss—then here's the trick you've been waiting for: Pour an 8-ounce can of condensed milk, 1 tablespoon of corn syrup, and 2 cups of moss into an old blender, and whirl it up into a slurry. Paint it onto your pots or stones, and in just a couple of weeks, they'll look like they've been in the family for generations!

Nourish your container plants. This hearty meal will keep your potted plants well fed and growing strong all season long—indoors or out. Here's how to make it: In a 1-gallon milk jug, mix 1 tablespoon of 15-30-13 fertilizer, $1/4$ teaspoon of instant tea granules, and $1/2$ teaspoon each of corn syrup, unflavored gelatin, and whiskey (any kind will do). Fill the balance of the jug with water. Then add $1/2$ cup of this mixture to every gallon of water you use to water your flowers, vegetables, or any other plants that you grow in pots, planters, hanging baskets, or window boxes.

Perk up annual flowers. When the summer weather turns steamy, even tough customers like zinnias, cosmos, and cleome can knuckle under. If your treasured annuals have stopped blooming, don't give them up for lost. You can get the show back on the road with this refreshing routine: Cut the plants back by about half, and water them thoroughly. Then pour 1 gallon of water into a sprinkling can, and add $1/4$ cup of beer and 1 tablespoon each of clear corn syrup, baby shampoo, and 15-30-15 fertilizer. Mix the ingredients thoroughly, and dribble the solution onto the soil around all of your annuals. Within a couple of weeks, they'll spring back to their full glory, and they'll keep churning out lush leaves and beautiful blooms until Jack Frost pulls down the curtain.

Christmas-Tree Survival Tonic

Every year, without fail, my Grandma Putt poured this elixir into our Christmas tree stand to keep that ol' tree fresh and green throughout the year-end holidays. I still use it—I've never found a better formula!

> 4 multivitamin-plus-iron tablets (crushed)
> 2 cups of clear corn syrup
> 4 tbsp. of household bleach
> 1 gal. of very hot water

As soon as you bring your tree indoors and set it up, mix all of the ingredients in a bucket and pour the mixture into the stand. Deliver a fresh dose whenever the water level starts going down, and your evergreen will stay as fresh as a daisy right into the new year.

Revive old shrubs. You've always taken good care of your shrubs, but lately they've seemed somehow…well…lackluster, as though they're just running out of steam. Don't blame yourself! That happens to most shrubs after they reach a certain age. But you can breathe new life into your senior citizens with a bracing potion made from 1 can of beer, 1 cup of ammonia, and 1/2 cup each of clear corn syrup and dishwashing liquid. Mix the ingredients thoroughly in a bucket, and pour the solution into a 20 gallon hose-end sprayer. Drench your shrubs to the point of runoff, making sure to get the undersides of all the leaves. Repeat the procedure each spring, and those old-timers will bounce back with plenty of fresh new growth. *Note:* Anytime a recipe calls for dishwashing liquid, do not use detergent or any product that contains antibacterial agents.

Corn Syrup

319

Rejuvenate vines and groundcovers. You say your shrubs are growin' and bloomin' to beat the band, but your climbers and sprawlers look a little limp and tired? Well, then, this timely tonic is just the ticket—it's like a breath of fresh air for weary, hardworking plants. To make it, mix 1 cup of hydrogen peroxide, $1/4$ cup of clear corn syrup, and 2 tablespoons each of whiskey and baby shampoo with $1^1/2$ cups of warm water in a bucket. Pour the solution into a 20 gallon hose-end sprayer, and apply it to your plants to the point of runoff just as new growth begins in the spring. You won't believe the difference!

Make cut evergreens last longer. If you like to make wreathes or centerpieces from fresh greens, here's a trick you should know: Before you start creating your masterpieces, soak the stems overnight in a mixture of $1/4$ cup of corn syrup and 1 tablespoon of dry bleach. In the morning, spray them with an antidesiccant. When they're dry to the touch, make fresh, sharp cuts on the ends. Then go to town!

Perform first aid on a potted plant. If one of your container plants starts looking kinda sickly, but there's no sign of pests or diseases, it could be that the potting mix simply needs a jolt of energy. Before you resort to more compli-

Plastic bottles, emptied of their contents, make terrific traps for all kinds of pests. Just coat the bottles with corn syrup; then either hang them from trees, or stick them upside down on stakes that you've pounded into the ground among your troubled plants. As for color, most insects zero in on yellow, but there are exceptions. You can find the roster in Chapter 1 (see "Color Them Gone," on page 17).

cated tactics, try this ultra-simple pick-me-up: Drizzle 2 tablespoons of corn syrup onto the soil at the base of the plant. Repeat the procedure once a month until the patient is back in the pink of health. (It shouldn't take more than one or two treatments.)

Give your herbs a drink. Just like people, herbs enjoy a nice, cool beverage when the going gets hot. I've found that they especially like this thirst-quencher: In a bucket, thoroughly mix 1 can of beer, 1 cup of ammonia, and ½ cup each of clear corn syrup and Murphy® Oil Soap. Pour the solution into a 20 gallon hose-end sprayer, and give your herbs a good dousing every six weeks throughout the growing season. They'll stay as cool as cucumbers and as happy as clams!

Keep cut flowers fresh longer. One of the best ways to prolong the lives of your homegrown or store-bought flowers is also one of the easiest: Just fill your vases with a solution of 2 tablespoons of clear corn syrup per quart of water.

Say "Stay out!" to stinging bugs. When you're hosting a barbecue, garden wedding reception, or other outdoor event, the last thing you want is a bunch of bees, wasps, and yellow jackets swarming around your guests. So bar the door with this simple trick: Coat pieces of cardboard or plastic with corn syrup, and set them around the perimeter of your yard. The stinging so-and-so's will be attracted to the sweet stuff and leave your partygoers in peace.

Make sticky traps. These dandy devices are a great, hands-off way to wipe out insect pests. They're also helpful when you simply want to monitor the population, so that you can find out what kinds of bugs are buggin' your plants. Whatever your reason for using them, they're a snap to make. Just spread corn syrup on sheets of cardboard that you've tacked to wooden stakes, and pound the stakes into the ground among your troubled plants.

Fabricate your own flypaper. In the days before pesticide sprays came along, every screened-in porch and pantry had a strip or two of sticky paper hanging from the ceiling. You can still buy these old-time fly traps, but it's a snap to make your own. Here's all you need to do: Mix 1 cup of corn syrup, 1 tablespoon of brown sugar, and 1 tablespoon of white sugar. Then cut strips from a brown paper bag, poke a hole in the top of each strip, and put a string through it. Brush the syrup mixture on your strips, and hang them wherever flies are flying.

 # Honey

Close the aphid ranch in your tree. If you've tried time and time again to get the sap-sucking pests out of a tree, and they just keep coming back, chances are it's because a colony of ants keeps drivin' 'em back up there and watchin' over them like cowboys tendin' a herd of cattle. To solve your aphid problem for good, you need to eliminate the trail drivers. There are a whole lot of ways to do that, but one of the best (and easiest) is to fill jar lids with honey and set them out on the ground around the base of the tree. The ants will make a beeline to the dessert bar, fall in, and die happy. As a bonus, you can rest easy knowing that only the mischief makers will be harmed—not any small children, pets, or innocent wildlife who may be tempted to sample the sweet stuff.

Head off wireworm woes. These villains tunnel into the roots of many fruits, vegetables, and ornamental plants, causing them to weaken, wilt, and often die. The worms' parents are click beetles (so called because they have a tendency to roll over on their backs, and in the process of flipping themselves right-side up—which can take several tries—

they make a clicking sound). Like many other insects, click beetles are drawn to sweet-tasting substances, and that gives you an ultra-simple way to practice planned unparenthood: Just drizzle honey on fence posts or thick wooden stakes. Then when the beetles fly in to sip the stuff, pick 'em off and drop 'em into soapy water. Whatever you do, though, don't lace the bait with poison! It'll kill the click beetles all right, but it'll also kill honeybees, butterflies, and other good-guy bugs that show up for a snack. *Note:* If you don't have any honey on hand, you can substitute corn syrup or molasses.

Trap pesky pests. Got cucumber beetles clobbering your cucurbit crops? Cabbage worms bashing your brassicas? Or maybe slugs are slashing their way through every plant in sight? Well, don't lose any sleep over it. Even if you're not sure what kind of villains are vandalizing your garden, this old-time technique will lure 'em in: In the early evening, gather some small boards, coat one side of each one with honey, and set them out near the infested plants. Prop up one corner of each board just enough so that the pests can crawl underneath it. And will they ever! By morning, your traps should be packed with thugs who've abandoned the salad bar in favor of dessert. Then you can simply scoop up the boards and dump them into a tub of soapy water.

Soothe your sunburn. You've gone and done it again! You started puttering in your garden and got so caught up in your chores that you completely lost track of the time. Now your skin is showing—and feeling—the results. Don't worry! This potion will have you feeling as cool as a cucumber in no time flat. To make it, mix $1/2$ cup of honey with 1 cup of vegetable oil, $1/2$ cup of liquid hand soap, and 1 tablespoon of pure vanilla extract (not artificial). Pour $1/4$ cup of the potion under running bath water, ease into the tub, and soak the flames away.

A Honey of a Health-Care Helper

Since at least as far back as the days of the pharaohs in Egypt, people have known about the amazing healing powers of honey. And you know what? Even today, when the supermarket shelves are packed with cure-alls for every ailment under the sun, old-fashioned bee juice is just what the doctor ordered for a whole lot of problems—including these.

THE PROBLEM	THE SWEET SOLUTION
Acid indigestion*	For immediate relief, take 1 to 3 teaspoons of honey. To ease a chronic problem, take 1 tablespoon each night at bedtime, on an empty stomach, until you feel better.
Bug bites and bee stings	Smooth a dab of honey onto the spot to eliminate the pain and itch.
Cough*	Mix 1 cup of honey with 4 tablespoons of lemon juice and 1/2 cup of olive oil. Heat the mixture for 5 minutes, then stir vigorously for 2 minutes. Take one teaspoon every 2 hours, and before you know it, your hacking will be history!
Cuts and scrapes	Wash the wound and spread honey over it. It'll dry to form a natural bandage and also hasten the healing process.
Hangover	Take 1 teaspoon of honey every hour until you feel better—which will be a lot sooner than you probably think.
Insomnia	Take 1 teaspoon of honey at bedtime, and you'll have a restful sleep.
Migraine headaches	To relieve an existing migraine, take 2 teaspoons of honey with each meal until your headache subsides. To stop a migraine before it starts, take 1 teaspoon of honey the minute you feel the early-warning signs.

*If your discomfort continues for more than a few days, or if you experience other symptoms, call your doctor immediately. *Caution:* Never give honey to a baby or young child who's under 2 years old.

Molasses

Simplify plant feeding. Plain old molasses, straight from the bottle, makes a dandy all-purpose, organic fertilizer. Apply it at a rate of 4 or 5 tablespoons per gallon of water, and your flowers and vegetables will stand up and say "Yum!" (in a manner of speaking).

Cook your compost faster. Whether you make your "black gold" in a plastic bin or a traditional pile, sprinkle it every few weeks with a half-and-half mix of molasses and water. (Either a bucket or a watering can makes a fine delivery mechanism.) Molasses increases microbial activity, thereby helping the organic matter break down more quickly. The water simply makes the gooey stuff a whole lot easier to handle.

Say "No!" to nematodes. These almost-microscopic worms run roughshod through sandy soil in warm coastal regions, where they invade the roots of many kinds of flowers and vegetables. If your garden beds are hosting the dastardly demons, combine 1 cup of molasses and 1 can of beer in a bucket, pour into your 20 gallon hose-end sprayer, and thoroughly soak the problem area. Your nematode nightmares will soon be over.

Toss earwigs out on their ear. Much of the time, earwigs are garden-variety heroes, helping turn dead plant material into valuable humus and wiping out bad-guy bugs, such as aphids, fleas, and grubs. Sometimes, though, these good guys go bad and chew the daylights out of living roots, leaves, flowers, and vegetables. Left unchecked, they can demolish a bed of seedlings. Fortunately, like many other insects, earwigs have a sweet tooth that rivals a 10-year-old's. So when trouble strikes, all you need to do is pour about half an inch of molasses into some glass jars, then

Hop to It!

Some years, grasshoppers just go about their business, not bothering anybody. Then one day, out of the blue, BAM! They descend in swarming masses, and almost before you can blink, every speck of green has vanished from your garden. These scourges happen most often on the hot, dry western plains, but grasshoppers can gang up on any patch of green in the country. When it comes to controlling them, there's bad news and good news. The bad news is that they stand up and say "Boo!" to Marvelous Mixes and other sprays that knock most other bugs flat. The good news is that 'hoppers flock to molasses the way bears flock to honey. You can put their craving to work in two ways:

1. Bury a jar up to its rim and fill it with a mixture of equal parts of molasses and water. The hellions will dive right in, and they won't get out—not alive, that is.

2. Mix 1 part molasses to 9 parts water, and pour the stuff into shallow containers, such as cat food or tuna fish cans. Set the cans in your garden, and sprinkle bread crumbs or sunflower seeds around them. Grasshoppers will zero in on the sweet water, and in the blink of an eye, birds will pounce on them and then hang around to help with your other pest-control chores.

add enough water to reach about three quarters of the way up. Stir until the water and molasses are thoroughly mixed, and set the beverages among your troubled plants. The earwigs will drop in for a drink, and they'll stay there!

Bring down flies. To put your fly frustrations firmly in the past, use my Grandma Putt's favorite good-riddance method: Beat an egg yolk with 1 tablespoon of molasses and a pinch of black pepper, and serve up the concoction in shallow cans or jar lids. The flies will glide in for a three-point landing, and they won't take off again!

Curtail codling moths. These are the culprits responsible for the old joke that goes, "What's worse than biting into an apple and finding a worm? Finding half a worm!" Although codling moths are most famous for ruining apple harvests from coast to coast, they also target crab apple, pear, quince, and sometimes plum and walnut trees. Once the worms are inside your fruit, there's nothing you can do about it; but you *can* prevent the next generation (or at least a sizeable part of it) from seeing the light of day. Here's your birth-control plan: Gather up some 1-gallon plastic milk jugs, and make a solution that's 1 part molasses to 1 part apple cider vinegar. Pour 1 to 2 inches of mix into each jug, tie a cord around the handle, and cover the opening with $\frac{1}{8}$- to $\frac{1}{4}$-inch mesh screen to keep honeybees out. Then hang the trap from a branch. The moths will fly in for a sip and not fly out.

MARVELOUS MIX

Fabulous Foliage Formula

Perennials with superstar foliage—like yuccas, hostas, and bearded irises—deserve TLC. So feed them this treat every three weeks, and they'll reward you with big, bright, shiny leaves.

> **1 can of beer**
> **$\frac{1}{2}$ cup of fish emulsion**
> **$\frac{1}{2}$ cup of ammonia**
> **$\frac{1}{4}$ cup of blackstrap molasses**
> **$\frac{1}{4}$ cup of instant tea granules**

Mix all of the ingredients in a bucket, pour into a 20 gallon hose-end sprayer, and apply until it runs off the leaves. *Note:* Aim the spray carefully so that it touches only the foliage, *not* the flowers.

Molasses

Get moles out of your yard. Over the years, lawn tenders have come up with a zillion ways to make these tiny, tunneling terrors turn tail and run (or at least toddle off). Here's another highly effective—and simple—trick: Just pour molasses into the moles' runs. It'll gum up their fur and send them off in search of less-sticky quarters. (If you want, you can add just a little water to make the molasses easier to handle.)

Fend off fungal diseases. These include many different plant ailments, and they can strike any part of a plant—roots, stems, leaves, flowers, or fruits. Once foul fungi start romping through your yard or garden, they're a royal pain in the grass. But there is a simple way to stop them before they get started. This routine works like a charm on ornamental

and edible plants: Mix $\frac{1}{2}$ cup of molasses, $\frac{1}{2}$ cup of powdered milk, and 1 teaspoon of baking soda into a paste. Stuff the mixture into an old panty hose leg, and let it steep in 1 gallon of warm water for several hours. Strain, pour the remaining liquid into a handheld sprayer bottle, and spritz your plants every week during the growing season.

Make your Christmas tree last longer. As you've seen throughout this book, folks have come up with a whole lot of ways to keep that old evergreen looking its festive best all through the holiday season. Here's another winner: When you bring the tree home, cut an inch or two off the bottom of the trunk, and immediately set it into a bucket of cold water with 1 cup of molasses added to it. Let the tree soak for two or three days before you move it indoors to its stand and start trimming it.

Remove grass stains. As unlikely as it may sound, molasses can take those annoying green splotches out of your clothes or canvas sneakers. Just rub the molasses into the spots, let the garments sit overnight, and wash them with mild soap (not detergent). The stains will vanish like magic! *Note:* If you're fresh out of molasses, you can perform this same fabulous feat using corn syrup.

 # Peanut Butter

Produce more bird-pleasing goodies. Here's an even easier way to say "Y'all come back now, y'hear!" Mix 2 parts peanut butter and 1 part black oil sunflower seed, and pack it into the rind of a grapefruit or large orange half. Make a sling out of twine, and hang the little feeder from a tree limb or a hook in your porch roof. Then get ready for action!

"Finger" the crooks. Not sure what kind of bugs, slugs, or other thugs are eating your plants? This terrific trick will help you find the answer: Bait a paper-towel or toilet-paper tube with a spoonful of peanut butter and a few drops of olive oil. Lay down the roll in your garden in the evening, and check it first thing each morning. After a couple of nights, you should find the culprits inside, and you can haul out the appropriate weaponry.

Trap mice. For such tiny critters, Mickey's clan can get into mighty big mischief around the old homestead—indoors and out. Fortunately, when you need to enforce the law, one of the best baits you can find is good ol' peanut butter. No matter what kind of mousetraps you favor, you'll draw a capacity crowd if you load 'em up with a dollop of the crunchy variety. Keep dishing the yummy stuff up until it has no more takers, and you can kiss your mouse miseries goodbye!

Make bird-food balls. You (and any youngsters in your house) will have a ball making these treats for your fine-feathered friends. Here's all there is to it: Mix peanut butter with enough whole-wheat flour to form a dough. (If you really want to turn your yard into an avian dining hot spot, add raisins, chopped fruit, or nuts to the mix.) Shape the dough into baseball-sized balls, and pop them into the freezer. When you want to serve one up, cut a section from a mesh produce bag, and wrap it around the ball. Tie the wrapping closed with twine or wire, and hang it from a sturdy tree branch.

Remove eau de garlic. Your garden offered up bumper crops of basil and garlic, and with the help of your food processor, you've spent a whole day making pesto. There's just one problem: Peeling all that garlic has left your hands reeking with the odor. The simple solution: Rub a dollop of peanut butter into your skin. When you wipe the creamy stuff off, the aroma will go along with it.

Lubricate your lawn mower. It'll never replace WD-40®, but in a real pinch, this works: Spread a little creamy peanut butter onto the blade shaft. The peanut oil will keep the blade cutting smoothly until you have time to visit your local hardware store.

Here's to YOU!

You've worked your tail off putting in a beautiful vegetable garden, but the local deer just won't leave it alone. The greedy gluttons have you so boiling mad that your blood pressure's skyrocketing. Well, just calm down (or try to, anyway). Dr. Jerry has a prescription that'll solve your deer problems for good. I call it my "gotcha" fence. It works by luring the critters with the tantalizing aroma of peanut butter. When they reach out for a bite, they get a light, but unwelcome, zap on the nose or tongue. Try it—it really works! Here's all you (or your hired helpers) need to do:

1. Attach insulators to 4-foot metal stakes.

2. Pound a stake into the ground at each corner of your garden and about 10 feet apart along the sides and ends.

3. String a line of 50-pound-tension hot wire from post to post at the top, and run the wire into a battery-charged generating unit.

4. Spread peanut butter all along the wire.

5. Turn on the electric current.

6. Watch the deer come running when they get a whiff of that peanut butter. And take a good, long look, because you won't see them coming back anytime soon!

Peanut Butter

Get rid of sap. I had a devil of a time scrubbing sticky sap off my hands after pruning my evergreens—until I discovered this trick. Just smooth peanut butter onto your hands, and clean it off with paper towels. Then de-sap your pruners by wiping the blades with a few dabs of peanut butter on a soft, clean cloth. The secret lies in the peanut oil: It dissolves the gums in the sap.

A Peanut Butter Timeline

Archeologists tell us that the peanut as we know it has been around since the Cretaceous period (65 million to 136 million years ago). For centuries, folks have been grinding those goobers up to make soups, sauces, and stews. (Civil War soldiers dined on what they called "Peanut Porridge.") But it wasn't until close to the dawn of the 20th century that peanut butter appeared on the scene. Here are some highlights in the history of one of America's favorite supermarket staples.

ON THIS DATE IN HISTORY	THIS IS WHAT HAPPENED
1890	A St. Louis physician named Ambrose W. Straub crushes peanuts into a paste as a protein source for his geriatric patients with bad (or no) teeth. Three years later, in 1893, the product is introduced to the public at the World's Columbian Exposition in Chicago.
1895	Dr. John Harvey Kellogg and his brother, W. K. Kellogg, of Battle Creek, Michigan, patent "the Process of Preparing Nut Meal," which they described as "a pasty adhesive substance that is for convenience of distinction termed nut butter." The product may have been healthful, but it lacked much taste appeal, probably because the peanuts were steamed, instead of roasted, prior to grinding. So the Kellogg brothers dropped the idea and turned their attention to breakfast cereals.

ON THIS DATE IN HISTORY	THIS IS WHAT HAPPENED
1903	Dr. Straub received Patent No. 721,651 for a "mill for grinding peanuts for butter." He encouraged George A. Bayle, Jr., the owner of a food products company, to process and package ground peanut paste. Bayle Food Products of St. Louis purchased all commercial rights to the peanut spread, making Mr. Bayle America's first peanut butter vendor.
1904	C. H. Sumner introduces peanut butter to the world at the Universal Exposition of 1904 in St. Louis. Eager customers at his concession stand snatch up the treat to the tune of $705.11, which was a whopping sum in those days.
1908	Krema Products Company in Columbus, Ohio, begins selling peanut butter. It is the oldest peanut butter company that's still in operation in the United States today.
1922	Joseph L. Rosefield of California receives the first patent for a shelf-stable peanut butter that is churned like butter, instead of simply ground and mixed like earlier versions. The result: a smoother product that stays fresh for up to a year, because the oil doesn't separate from the peanut mixture.
1932	Mr. Rosefield begins marketing his smooth recipe under the Skippy label. Two years later, in 1934, he creates the first crunchy-style peanut butter by mixing in chopped peanuts at the end of the manufacturing process.
1941–1945	Both peanut butter and jelly are included in ration kits for the U.S. military. The GIs begin adding jelly to their sandwiches to jazz up the peanut butter, and a lunchbox superstar is born.

 **Sugar**

Sow tiny seeds. Many flowers and vegetables, such as snapdragons, lettuce, and carrots, have itty-bitty seeds that are the dickens to plant where you want them to grow. Either they blow away in the wind, or they stick together and fall out of the packet in one big clump. You can put an end to that foolishness (and your frustration) by mixing the seeds with a tablespoon or two of granulated sugar. Besides making the little things easier to handle, the sugar will add nourishment to the soil.

Feed shade trees. Maples, elms, sycamores, and other big trees use a lot of energy during the growing season. When they wake up after their long winter's nap, they want breakfast—*now*! Here's how to serve it up: Start by mixing 25 pounds of dry, organic fertilizer (5-10-5) with 1 pound of sugar and 1/2 pound of Epsom salts. Then drill holes in the ground out at the weep line (at the tip of the farthest branch). Make the holes 8 to 10 inches deep and 18 to 24 inches apart. Pour 2 tablespoons of the breakfast mix into each hole, and sprinkle the remainder over the soil.

Grow sweeter tomatoes. The folks who keep such statistics tell us that 90 percent of American gardeners grow tomatoes. But I'll wager that not many of them know this secret: If you add a spoonful of sugar to each hole at planting time, your fruits will be so sweet and juicy, you'll want to eat them for dessert!

Raise tastier rhubarb. My Grandma Putt's rhubarb pies, cobblers, and sauces were the most delicious treats in town. Yours will be, too, if you use her special trick: Several times during the growing season, give your plants a quality brand of dry, balanced organic fertilizer (15-15-15 is good) at the rate recommended on the label, and mix in 1/2 cup of sugar per 5 pounds of food. Broadcast this mixture over the planting bed, and water it in well. Then sit back and wait for a heavenly harvest!

MARVELOUS MIX

Vegetable Power Powder

In this world-famous formula, sugar adds the punch that will help get your garden off to the best start possible.*

15 lbs. of dry, organic fertilizer (either 4-12-4 or 5-10-5)
5 lbs. of gypsum
2 lbs. of diatomaceous earth
1 lb. of sugar

Mix these ingredients together, and put them into a hand-held broadcast spreader. Set the spreader on medium, apply the mixture over the top of your garden, and work it into the soil. Follow up by immediately overspraying the area with this energizing tonic:

1 can of beer
1 cup of mild dishwashing liquid**
1 cup of antiseptic mouthwash
1 cup of regular cola (not diet)
1 tsp. of instant tea granules

Mix these ingredients in a bucket, fill a 20 gallon hose-end sprayer with the solution, and apply it to the soil to the point of runoff. Then let the area sit for two weeks before you start planting.

*This recipe makes enough to cover 100 square feet of garden area.
**Do not use detergent or any product that contains antibacterial agents.

Sugar

Root houseplant cuttings. Ivy, philodendrons, coleus, and many other indoor plants are a snap to propagate by taking stem cuttings and plunking them in a glass of water. But those plant parts will form roots faster if you add a pinch of $C_{12}H_{22}O_{11}$ (a.k.a. table sugar) to the H_2O.

Pollinate your cucurbits. If your cuke-family plants are producing flowers galore but few, if any, fruits, there could be a four-letter reason: b-e-e-s. Or, rather, the lack of them. Cucumbers, melons, and squash (including gourds and pumpkins) bear both male and female flowers on the same plant. Then it's up to insects—primarily honeybees—to collect the pollen offered up by the boys and carry it to the girls, who produce the fruit. If the buzzers aren't showing up in big enough numbers, the pollination rate—and therefore, your yield—will suffer. But don't worry. Here's a sweet way to lure bees to your plants. Put 2 cups of water in a cooking pot, add $^1/_2$ cup of sugar, and boil, stirring, until the sugar is completely dissolved. Let the mixture cool, dilute it with 1 gallon of water, and pour the solution into a handheld sprayer bottle. Then spritz your bloomin' plants. Before you know it, willing winged workers will fly to your rescue!

Polish off aphids. Or rather, enlist a posse of good-guy bugs to do the job for you. How? It's simple: Just spray your target plants with the same sugar-water solution described above (see "Pollinate your cucurbits"). It'll attract ladybugs, lacewings, damselflies, and hordes of other beneficial insects that eat aphids by the bucketload.

Snag slugs and snails. Beer is a classic bait for slug and snail traps. But if you've got a lot of slimy pests to get rid of, even the cheapest brews will cost you a pretty penny. And why spend your hard-earned cash on the enemy? Instead, pour 1 pound of brown sugar and $^1/_2$ package ($1^1/_2$ teaspoons) of dry yeast into a 1-gallon jug, fill it with warm water, and let it sit for two days, uncovered. Then pour it into your slug traps, and watch the culprits belly up to the bar!

If you ordered some ladybugs from a catalog and set them out in your garden, only to have them fly the coop, you're not alone. That's a problem I hear about from a lot of folks. The reason is that the ladybugs most often sold commercially are collected while they're hibernating, and when they wake up, they usually move on to fresh territory. The key to success with mail-order lady-bugs is to get them to hang around long enough to lay eggs. Then it won't matter if they take off because when the larvae hatch, they'll start gobbling up pesky pests like there's no tomorrow. Here's a handful of hints for providing hospitality, ladybug style:

* Put the package in the refrigerator for a few hours before you open it. That'll make the bugs sluggish and less likely to take off.

* Give your garden a thorough sprinkling, from top to bottom, just before you release the bugs. They need humidity and moisture to survive.

* Release your hired guns in the evening, because they don't usually fly away in the dark.

* Handle the little critters *very* gently. If they're agitated or feel threatened, they'll fly away to safety.

* Put about a tablespoon of the ladies at the base of each plant. Then spray your plants with a solution made of 1 part sugar to 9 parts water. That way, when the girls wake up in the morning, they'll have something to snack on right away, and they won't have to fly off in search of breakfast.

Sugar

Send flies to their doom. It never fails: You no sooner sit down to enjoy a nice, relaxing lunch on your deck than a bunch of pesky flies appear from out of nowhere. Well, don't spend all of your time waving the pests away—and don't reach for one of those toxic aerosol sprays! Instead, dash the dirty devils with this food-safe formula: Mix 2 cups of milk, 1/2 cup of sugar, and 2 tablespoons of ground black pepper in a pan, and let the mixture simmer for about 10 minutes, stirring occasionally. Then pour it into shallow bowls or plastic margarine tubs, and set them around the perimeter of the plagued area. The flies will zero in on the sweet bait, fall into the trap, and drown!

Rout out root aphids. When your flowers or vegetables wilt during sunny weather, even though you know they're getting plenty of water, you could be entertaining a crowd of root aphids. These tiny suckers are kissin' cousins to the aphids that drain sap from leaves and flowers, but they do their

Do Tell!

Unlike many of the products on supermarket shelves, sugar has been around in its present form for a *long* time. In fact, folks in India were growing and refining sugar cane at least as far back as 3000 B.C. From there, the sweet treasure (known as *sarkara* or *sakara* in Sanskrit) spread first to Indochina and Arabia, and then to Europe (thanks to Nearcus, one of Alexander the Great's gallivanting Greek generals). At each stop, the name was tweaked slightly. *Sarkara* became *sukkar* in Arabic, *sakharon* in Greek, *zucchero* in Italian, and *sucre* in French. But no matter what people called sugar, they gleefully gobbled it up, and they still do. Are you ready for this? In 2006, worldwide sugar consumption topped 152 million metric tons. The U.S. accounted for roughly 10.5 million tons of that total. How sweet it is!

dirty deeds underground, where you can't see them. If their shenanigans go on unchecked, plants will lose their get-up-and-grow power, and may eventually die. To make a positive I.D., pull up one of the victims. If root aphids are at work, you'll see a white, fluffy or powdery wax on the roots and soil—and your mission is clear: Sprinkle about 1/4 cup of sugar around each afflicted plant, and water it into the soil. If the sweet stuff doesn't wipe out all of the rooting rascals, it'll at least put a big dent in the population.

Stop root-knot nematodes in their tracks. Here's a sweet—and sweetly simple—way to keep these nasty Nellies from demolishing the roots of your flowers and vegetables: Just work sugar into the soil at a rate of 5 pounds per 50 square feet of planting area. The tiny worms will gobble the stuff up, and it'll choke them to death! As a bonus, the sugar will feed the beneficial bacteria in the soil, and make all of your plants generally healthier.

Clobber cockroaches. These obnoxious pests are infamous far and wide for the mischief they cause in kitchens and other indoor rooms, but they also invade garden sheds and workshops. Fortunately, no matter where the roaches are roaming, it's a snap to get rid of them—without resorting to smelly and possibly dangerous pesticides. All you need to do is make a half-and-half mixture of sugar and baking powder, and sprinkle it over the infested territory. The bugs will scurry to gobble up the sugar, and the baking powder will kill them. Replace the supply as needed to prevent further invasions.

Make cut rosebuds open faster. If your idea of a heavenly sight is a vase filled with perfect rosebuds from your garden, you can skip this tip. On the other hand, if you prefer roses that have opened into their full, fluffed-out glory, take note: To make those buds unfurl lickety-split, simply stir a spoonful of sugar into their water. They'll unfold almost before your very eyes!

Attract hummingbirds. The places that sell nectar feeders can also provide you with the sweet stuff to put inside of them. But for a fraction of the cost, you can make your own, using 4 parts water to 1 part granulated sugar. Heat the water in a pan until it's almost boiling, then remove the pan from the heat and stir in the sugar. Continue stirring until the sugar is completely dissolved. Cool, and fill your freshly cleaned feeder. Store any extra solution in the refrigerator in a tightly capped bottle or jar. It will keep for about three days. *Note:* If hummers are on the scene when a late-spring cold snap or an early fall frost hits your region, boost the sugar-to-water ratio by adding an extra 2 to 4 tablespoons of sugar per cup of water. That way, these heat-loving birds will get enough calories to keep on buzzin'. Just one word of caution: Never use honey in your feeder—it can infect hummingbirds with a fatal fungus.

Beckon orioles, too. These snazzy songbirds go for sugar just as much as their hovering cousins do, but they prefer their nectar a tad less sweet. Make their supply with 6 parts water to 1 part sugar, and pour it into a feeder that's specially made for orioles. They're similar to the ones sold for hummingbirds, but they're bigger and have sturdier perches. Also, instead of red, they're bright orange—the color orioles prefer over all others.

Bring on the butterflies. The same sugar water that draws hummingbirds and orioles from near and far will also attract flocks of these winged jewels to your yard. Use the classic hummers' ratio of 4 parts water to 1 part sugar, but serve it up a little bit differently: Grab a thin, green, plastic-fiber scrubbing pad from your kitchen drawer, and saturate it with the sweet syrup. Set the pad on a plastic plate that you've screwed to a post or other flat surface. Then sit back and wait for the show to begin. *Note:* Whatever you do, don't go out and buy a commercial butterfly feeder! Nearly all of them come equipped with a moat that you fill with water, thereby keeping crawling insects out of the nectar. But a lot of small butterflies also get trapped in the water, with fatal results.

Here's to
YOU!

Wasps and yellow jackets can sure put a damper on your summertime fun. But you can stop 'em in their tracks, using any of these sweet tricks:

✳ Dissolve 1/2 cup of sugar in 1/2 cup of water in a half-gallon milk jug, then add 1 cup of apple cider vinegar and a banana peel. Pour in enough cold water to fill the jug about halfway. Screw on the cap, and shake the bottle to mix the ingredients thoroughly. Remove the cap, and hang your trap by the handle from a tree branch.

✳ Drill three or four 1/2-inch holes in the lid of a large, plastic food-storage container. Mix 1/3 cup of sugar, 3 tablespoons of lemon juice, and 2 cups of water in the container, snap on the lid, and set it where the pests are causing problems.

✳ Poke a hole in a strip of duct tape or a sheet of adhesive-backed paper, and run a piece of twine or wire through the hole. Sprinkle sugar on the sticky side of the tape or paper, and hang it in the infested area.

Just one note of caution: Honeybees will also be attracted to the sugary devices, so keep close watch. If you find that the good guys are getting caught in your traps, take them down immediately.

Sugar

Keep cut flowers fresh longer. No matter what kind of flowers you've gathered from your garden (or bought at the super-market), you want them to look their best for as long as possible. And they will if you simply fill your vases with a solution made from 3 tablespoons of sugar and 2 table-spoons of white vinegar per quart of warm water. The sugar will provide nourishment for the blooms, and the vinegar will stem the growth of bacteria. You'll be aston-ished at how long your bouquet keeps its youthful beauty!

Treat a wasp sting. Ouch! You were setting out your wasp traps, and one of the early arrivals planted his business end in your arm! Well, if you've still got the sugar close at hand, you're in luck. Quickly mix a teaspoon of the white gran-ules with just enough water to make a paste, and rub it over the sting site for a few minutes. The sugar will neu-tralize the toxin and head off the pain and swelling.

Clean up gasoline spills. When you're filling up your lawn mower and some fuel slops onto the grass, don't panic—you can save that turf. Just mix 6 cups of gypsum with 1 cup of sugar, spread the mixture over the scene of the spill, and water it in well. And next time, fill your mower in the mid-dle of the driveway, not on the lawn!

Wash your hardworking hands. You can buy special, super-powered soaps to accomplish this task, but don't bother! To get rid of grease, paint, or ground-in dirt, just pour equal amounts of sugar and olive oil into the palm of one hand, and rub your paws together for a few minutes. Rinse with clear water, and your skin will be as clean as a whistle!

Get grass stains out of your clothes. Will there *ever* be a time when you come in from working in your yard without sport-ing green splotches on your pants? Probably not. It's a good thing those marks are so easy to remove! Here's one of my favorite, surefire methods: Heat 1 cup of water in a pan until it's almost boiling, then remove the pan from the heat and stir in 1/2 cup of sugar. Continue stirring until the sugar is completely dissolved, and pour the syrup over the stains. Let the garment sit for an hour, then launder it as usual.

Quench your thirst. Working in the garden is mighty thirsty business—and it always has been. Nowadays, the supermarket shelves are crammed with fancy sports drinks. Back in the "good old days," folks didn't have all of those choices, but they had some mighty good homemade alternatives. This is one of the best: In a big jug or very large bowl, mix 2 1/2 cups of sugar, 1 cup of dark molasses, and 1/2 cup of apple cider vinegar in 1 gallon of water. Stash the libation in the refrigerator. Then when your outdoor-chore team needs a break, get 'em out of the sun, and pour everyone a tall, cool, refreshing glass.

MARVELOUS MIX

Sweet Salve

Sugar helps cuts and scrapes heal faster, and helps lessen the risk of infection by keeping the wounds dry. So the next time you have a minor mishap, slather on some of this healthful ointment.

> 4 parts sugar
> 1 part Betadine® ointment (available in the supermarket's pharmacy or first-aid section)

First, wash and dry the wound, and make sure it has stopped bleeding (otherwise, the sugar will make it bleed more). Mix the sugar and Betadine together, dab a thick layer onto the cut, and cover it with a bandage. Repeat the procedure three or four times a day in the beginning, decreasing to once a day as the healing progresses.

Paper Products

| PAPER CUPS |
| PAPER PLATES |
| PAPER TOWELS |
| STRAWS |
| TOOTHPICKS |

Paper Cups

Fend off cutworms. No flower or vegetable seedling is safe from the jaws of these creepy crawlers, but protection is as close as the Paper Products aisle. Just grab a package of paper cups, and turn them into anti-cutworm collars. (The 8-ounce cups, which measure roughly 5 inches high, are perfect.) Punch out the bottoms, set a cup over each baby plant, and push the cup about 2 inches into the soil, leaving the rest showing above ground.

Start seeds. Small, unwaxed paper cups make some of the finest seed-starter pots you could ever ask for. Simply poke a couple of drainage holes in the bottoms of the cups, and group them on a waterproof tray. Then add seed-starting mix and sow your seeds. Come transplant time, set your young plants into the ground, pots and all. (For best results, tear off the bottom of each cup at planting time to give the roots more growing room.) The paper will quickly decompose, enriching the soil in the process.

If you use disposable plastic cups and you grow tall plants that need staking, this tip has your name written all over it! You can turn those pieces of Paper Product aisle trash into genuine treasure. How? Just put a piece of double-sided tape on the top of each stake and push a plastic cup, upside down, over the top of it. When you're working in your garden, those toppers will keep you from hitting your face or, worse, your eye on the sharp stakes. What's more, if you're using the transparent cups, you'll barely notice them.

Protect your deer deterrents. Rain, snow, and sleet can quickly destroy the odor of hair, powder-scented rags, perfumed soap, and other smelly repellents. So before you expose your critter-chaser of choice to the elements, give it a cozy shelter. To make it, put the material into an old panty hose foot, and tie it closed with a string. Poke a hole in the bottom of a 12-ounce waxed paper cup, tuck the pouch inside, pull the string through the hole, and fasten it to a tree or shrub branch. The aroma should stay fresh for about a year, no matter what kind of wild weather Mother Nature sends your way.

Scare away birds. And plenty of four-legged critters, too! Regardless of what kind of mischief-makers are helping themselves to your harvest (or your newly planted seeds), simple paper cups—slightly souped-up—will send 'em packin'. Here's all you need to do: Cut colorful plastic bags into strips about 1 inch wide, and staple them around the tops of waxed paper cups. Then nail the cups, upside down, to the tops of 4- to 6-foot-tall wooden posts that you've driven into the ground throughout your garden or your newly seeded lawn. I set mine in a random pattern, approximately 10 to 15 feet apart. When that shiny fringe flaps in the wind, voracious varmints will vamoose very fast!

 # Paper Plates

Say "Adios" to ants. Whether the tiny rascals are traipsing into your house, farming aphids in your trees, or making major mischief at your barbecue, it's a snap to get rid of them: Just whip up any one of the ultra-safe ant baits in this book, and serve up the goodies on snack-sized paper plates. When the "artillery" has done its job, toss the plate into the compost bin, or bury it in the garden. You'll solve your pest problem and improve your soil at the same time.

Make sticky traps. Paper plates come in just about every color of the rainbow—which makes them an ideal choice for snagging flying insects. First, choose a shade that your troublesome bugs find irresistible (see "Color Them Gone," on page 17). Then either tack the plate to a wooden stake or poke a hole near the edge of the plate, and thread a piece of twine or wire through it. Coat the paper surface with corn syrup, petroleum jelly, or a commercial stick-um, and hang the trap on or next to your plagued plant. Every few days, remove the bug-covered plate and replace it with a fresh one. *Note:* If your potential victims are container plants, use small, snack-sized plates.

Just one word of caution: If you find that your traps are catching beneficial insects like bees, butterflies, or ladybugs along with the bad guys, change your tactics. Throughout this book, you'll find plenty of ways to get rid of destructive pests without harming garden-variety heroes.

Make a quickie bird feeder. Yikes! The temperature has taken an early nosedive, and your regular feeder has more customers than it can handle. Well, don't fret—and don't let your fine-feathered friends go hungry, either. Just set extra places at the table using heavy-duty, pressed-paper plates, like the Chinet® brand. They'll last for weeks if you put them in a place that's protected from the rain. Use thumbtacks to attach the plates to your wooden porch railing or other sheltered spot, and scatter a handful of black oil sunflower seeds in each one. Then sit back and watch the eager diners fly in!

We all know that when you're eating on the run, paper plates can save you a whole lot of cleanup time. But that's not the only way these disposable, sturdy helpers can come to your aid. Here's just a small sampling of other chores that paper plates can perform for you:

Here's to **YOU!**

Catch paint drips. Time to paint a ceiling or some crown molding? Before you start, poke a hole in a paper plate, push your brush handle through it, and secure it with duct tape. Then you can be sure that the paint will dribble onto the paper and not onto your head, your hand, and/or your shirt.

Cushion your china. When ceramic plates are stacked on a shelf or in a cabinet, the bottom of one can scratch the surface of the plate below. To keep that from happening, put inexpensive paper plates between them. While you're at it, put paper plates inside large skillets so you can stack another pot or pan in each one.

Play the learning game. Flash cards are great teaching aids for young children (or even for adults who are learning a foreign language), but they can work even better if you spice up the action. How? Just write or draw the relevant letters, numbers, shapes, or words on paper plates. When the student gets the answer right, he or she can celebrate by flinging the plate across the room, Frisbee®-style.

Win the sweepstakes. The contest instructions say "Mail in your entry on a 3" × 5" card," but you don't have one. So make one in a flash by cutting a 3- × 5-inch rectangle from the center of a paper plate. It's that easy!

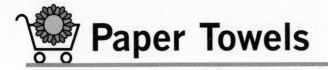

Paper Towels

Keep just-cut flowers fresh. A friend has invited you to help yourself to a big bouquet of flowers from her garden. The trouble is, you've got a long drive home, and those blooms are likely to turn as limp as wet dishrags on the way. Well, don't worry—here's the simple solution: Wrap the stems in a wet paper towel, slide the bundle into a plastic bag, and close the top up tight with a twist tie. (Or use a zip-top bag, and slide the zipper closed as far as possible.)

Germinate seeds. To get a jump on the growing season, wrap your flower or vegetable seeds in a moist paper towel, close it up in a zip-top plastic bag, and set it in a place where the temperature stays about 70°F. (On top of your refrigerator is perfect.) Every few days, open your homemade incubator and take a look: When you see little sprouts, remove the seeds and plant them, either directly in the garden, or in starter pots indoors (depending on the time of year and the type of seed).

Mulch early. When you plant heat-loving annuals and tender perennials, like zinnias, marigolds, and petunias, it's best to wait a few weeks after planting before you add mulch around them. This gives the soil time to warm up to the plants' comfort level. There's just one problem with this delay tactic: It also gives early-sprouting weeds a chance to gain a toehold. The simple solution: Spread a single layer of paper towels over the planting bed, cut holes in the paper, and set in your transplants. Finish up by adding an ultralight layer of soil or compost—just enough to conceal the towels and keep them from blowing away. The weeds won't be able to penetrate the blanket, but the sun's rays will. Within a couple of weeks, the soil should be warm enough so you can lay down an inch or two of compost, pine needles, or other weed-suppressing (and moisture-retaining) mulch.

Make seed tape. Seed tape is one of the best planting aids that any gardener could ask for. It's especially handy if you've got young helpers who tend to get the seeds everywhere but in the holes where they belong. Most garden centers and catalogs sell seed tape, but you'll have a much bigger choice of plants—and have a whole lot of fun, besides—if you make your own. (It's a great rainy-day project for kids.) Here's the routine: First, cut some paper towels into 1-inch-wide strips, and set them aside. Next, mix flour and water to make a paste that's thick enough to roll into pea-sized balls. Push a seed into each ball and set them on the paper-towel strips, spacing them according to the guidelines on the seed packet. Press the balls down just enough to make them stick to the paper. Wait until they've dried (it shouldn't take more than 15 minutes or so). Then carry your seed tape out to the garden, and plant it at the recommended depth for the type of plant. (Again, your seed packet will give you the details.)

Cover drainage holes. If you're still using pot shards to cover the holes in your planting containers, I have two words of advice for you: Stop it! Contrary to what we all used to think, those pieces of clay don't improve drainage. In fact, they can actually hinder it. Here's a better idea: Fold up a heavy-duty paper towel to form a pad that's several layers thick, and lay it over the bottom of the pot. It'll keep the soil from washing out, but still let excess moisture escape.

Water all the plants in a strawberry jar. These tall, beautiful pots are not just for strawberries. They also make perfect containers for any kind of trailing or sprawling plants, including thyme, impatiens, lobelia, tuberous begonias, and ivy—to name just a handful of choices. There's just one minor problem: Because the plants are all stacked up around the edges of the jar, getting enough moisture to all of the roots can be tricky. But an empty paper towel roll can help ease your watering worries. All you need to do is follow this routine before you insert any plants: Pour a few inches of fine gravel into the bottom of the pot, and set the cardboard tube on top, so the top of the tube will be flush with the soil surface. (Add or remove gravel as needed.) Fill the tube with more gravel. Then fill the rest of the container with potting mix, and tuck your plants into the pockets on the sides of the jar. When you water, aim your

MARVELOUS MIX

Homemade Baby Wipes

As we discussed back in Chapter 8, baby wipes have a zillion-and-one uses in your yard and garden. There's just one problem: If you use a lot of them, the cost can add up to a pretty penny. But you don't need to buy them. You probably already have everything you need to make your own. Here's how it's done.

> **1 roll of soft, absorbent paper towels (premium brands work best)**
> **1 tall plastic container with tight-fitting lid**
> **2 tbsp. of baby oil**
> **2 tbsp. of liquid baby bath soap**
> **2 cups of water**

Cut the roll of paper towels in half with a serrated knife, and remove the cardboard tube. Place half the roll, on end, in the plastic container. Mix the liquid ingredients, pour the solution into the container, and close the lid. The towels will absorb the liquid. As you need them, simply pull the wipes up from the center of the roll.

watering-can nozzle at the gravel circle on the soil surface. The moisture will flow out evenly all the way down to the bottom of the jar. Eventually, the cardboard will disintegrate, leaving a column of gravel to carry on the job.

Guard your garbage. Raccoons and other trash-can raiders will beat a hasty retreat if you use this simple trick: Dip a big wad of paper towels in ammonia, douse it with hot sauce (the hotter the better), and toss the paper on top of the garbage in the can. That's all there is to it!

 # Straws

Fence out cutworms. All winter long, you've been collecting paper towel rolls and toilet paper rolls to use as anti-cutworm collars for your homegrown seedlings. Now, spring has sprung, and you're down on your hands and knees in your garden, carefully setting your transplants into the ground, complete with their protective armor. Then suddenly you realize that you don't have enough cardboard rolls to go around. Are your baby plants doomed? Not if you have a box or two of straws in the kitchen—or you can make a quick trip to your local supermarket. Just cut each straw into 3-inch pieces and slit them lengthwise. After you've planted a seedling, slip a section of straw around its stem, pushing it only slightly into the ground (if you go too far, you'll damage the roots). As the plants grow, the cut tubes will expand to accommodate them.

Locate your bulbs. After the foliage dies down, it can be all but impossible to remember exactly where your tulips, daffodils, and other spring bloomers are sleeping. And that can make for mighty tricky planting when you're adding

Although most folks (at least those of a certain age) probably associate straws with old-time soda fountains, these sipping devices actually had their start in a Washington, D.C., tavern. It happened one day in 1888, when Marvin Stone, the owner of a company that made paper cigarette holders, stopped in to enjoy an after-work drink with his pals. He ordered his usual cocktail, an icy-cold mint julep. Because juleps lose their flavor when they're warm, people drank them through straws so they didn't have to touch the glass with their hands. In those days, straws were cut from natural grasses, generally rye, which tended to give the drink a distinct grassy taste. Mr. Stone, deciding that he'd had one grass-flavored julep too many, began building a better straw by winding long strips of paper around a pencil and fastening the end with a dab of glue. Before long, other julep-lovers started asking him to make these unflavored straws for them, too. And by 1890, the Stone Cigarette Holder Company was turning out a lot more straws than cigarette holders.

more bulbs or other plants to the bed. Fortunately, you can find the solution to this dilemma right in the Paper Products aisle. Just pick up a box of plastic straws, and stick them into the soil above the bulbs, leaving an inch or two of each straw showing above ground. When the leaves have vanished, those signposts will still point the way to your buried treasure.

Make cut flower stems taller. Phooey! You've just gathered a big bunch of flowers from your garden, but some (or maybe all) of the stems are too short for the vase you want to put them in. Well, don't give up—and don't go scrounging around for another vase. Instead, shove each of the too-short stems into a plastic straw that you've cut to the length you want. Presto: a floral growth spurt!

Straws

Create a mini greenhouse. When you're getting ready to grow new perennials or shrubs from stem cuttings, drinking straws can help. Here's how: After you've filled your flat or pot with sterilized rooting medium and inserted your cuttings, push three or four straws into the soil. Then cover this support structure with plastic wrap or a clear plastic bag, and secure it to the top of the container with a rubber band. This will create the humid conditions that cuttings need for good growth. (They need ventilation, too, so poke a few holes in the plastic using a pin or small nail. Don't worry if the cover fogs up; but if water starts dripping from it, remove it for a few hours each day to fend off funky fungal diseases.)

See croquet wickets clearly. It's your turn to host your family's annual cutthroat croquet tournament, and you've started to set up the court. For some reason, though, the wickets don't seem to stand out against the green grass as vividly as they used to. (It couldn't possibly have anything to do with your aging eyeballs, could it?) No matter what's causing the wickets to fade from view, here's a fast way to make them more visible: Run each one through a plastic straw before you shove the ends into the ground. Then let the games begin!

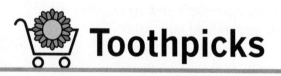 # Toothpicks

Stick it to cutworms. As you've seen throughout this book, there are oodles of supermarket products that you can turn into anti-cutworm collars. Well, here's a protective device that's even easier to make than a collar, and it's almost invisible, to boot! All you need to do is stick a couple of toothpicks into the soil on either side of each seedling. The mini stakes will prevent the worms from curling around the stem—and if they can't curl around their target, they can't eat it.

Get rid of mealybugs. Although these sap-sucking pests attack a wide range of outdoor plants, they're most common in sunrooms and home greenhouses. You'll most often see them massed on leaves or stems, looking like little piles of dirty cotton. If the afflicted plant is small, or you catch the invasion in its early stages, your good-riddance plan couldn't be simpler. Just use a toothpick to flick the bugs off the foliage. That act alone should kill the little fiends, but if you see any of them on the ground, put your foot down for good measure.

What on earth can you do with used toothpicks? Well, if you also have an avocado pit on hand, you can grow a lush, green houseplant for free. Here's how: Peel off the pit's brown covering, and stick three or four toothpicks into the middle, so that you can suspend it, flat end down, over a jar of water. The toothpicks rest on the rim of the jar, and the bottom of the pit should just touch the water. Place the jar in a dark, warm spot. As the water evaporates, add more to keep the bottom of the pit wet. In four to eight weeks, you'll see roots, and soon after that, a green stem and leaves will appear. When that happens, plant the seed in a container filled with commercial potting soil, and move it to a sunny location. As your seedling grows, keep pinching back the growing tip, and turn the pot around now and then, so your tree will grow bushy and even. When warm weather comes, move your tree outdoors. Summers in the sun will make it grow by leaps and bounds!

Label your seeds. When a future flower or vegetable sends up its first specks of green (technically known as cotyledons), it's all but impossible to tell what kind of plant you've got. So to avoid any confusion, make sure you label your flats when you sow your seeds. One quick way to do that is to write the relevant details on adhesive labels or pieces of masking tape, and fold them around toothpicks. Then stick the tiny banners into the appropriate containers. Now there's no chance of mistaking your peppers for your petunias, or your cauliflower for your cosmos!

Repair your garden hose. Dang! Somehow, your trusty rubber helper has picked up a puncture wound. Don't fret—with a little first aid, that hose'll be back on the job in no time flat. Just shove a wooden toothpick into the hole, and break it off flush with the surface of the hose. The wood will absorb moisture and swell up to fill the gap. (Use two or three toothpicks if one won't fill the opening). Wrap duct tape around the spot, and you're good to go.

Sow tiny seeds. These little buggers can be real bears to plant exactly where you want them. To keep your sanity, moisten the tip of a toothpick, and use it to pluck the tiny seeds from a small bowl and deposit them onto soil that's been dampened. The seeds will seem to magically jump from the toothpick tip to the damp ground, with little effort on your part.

Index

for disease control, 222
for fertilizing, 81, 215, 335
for killing moss, 102
for pruning wounds, 113
Mud stains, 208, 314
Muffin cups, 72–74
Mulch, 2, 4, 26, 86, 349–350
Murphy® Oil Soap
for fertilizing, 80, 209
for herbs, 321
for killing moss, 102, 231
for pest control, 75, 208, 210, 211
Muscle or joint pain, 32, 51, 76, 130, 313, 328
Mustard, dry, 120
Mustard stains, 170
Musty odors, 87

N
Nail clippers, 252
Nematodes (pests), 83, 150, 325, 339
Nuts and bolts, rusted, 100–101
Nut trees, 211

O
Oatmeal, 157
Oilcloth, 157
Oil lamps, 78
Oil spills, 58, 63, 97, 198
Old-Time Board Cleaner, 264
Onions, 303–307
for disease control, 166
for fertilizing, 309

for pest control, 111, 300, 310
storing, 25, 259
Orange extract, 122, 123
Oranges, 94, 273, 274, 282–291, 329
Organizing aids
baby wipe containers, 244
berry baskets, 284
dairy containers, 160
first-aid packaging, 188
food-storage bags, 16
food-storage containers, 21
spray can lids, 56
trash bags, 37
Oriole Cookies, 94
Orioles, 287, 340
Outdoor furniture
cleaning, 52, 55, 169, 199
covers for, 41
mildewed, 203
painting, 140
pets and, 6
staining, 85, 141
Outdoor lighting, 9

P
Packing materials, 29, 30, 219, 284
Paint, 31, 235
Paint brushes, 220
Paint buckets, 223
Painted daisies, 168
Painting techniques, 140, 169, 290, 348
Paint odors, 125, 273
Paint thinner, 90
Panty hose, 18, 245, 257–260
Paper cups, 345–346

Paper plates, 346–348
Paper towels, 349–352
Paperwork, 16, 257
Papier-mâché, 65
Paprika, 117
Parsley, 118, 119, 298
Party decorations, 29
Patios, cleaning, 52, 95, 141
Peanut butter, 278, 288, 329–333
Pears, 15
Pecans, 60
Pepper, ground, 121, 146, 156, 326, 338
Peppercorns, 298
Peppermint oil, 104, 123, 215, 245, 246. *See also* Mint
Peppers, hot, 300, 307–310
Pepto-Bismol®, 172
Perennials
bare-root, 102–103
cleaning, 92
from cuttings, 2–3, 189, 354
disease control for, 241
fertilizing, 109, 327
pest control for, 154
from seed, 88
Perspiration control, 51
Pest control agents.
See also specific pests; specific plants
alcohol, 165–166
ammonia, 195, 196
aspirin, 172–173
athlete's foot powder, 164
bags and wraps, 11, 16, 28, 346
citrus fruit, 286

Index